We Hold These Truths

Historic Documents, Essays, and Speeches in American Government

---

Edited by

Ray Notgrass

Curriculum That Teaches the Heart, Soul, and Mind

Cover Design by Mary Evelyn Notgrass
Interior Design by Charlene Notgrass and Mary Evelyn Notgrass

Pictured on the cover (© 2008 JupiterImages Corporation unless otherwise noted):
Articles of Confederation
Members of the Continental Congress
Woodrow Wilson (courtesy Library of Congress)
The White House (courtesy Department of Defense)
John Jay
U.S. House of Representatives chamber (courtesy Library of Congress)
Statue of John Marshall
American flag (courtesy Department of Defense)

Notgrass Company
370 South Lowe Avenue, Suite A
PMB 211
Cookeville, Tennessee 38501

1-800-211-8793
www.notgrass.com
books@notgrass.com

ISBN 978-1-933410-89-0

Scripture quotations taken from the New American Standard Bible®,
Copyright © 1960, 1962, 1963, 1968, 1971, 1972, 1973, 1975, 1977, 1995
by The Lockman Foundation. Used by permission.

Published in the United States by the Notgrass Company.

Table of Contents

Introduction...1

Exodus 20:1-17...3

Ezekiel 34...4

Romans 13...6

Declaration of Independence *(1776)*...7

Articles of Confederation *(1777)*...11

Constitution of the United States *(1787)*..18

Twelve Tables of Roman Law (excerpt) *(c. 451 BC)*..36

Magna Carta (excerpt) *(1215)*..37

On the Divine Right of Kings (excerpt), James I of England *(1609)*..................41

English Bill of Rights (excerpt) *(1689)*..42

Two Treatises of Government (excerpt), John Locke *(1690)*................................44

Preamble of the Frame of Government of Pennsylvania, William Penn *(1682)*......47

Thoughts on Government, John Adams *(1776)*...50

The Federalist Number 2, John Jay *(1787)*..56

Speech by Patrick Henry Opposing Ratification of the Constitution (excerpt) *(1788)*............60

Exchange of Letters between the Danbury (Connecticut) Baptist Association and President
      Thomas Jefferson *(1801-1802)*...65

McCulloch v. Maryland (excerpt) *(1819)*...67

Wesberry v. Sanders (excerpt) *(1964)*...73

Tonkin Gulf Resolution *(1964)*...77

Joint Resolution to Authorize the Use of United States Armed Forces Against Iraq *(2002)*...78

2004 State of the Union Address, George W. Bush..84

South Dakota 2006 Law Regarding Abortion..94

"The U.S. Supreme Court" from *Democracy in America*, Alexis de Tocqueville *(1835)*...........97

"On a Visit to the Senate When He Was Twelve" from *The Education of Henry Adams*,
      Henry Adams *(1907)*...99

"The House of Representatives" from *Congressional Government*,
      Woodrow Wilson *(1885)*...101

Can We Be Good Without God?, Chuck Colson..107

The Religious Roots of Freedom, M. Stanton Evans..113

It's Time to End the Filibuster Rule, Ray Notgrass...120

Our Unconstitutional Congress, Stephen Moore..122

The Real Cost of Regulation, John Stossel...129

The Threat from Lawyers is No Joke, Walter Olson..135

The Liberal Assault on Freedom of Speech, Thomas G. West.............................141

Constitutional Myths and Realities, Stephen Markman...149

The Late, Great Doctrine of States' Rights, Ray Notgrass...155

The Moral Case for the Flat Tax, Steve Forbes..158

Morality and Foreign Policy: Reagan and Thatcher, Edwin Meese III....................163

American Unilateralism, Charles Krauthammer...168

America and the United Nations, Mark Steyn..175

Immigration, the War on Terror and the Rule of Law, Michelle Malkin..................182

Frank Talk About 'Mexifornia,' Victor Davis Hanson..189

The Ten Commandments Controversy, Michael Novak..195

Rolling Back Government: Lessons from New Zealand, Maurice P. McTigue........201

Something Higher Than Incumbency, James E. Rogan..208

Statesmanship and Its Betrayal, Mark Helprin...212

Introduction

We Hold These Truths is a compilation of Biblical texts, historic documents, speeches, essays, excerpts from Supreme Court opinions, and other writings, all of which help to inform our understanding of American government. It is designed to be used in conjunction with the text *Exploring Government*. The student who is using that text will find references in the lessons to the documents in this volume that he or she is to read in conjunction with those lessons.

The organization of this volume is in this order: Biblical texts; foundational documents of American government; ancient, medieval, and colonial documents; and finally modern essays and other commentaries on government. The purpose of this collection is to give the reader handy access to significant original documents and to provide the opinions and ideas of others so that the reader can develop his or her own informed thinking about government.

Several entries are taken from *Imprimis*, the monthly speech journal published by Hillsdale College. The title is pronounced im-PRY-mis. It comes from the Latin and means "in the first place." Hillsdale is a private, liberal arts college in Michigan that accepts no government money of any kind, not even Federal loans and grants to students. The college decided some years ago that it did not want to deal with the strings that are attached to accepting Federal money. Each month, *Imprimis* presents the essence of a speech given at a recent Hillsdale-sponsored function. The publication is offered free of charge, and it is also available on the Internet at www.hillsdale.edu. Several years of *Imprimis* issues are archived on the website.

Hillsdale provides a valuable service with *Imprimis* by presenting thoughtful, relevant, conservative thinking; by offering the publication free; and by generously giving permission for the material to be reproduced without charge provided that the appropriate credit line is given. The *Imprimis* material is copyrighted as of the date of original publication by Hillsdale College and is used here by permission of Hillsdale. Occasionally a speech will include a few comments that are inappropriate; but generally *Imprimis* is worth reading every month. I strongly encourage anyone who is interested in government and politics to subscribe to it or to read it online every month.

In editing the entries in this volume, I have left out some sections that I thought best to omit. These are indicated by ellipses. I have also added some explanations that are enclosed in brackets. For the most part, I have left variations in spelling and the citations of other works as they appear in the originals.

Ray Notgrass

Exodus 20:1-17

1 Then God spoke all these words, saying,

2 "I am the LORD your God, who brought you out of the land of Egypt, out of the house of slavery.

3 "You shall have no other gods before Me.

 4 "You shall not make for yourself an idol, or any likeness of what is in heaven above or on the earth beneath or in the water under the earth.

5 "You shall not worship them or serve them; for I, the LORD your God, am a jealous God, visiting the iniquity of the fathers on the children, on the third and the fourth generations of those who hate Me,

6 but showing lovingkindness to thousands, to those who love Me and keep My commandments.

7 "You shall not take the name of the LORD your God in vain, for the LORD will not leave him unpunished who takes His name in vain.

8 "Remember the sabbath day, to keep it holy.

9 "Six days you shall labor and do all your work,

10 but the seventh day is a sabbath of the LORD your God; in it you shall not do any work, you or your son or your daughter, your male or your female servant or your cattle or your sojourner who stays with you.

11 "For in six days the LORD made the heavens and the earth, the sea and all that is in them, and rested on the seventh day; therefore the LORD blessed the sabbath day and made it holy.

12 "Honor your father and your mother, that your days may be prolonged in the land which the LORD your God gives you.

13 "You shall not murder.

14 "You shall not commit adultery.

15 "You shall not steal.

16 "You shall not bear false witness against your neighbor.

17 "You shall not covet your neighbor's house; you shall not covet your neighbor's wife or his male servant or his female servant or his ox or his donkey or anything that belongs to your neighbor."

Ezekiel

1 Then the word of the LORD came to me saying,

2 "Son of man, prophesy against the shepherds of Israel. Prophesy and say to those shepherds, 'Thus says the Lord GOD, "Woe, shepherds of Israel who have been feeding themselves! Should not the shepherds feed the flock?

3 "You eat the fat and clothe yourselves with the wool, you slaughter the fat sheep without feeding the flock.

4 "Those who are sickly you have not strengthened, the diseased you have not healed, the broken you have not bound up, the scattered you have not brought back, nor have you sought for the lost; but with force and with severity you have dominated them.

5 "They were scattered for lack of a shepherd, and they became food for every beast of the field and were scattered.

6 "My flock wandered through all the mountains and on every high hill; My flock was scattered over all the surface of the earth, and there was no one to search or seek for them."'"

7 Therefore, you shepherds, hear the word of the LORD:

8 "As I live," declares the Lord GOD, "surely because My flock has become a prey, My flock has even become food for all the beasts of the field for lack of a shepherd, and My shepherds did not search for My flock, but rather the shepherds fed themselves and did not feed My flock;

9 therefore, you shepherds, hear the word of the LORD:

10 'Thus says the Lord GOD, "Behold, I am against the shepherds, and I will demand My sheep from them and make them cease from feeding sheep. So the shepherds will not feed themselves anymore, but I will deliver My flock from their mouth, so that they will not be food for them."'"

11 For thus says the Lord GOD, "Behold, I Myself will search for My sheep and seek them out.

12 "As a shepherd cares for his herd in the day when he is among his scattered sheep, so I will care for My sheep and will deliver them from all the places to which they were scattered on a cloudy and gloomy day.

13 "I will bring them out from the peoples and gather them from the countries and bring them to their own land; and I will feed them on the mountains of Israel, by the streams, and in all the inhabited places of the land.

14 "I will feed them in a good pasture, and their grazing ground will be on the mountain heights of Israel. There they will lie down on good grazing ground and feed in rich pasture on the mountains of Israel.

15 "I will feed My flock and I will lead them to rest," declares the Lord GOD.

16 "I will seek the lost, bring back the scattered, bind up the broken and strengthen the sick; but the fat and the strong I will destroy. I will feed them with judgment.

17 "As for you, My flock, thus says the Lord GOD, 'Behold, I will judge between one sheep and another, between the rams and the male goats.

18 'Is it too slight a thing for you that you should feed in the good pasture, that you must tread down with your feet the rest of your pastures? Or that you should drink of the clear waters, that you must foul the rest with your feet?

19 'As for My flock, they must eat what you tread down with your feet and drink what you foul with your feet!"

20 Therefore, thus says the Lord GOD to them, "Behold, I, even I, will judge between the fat sheep and the lean sheep.

21 "Because you push with side and with shoulder, and thrust at all the weak with your horns until you have scattered them abroad,

22 therefore, I will deliver My flock, and they will no longer be a prey; and I will judge between one sheep and another.

23 "Then I will set over them one shepherd, My servant David, and he will feed them; he will feed them himself and be their shepherd.

24 "And I, the LORD, will be their God, and My servant David will be prince among them; I the LORD have spoken.

25 "I will make a covenant of peace with them and eliminate harmful beasts from the land so that they may live securely in the wilderness and sleep in the woods.

26 "I will make them and the places around My hill a blessing And I will cause showers to come down in their season; they will be showers of blessing.

27 "Also the tree of the field will yield its fruit and the earth will yield its increase, and they will be secure on their land. Then they will know that I am the LORD, when I have broken the bars of their yoke and have delivered them from the hand of those who enslaved them.

28 "They will no longer be a prey to the nations, and the beasts of the earth will not devour them; but they will live securely, and no one will make them afraid.

29 "I will establish for them a renowned planting place, and they will not again be victims of famine in the land, and they will not endure the insults of the nations anymore.

30 "Then they will know that I, the LORD their God, am with them, and that they, the house of Israel, are My people," declares the Lord GOD.

31 "As for you, My sheep, the sheep of My pasture, you are men, and I am your God," declares the Lord GOD.

1 Every person is to be in subjection to the governing authorities. For there is no authority except from God, and those which exist are established by God.

2 Therefore whoever resists authority has opposed the ordinance of God; and they who have opposed will receive condemnation upon themselves.

3 For rulers are not a cause of fear for good behavior, but for evil. Do you want to have no fear of authority? Do what is good and you will have praise from the same;

4 for it is a minister of God to you for good. But if you do what is evil, be afraid; for it does not bear the sword for nothing; for it is a minister of God, an avenger who brings wrath on the one who practices evil.

Paul Teaching in a Synagogue

5 Therefore it is necessary to be in subjection, not only because of wrath, but also for conscience' sake.

6 For because of this you also pay taxes, for rulers are servants of God, devoting themselves to this very thing.

7 Render to all what is due them: tax to whom tax is due; custom to whom custom; fear to whom fear; honor to whom honor.

8 Owe nothing to anyone except to love one another; for he who loves his neighbor has fulfilled the law.

9 For this, "YOU SHALL NOT COMMIT ADULTERY, YOU SHALL NOT MURDER, YOU SHALL NOT STEAL, YOU SHALL NOT COVET," and if there is any other commandment, it is summed up in this saying, "YOU SHALL LOVE YOUR NEIGHBOR AS YOURSELF."

10 Love does no wrong to a neighbor; therefore love is the fulfillment of the law.

11 Do this, knowing the time, that it is already the hour for you to awaken from sleep; for now salvation is nearer to us than when we believed.

12 The night is almost gone, and the day is near. Therefore let us lay aside the deeds of darkness and put on the armor of light.

13 Let us behave properly as in the day, not in carousing and drunkenness, not in sexual promiscuity and sensuality, not in strife and jealousy.

14 But put on the Lord Jesus Christ, and make no provision for the flesh in regard to its lusts.

Declaration of Independence *(1776)*

IN CONGRESS, July 4, 1776.

The unanimous Declaration of the thirteen
United States of America

When in the Course of human events, it becomes necessary for one people to dissolve the political bands which have connected them with another, and to assume among the powers of the earth, the separate and equal station to which the Laws of Nature and of Nature's God entitle them, a decent respect to the opinions of mankind requires that they should declare the causes which impel them to the separation.

We hold these truths to be self-evident, that all men are created equal, that they are endowed by their Creator with certain unalienable Rights, that among these are Life, Liberty and the pursuit of Happiness.—That to secure these rights, Governments are instituted among Men, deriving their just powers from the consent of the governed,—that whenever any Form of Government becomes destructive of these ends, it is the Right of the People to alter or to abolish it, and to institute new Government, laying its foundation on such principles and organizing its powers in such form, as to them shall seem most likely to effect their Safety and Happiness. Prudence, indeed, will dictate that Governments long established

Members of the Continental Congress

should not be changed for light and transient causes; and accordingly all experience hath shewn, that mankind are more disposed to suffer, while evils are sufferable, than to right themselves by abolishing the forms to which they are accustomed. But when a long train of abuses and usurpations, pursuing invariably the same Object evinces a design to reduce them under absolute Despotism, it is their right, it is their duty, to throw off such Government, and to provide new Guards for their future security.—Such has been the patient sufferance of these Colonies; and such is now the necessity which constrains them to alter their former Systems of Government. The history of the present King of Great Britain is a history of repeated injuries and usurpations, all having in direct object the establishment of an absolute Tyranny over these States. To prove this, let Facts be submitted to a candid world.

He has refused his Assent to Laws, the most wholesome and necessary for the public good.

He has forbidden his Governors to pass Laws of immediate and pressing importance, unless suspended in their operation till his Assent should be obtained; and when so suspended, he has utterly neglected to attend to them.

He has refused to pass other Laws for the accommodation of large districts of people, unless those people would relinquish the right of Representation in the Legislature, a right inestimable to them and formidable to tyrants only.

He has called together legislative bodies at places unusual, uncomfortable, and distant from the depository of their public Records, for the sole purpose of fatiguing them into compliance with his measures.

He has dissolved Representative Houses repeatedly, for opposing with manly firmness his invasions on the rights of the people.

He has refused for a long time, after such dissolutions, to cause others to be elected; whereby the Legislative powers, incapable of Annihilation, have returned to the People at large for their exercise; the State remaining in the mean time exposed to all the dangers of invasion from without, and convulsions within.

He has endeavoured to prevent the population of these States; for that purpose obstructing the Laws for Naturalization of Foreigners; refusing to pass others to encourage their migrations hither, and raising the conditions of new Appropriations of Lands.

He has obstructed the Administration of Justice, by refusing his Assent to Laws for establishing Judiciary powers.

He has made Judges dependent on his Will alone, for the tenure of their offices, and the amount and payment of their salaries.

He has erected a multitude of New Offices, and sent hither swarms of Officers to harrass our people, and eat out their substance.

He has kept among us, in times of peace, Standing Armies without the Consent of our legislatures.

He has affected to render the Military independent of and superior to the Civil power.

He has combined with others to subject us to a jurisdiction foreign to our constitution, and unacknowledged by our laws; giving his Assent to their Acts of pretended Legislation:

For Quartering large bodies of armed troops among us:

For protecting them, by a mock Trial, from punishment for any Murders which they should commit on the Inhabitants of these States:

For cutting off our Trade with all parts of the world:

For imposing Taxes on us without our Consent:

For depriving us in many cases, of the benefits of Trial by Jury:

For transporting us beyond Seas to be tried for pretended offences:

For abolishing the free System of English Laws in a neighbouring Province, establishing therein an Arbitrary government, and enlarging its Boundaries so as to render it at once an example and fit instrument for introducing the same absolute rule into these Colonies:

For taking away our Charters, abolishing our most valuable Laws, and altering fundamentally the Forms of our Governments:

For suspending our own Legislatures, and declaring themselves invested with power to legislate for us in all cases whatsoever.

He has abdicated Government here, by declaring us out of his Protection and waging War against us.

He has plundered our seas, ravaged our Coasts, burnt our towns, and destroyed the lives of our people.

He is at this time transporting large Armies of foreign Mercenaries to compleat the works of death, desolation and tyranny, already begun with circumstances of Cruelty & perfidy scarcely paralleled in the most barbarous ages, and totally unworthy the Head of a civilized nation.

He has constrained our fellow Citizens taken Captive on the high Seas to bear Arms against their Country, to become the executioners of their friends and Brethren, or to fall themselves by their Hands.

He has excited domestic insurrections amongst us, and has endeavoured to bring on the inhabitants of our frontiers, the merciless Indian Savages, whose known rule of warfare, is an undistinguished destruction of all ages, sexes and conditions.

In every stage of these Oppressions We have Petitioned for Redress in the most humble terms: Our repeated Petitions have been answered only by repeated injury. A Prince whose character is thus marked by every act which may define a Tyrant, is unfit to be the ruler of a free people.

Nor have We been wanting in attentions to our British brethren. We have warned them from time to time of attempts by their legislature to extend an unwarrantable jurisdiction over us. We have reminded them of the circumstances of our emigration and settlement here. We have appealed to their native justice and magnanimity, and we have conjured them by the ties of our common kindred to disavow these usurpations, which, would inevitably interrupt our connections and correspondence. They too have been deaf to the voice of justice and of consanguinity. We must, therefore, acquiesce in the necessity, which denounces our Separation, and hold them, as we hold the rest of mankind, Enemies in War, in Peace Friends.

We, therefore, the Representatives of the united States of America, in General Congress, Assembled, appealing to the Supreme Judge of the world for the rectitude of our intentions, do, in the Name, and by Authority of the good People of these Colonies, solemnly publish and declare, That these United Colonies are, and of Right ought to be Free and Independent States; that they are Absolved from all Allegiance to the British Crown, and that all political connection between them and the State of Great Britain, is and ought to be totally dissolved; and that as Free and Independent States, they have full Power to levy War, conclude Peace, contract Alliances, establish Commerce, and to do all other Acts and Things which Independent States may of right do. And for the support of this Declaration, with a firm reliance on the protection of divine Providence, we mutually pledge to each other our Lives, our Fortunes and our sacred Honor.

Signers of the Declaration of Independence

[Georgia:]
Button Gwinnett
Lyman Hall
George Walton

[North Carolina:]
William Hooper
Joseph Hewes
John Penn

[South Carolina:]
Edward Rutledge
Thomas Heyward, Jr.
Thomas Lynch, Jr.
Arthur Middleton

[Maryland:]
Samuel Chase
William Paca
Thomas Stone
Charles Carroll
   of Carrollton

[Virginia:]
George Wythe
Richard Henry Lee
Thomas Jefferson
Benjamin Harrison
Thomas Nelson, Jr.
Francis Lightfoot Lee
Carter Braxton

[Pennsylvania:]
Robert Morris
Benjamin Rush
Benjamin Franklin
John Morton
George Clymer
James Smith
George Taylor
James Wilson
George Ross

[Delaware:]
Caesar Rodney
George Read
Thomas McKean

[New York:]
William Floyd
Philip Livingston
Francis Lewis
Lewis Morris

[New Jersey:]
Richard Stockton
John Witherspoon
Francis Hopkinson
John Hart
Abraham Clark

[New Hampshire:]
Josiah Bartlett
William Whipple
Matthew Thornton

[Massachusetts:]
John Hancock
Samuel Adams
John Adams
Robert Treat Paine
Elbridge Gerry

[Rhode Island:]
Stephen Hopkins
William Ellery

[Connecticut:]
Roger Sherman
Samuel Huntington
William Williams
Oliver Wolcott

Articles of Confederation (1777)

To all to whom these Presents shall come, we the undersigned Delegates of the States affixed to our Names send greeting.

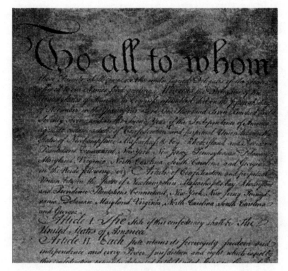

Articles of Confederation

Articles of Confederation and perpetual Union between the states of New Hampshire, Massachusetts-Bay, Rhode Island and Providence Plantations, Connecticut, New York, New Jersey, Pennsylvania, Delaware, Maryland, Virginia, North Carolina, South Carolina and Georgia.

I. The Stile of this Confederacy shall be "The United States of America."

II. Each state retains its sovereignty, freedom, and independence, and every power, jurisdiction, and right, which is not by this Confederation expressly delegated to the United States, in Congress assembled.

III. The said States hereby severally enter into a firm league of friendship with each other, for their common defense, the security of their liberties, and their mutual and general welfare, binding themselves to assist each other, against all force offered to, or attacks made upon them, or any of them, on account of religion, sovereignty, trade, or any other pretense whatever.

IV. The better to secure and perpetuate mutual friendship and intercourse among the people of the different States in this Union, the free inhabitants of each of these States, paupers, vagabonds, and fugitives from justice excepted, shall be entitled to all privileges and immunities of free citizens in the several States; and the people of each State shall enjoy free ingress and regress to and from any other State, and shall enjoy therein all the privileges of trade and commerce, subject to the same duties, impositions, and restrictions as the inhabitants thereof respectively, provided that such restrictions shall not extend so far as to prevent the removal of property imported into any State, to any other State, of which the owner is an inhabitant; provided also that no imposition, duties or restriction shall be laid by any State, on the property of the United States, or either of them.

If any person guilty of, or charged with, treason, felony, or other high misdemeanor in any State, shall flee from justice, and be found in any of the United States, he shall, upon demand of the Governor or executive power of the State from which he fled, be delivered up and removed to the State having jurisdiction of his offense.

Full faith and credit shall be given in each of these States to the records, acts, and judicial proceedings of the courts and magistrates of every other State.

V. For the most convenient management of the general interests of the United States, delegates shall be annually appointed in such manner as the legislatures of each State shall direct, to meet in Congress on the first Monday in November, in every year, with a power reserved to each State to recall its delegates, or any of them, at any time within the year, and to send others in their stead for the remainder of the year.

No State shall be represented in Congress by less than two, nor more than seven members; and no person shall be capable of being a delegate for more than three years in any term of six years; nor shall any person, being a delegate, be capable of holding any office under the United States, for which he, or another for his benefit, receives any salary, fees or emolument of any kind.

Each State shall maintain its own delegates in a meeting of the States, and while they act as members of the committee of the States.

In determining questions in the United States in Congress assembled, each State shall have one vote.

Freedom of speech and debate in Congress shall not be impeached or questioned in any court or place out of Congress, and the members of Congress shall be protected in their persons from arrests or imprisonments, during the time of their going to and from, and attendance on Congress, except for treason, felony, or breach of the peace.

VI. No State, without the consent of the United States in Congress assembled, shall send any embassy to, or receive any embassy from, or enter into any conference, agreement, alliance or treaty with any King, Prince or State; nor shall any person holding any office of profit or trust under the United States, or any of them, accept any present, emolument, office or title of any kind whatever from any King, Prince or foreign State; nor shall the United States in Congress assembled, or any of them, grant any title of nobility.

No two or more States shall enter into any treaty, confederation or alliance whatever between them, without the consent of the United States in Congress assembled, specifying accurately the purposes for which the same is to be entered into, and how long it shall continue.

No State shall lay any imposts or duties, which may interfere with any stipulations in treaties, entered into by the United States in Congress assembled, with any King, Prince or State, in pursuance of any treaties already proposed by Congress, to the courts of France and Spain.

No vessel of war shall be kept up in time of peace by any State, except such number only, as shall be deemed necessary by the United States in Congress assembled, for the defense of such State, or its trade; nor shall any body of forces be kept up by any State in time of peace, except such number only, as in the judgement of the United States in Congress assembled, shall be deemed requisite to garrison the forts necessary for the defense of such State; but every State shall always keep up a well-regulated and disciplined militia, sufficiently armed and accoutered, and shall provide and constantly have ready for use, in public stores, a due number of field pieces and tents, and a proper quantity of arms, ammunition and camp equipage.

No State shall engage in any war without the consent of the United States in Congress assembled, unless such State be actually invaded by enemies, or shall have received certain advice of a resolution being formed by some nation of Indians to invade such State, and the danger is so imminent as not to admit of a delay till the United States in Congress assembled can be consulted; nor shall any State grant commissions to any ships or vessels of war, nor letters of marque or reprisal, except it be after a declaration of war by the United States in Congress assembled, and then only against the Kingdom or State and the subjects thereof, against which war has been so declared, and under such regulations as shall be established by the United States in Congress assembled, unless such State be infested by pirates, in which case vessels of war may be fitted out for that occasion, and kept so long as the danger shall continue, or until the United States in Congress assembled shall determine otherwise.

VII. When land forces are raised by any State for the common defense, all officers of or under the rank of colonel, shall be appointed by the legislature of each State respectively, by whom such forces shall be raised, or in such manner as such State shall direct, and all vacancies shall be filled up by the State which first made the appointment.

VIII. All charges of war, and all other expenses that shall be incurred for the common defense or general welfare, and allowed by the United States in Congress assembled, shall be defrayed out of a common treasury, which shall be supplied by the several States in proportion to the value of all land within each State, granted or surveyed for any person, as such land and the buildings and improvements thereon shall be estimated according to such mode as the United States in Congress assembled, shall from time to time direct and appoint.

The taxes for paying that proportion shall be laid and levied by the authority and direction of the legislatures of the several States within the time agreed upon by the United States in Congress assembled.

IX. The United States in Congress assembled, shall have the sole and exclusive right and power of determining on peace and war, except in the cases mentioned in the sixth article

—of sending and receiving ambassadors

—entering into treaties and alliances, provided that no treaty of commerce shall be made whereby the legislative power of the respective States shall be restrained from imposing such imposts and duties on foreigners, as their own people are subjected to, or from prohibiting the exportation or importation of any species of goods or commodities whatsoever

—of establishing rules for deciding in all cases, what captures on land or water shall be legal, and in what manner prizes taken by land or naval forces in the service of the United States shall be divided or appropriated

—of granting letters of marque and reprisal in times of peace

—appointing courts for the trial of piracies and felonies commited on the high seas and establishing courts for receiving and determining finally appeals in all cases of captures, provided that no member of Congress shall be appointed a judge of any of the said courts.

The United States in Congress assembled shall also be the last resort on appeal in all disputes and differences now subsisting or that hereafter may arise between two or more States concerning boundary, jurisdiction or any other causes whatever; which authority shall always be exercised in the manner following. Whenever the legislative or executive authority or lawful agent of any State in controversy with another shall present a petition to Congress stating the matter in question and praying for a hearing, notice thereof shall be given by order of Congress to the legislative or executive authority of the other State in controversy, and a day assigned for the appearance of the parties by their lawful agents, who shall then be directed to appoint by joint consent, commissioners or judges to constitute a court for hearing and determining the matter in question: but if they cannot agree, Congress shall name three persons out of each of the United States, and from the list of such persons each party shall alternately strike out one, the petitioners beginning, until the number shall be reduced to thirteen; and from that number not less than seven, nor more than nine names as Congress shall direct, shall in the presence of Congress be drawn out by lot, and the persons whose names shall be so drawn or any five of them, shall be commissioners or judges, to hear and finally determine the controversy, so always as a major part of the judges who shall hear the cause shall agree in the determination: and if either party shall neglect to attend at the day appointed, without showing reasons, which Congress shall judge sufficient, or being present shall refuse to strike, the Congress shall proceed to nominate three persons out of each State, and the secretary of Congress shall strike in behalf of such party absent or refusing; and the judgement and sentence of the court to be appointed, in the manner before prescribed, shall be final and conclusive; and if any of the parties shall refuse to submit to the authority of such court, or to appear or defend their claim or cause, the court shall nevertheless proceed to pronounce sentence, or judgement, which shall in like manner be final and decisive, the judgement or sentence and other proceedings being in either case transmitted to Congress, and lodged among the acts of Congress for the security of the parties concerned: provided that every commissioner, before he sits in judgement, shall take an oath to be administered by one of the judges of the supreme or superior court of the State, where the cause shall be tried, 'well and truly to hear and determine the matter in question, according to the best of his judgement, without favor, affection or hope of reward': provided also, that no State shall be deprived of territory for the benefit of the United States.

All controversies concerning the private right of soil claimed under different grants of two or more States, whose jurisdictions as they may respect such lands, and the States which passed such grants are adjusted, the said grants or either of them being at the same time claimed to have originated antecedent to such settlement of jurisdiction, shall on the petition of either party to the Congress of the United States, be finally determined as near as may be in the same manner as is before prescribed for deciding disputes respecting territorial jurisdiction between different States.

The United States in Congress assembled shall also have the sole and exclusive right and power of regulating the alloy and value of coin struck by their own authority, or by that of the respective States

—fixing the standards of weights and measures throughout the United States

—regulating the trade and managing all affairs with the Indians, not members of any of the States, provided that the legislative right of any State within its own limits be not infringed or violated

—establishing or regulating post offices from one State to another, throughout all the United States, and exacting such postage on the papers passing through the same as may be requisite to defray the expenses of the said office—appointing all officers of the land forces, in the service of the United States, excepting regimental officers—appointing all the officers of the naval forces, and commissioning all officers whatever in the service of the United States—making rules for the government and regulation of the said land and naval forces, and directing their operations.

The United States in Congress assembled shall have authority:

—to appoint a committee, to sit in the recess of Congress, to be denominated 'A Committee of the States', and to consist of one delegate from each State; and to appoint such other committees and civil officers as may be necessary for managing the general affairs of the United States under their direction

—to appoint one of their members to preside, provided that no person be allowed to serve in the office of president more than one year in any term of three years; to ascertain the necessary sums of money to be raised for the service of the United States, and to appropriate and apply the same for defraying the public expenses—to borrow money, or emit bills on the credit of the United States, transmitting every half-year to the respective States an account of the sums of money so borrowed or emitted.

—to build and equip a navy

—to agree upon the number of land forces, and to make requisitions from each State for its quota, in proportion to the number of white inhabitants in such State; which requisition shall be binding, and thereupon the legislature of each State shall appoint the regimental officers, raise the men and clothe, arm and equip them in a solid-like manner, at the expense of the United States; and the officers and men so clothed, armed and equipped shall march to the place appointed, and within the time agreed on by the United States in Congress assembled. But if the United States in Congress assembled shall, on consideration of circumstances judge proper that any State should not raise men, or should raise a smaller number of men than the quota thereof, such extra number shall be raised, officered, clothed, armed and equipped in the same manner as the quota of each State, unless the legislature of such State shall judge that such extra number cannot be safely spread out in the same, in which case they shall raise, officer, clothe, arm and equip as many of such extra number as they judge can be safely spared. And the officers and men so clothed, armed, and equipped, shall march to the place appointed, and within the time agreed on by the United States in Congress assembled.

The United States in Congress assembled shall never engage in a war, nor grant letters of marque or reprisal in time of peace, nor enter into any treaties or alliances, nor coin money, nor regulate the value thereof, nor ascertain the sums and expenses necessary for the defense and welfare of the United States, or any of them, nor emit bills, nor borrow money on the credit of the United States, nor appropriate money, nor agree upon the number of vessels of war, to be built or purchased, or the number of land or sea forces to be raised, nor appoint a commander in chief of the army or navy, unless nine States assent to the same: nor shall a question on any other point, except for adjourning from day to day be determined, unless by the votes of the majority of the United States in Congress assembled.

The Congress of the United States shall have power to adjourn to any time within the year, and to any place within the United States, so that no period of adjournment be for a longer duration than the space of six months, and shall publish the journal of their proceedings monthly, except such parts thereof relating to treaties, alliances or military operations, as in their judgement require secrecy; and the yeas and nays of the delegates of each State on any question shall be entered on the journal, when it is desired by any delegates of a State, or any of them, at his or their request shall be furnished with a transcript of the said journal, except such parts as are above excepted, to lay before the legislatures of the several States.

X. The Committee of the States, or any nine of them, shall be authorized to execute, in the recess of Congress, such of the powers of Congress as the United States in Congress assembled, by the consent of the nine States, shall from time to time think expedient to vest them with; provided that no power be delegated to the said Committee, for the exercise of which, by the Articles of Confederation, the voice of nine States in the Congress of the United States assembled be requisite.

XI. Canada acceding to this confederation, and adjoining in the measures of the United States, shall be admitted into, and entitled to all the advantages of this Union; but no other colony shall be admitted into the same, unless such admission be agreed to by nine States.

XII. All bills of credit emitted, monies borrowed, and debts contracted by, or under the authority of Congress, before the assembling of the United States, in pursuance of the present confederation, shall be deemed and considered as a charge against the United States, for payment and satisfaction whereof the said United States, and the public faith are hereby solemnly pledged.

XIII. Every State shall abide by the determination of the United States in Congress assembled, on all questions which by this confederation are submitted to them. And the Articles of this Confederation shall be inviolably observed by every State, and the Union shall be perpetual; nor shall any alteration at any time hereafter be made in any of them; unless such alteration be agreed to in a Congress of the United States, and be afterwards confirmed by the legislatures of every State.

And Whereas it hath pleased the Great Governor of the World to incline the hearts of the legislatures we respectively represent in Congress, to approve of, and to authorize us to ratify the said Articles of Confederation and perpetual Union, Know Ye that we the undersigned delegates, by virtue of the power and authority to us given for that purpose, do by these presents, in the name and in behalf of our respective constituents, fully and entirely ratify and confirm each and every of the said Articles of Confederation and perpetual Union, and all and singular the matters and things therein contained: And we do further solemnly plight and engage the faith of our respective constituents, that they shall abide by the determinations of the United States in Congress assembled, on all questions, which by the said Confederation are submitted to them. And that the Articles thereof shall be inviolably observed by the States we respectively represent, and that the Union shall be perpetual.

In Witness whereof we have hereunto set our hands in Congress. Done at Philadelphia in the State of Pennsylvania the ninth day of July in the Year of our Lord One Thousand Seven Hundred and Seventy-Eight, and in the Third Year of the independence of America.

Finalized by the Continental Congress, November 15, 1777
In force after ratification by Maryland, March 1, 1781

Constitution of the United States *(1787)*

President and Mrs. Calvin Coolidge and others attended this 1924 ceremony when the Constitution was placed in a vault in the Library of Congress.

Preamble

We the People of the United States, in Order to form a more perfect Union, establish Justice, insure domestic Tranquility, provide for the common defence, promote the general Welfare, and secure the Blessings of Liberty to ourselves and our Posterity, do ordain and establish this Constitution for the United States of America.

Article I.

Section 1. All legislative Powers herein granted shall be vested in a Congress of the United States, which shall consist of a Senate and House of Representatives.

Section 2. The House of Representatives shall be composed of Members chosen every second Year by the People of the several States, and the Electors in each State shall have the Qualifications requisite for Electors of the most numerous Branch of the State Legislature.

No Person shall be a Representative who shall not have attained to the Age of twenty five Years, and been seven Years a Citizen of the United States, and who shall not, when elected, be an Inhabitant of that State in which he shall be chosen.

Representatives and direct Taxes shall be apportioned among the several States which may be included within this Union, according to their respective Numbers, which shall be determined by adding to the whole Number of free Persons, including those bound to Service for a Term of Years, and excluding Indians not taxed, three fifths of all other Persons. The actual Enumeration shall be made within three Years after the first Meeting of the Congress of the United States, and within every subsequent Term of ten Years, in such Manner as they shall by Law direct. The number of Representatives shall not exceed one for every thirty Thousand, but each State shall have at Least one Representative; and until such enumeration shall be made, the State of New Hampshire shall be entitled to chuse three, Massachusetts eight, Rhode-Island and Providence Plantations one, Connecticut five, New-York six, New Jersey four, Pennsylvania eight, Delaware one, Maryland six, Virginia ten, North Carolina five, South Carolina five, and Georgia three.

When vacancies happen in the Representation from any State, the Executive Authority thereof shall issue Writs of Election to fill such Vacancies.

The House of Representatives shall chuse their Speaker and other Officers; and shall have the sole Power of Impeachment.

Section 3. The Senate of the United States shall be composed of two Senators from each State, chosen by the Legislature thereof, for six Years; and each Senator shall have one Vote.

Immediately after they shall be assembled in Consequence of the first Election, they shall be divided as equally as may be into three Classes. The Seats of the Senators of the first Class shall be vacated at the Expiration of the second Year, of the second Class at the Expiration of the fourth Year, and of the third Class at the Expiration of the sixth Year, so that one third may be chosen every second Year; and if Vacancies happen by Resignation, or otherwise, during the Recess of the Legislature of any State, the Executive thereof may make temporary Appointments until the next Meeting of the Legislature, which shall then fill such Vacancies.

No Person shall be a Senator who shall not have attained to the Age of thirty Years, and been nine Years a Citizen of the United States, and who shall not, when elected, be an Inhabitant of that State for which he shall be chosen.

The Vice President of the United States shall be President of the Senate, but shall have no Vote, unless they be equally divided.

The Senate shall chuse their other Officers, and also a President pro tempore, in the Absence of the Vice President, or when he shall exercise the Office of President of the United States.

The Senate shall have the sole Power to try all Impeachments. When sitting for that Purpose, they shall be on Oath or Affirmation. When the President of the United States is tried, the Chief Justice shall preside: And no Person shall be convicted without the Concurrence of two thirds of the Members present.

Judgment in Cases of Impeachment shall not extend further than to removal from Office, and disqualification to hold and enjoy any Office of honor, Trust or Profit under the United States: but the Party convicted shall nevertheless be liable and subject to Indictment, Trial, Judgment and Punishment, according to Law.

Section 4. The Times, Places and Manner of holding Elections for Senators and Representatives, shall be prescribed in each State by the Legislature thereof; but the Congress may at any time by Law make or alter such Regulations, except as to the Places of chusing Senators.

The Congress shall assemble at least once in every Year, and such Meeting shall be on the first Monday in December, unless they shall by Law appoint a different Day.

Section 5. Each House shall be the Judge of the Elections, Returns and Qualifications of its own Members, and a Majority of each shall constitute a Quorum to do Business, but a smaller Number may adjourn from day to day, and may be authorized to compel the Attendance of absent Members, in such Manner, and under such Penalties as each House may provide.

Each House may determine the Rules of its Proceedings, punish its Members for disorderly Behaviour, and, with the Concurrence of two thirds, expel a Member.

Each House shall keep a Journal of its Proceedings, and from time to time publish the same, excepting such Parts as may in their Judgment require Secrecy; and the Yeas and Nays of the Members of either House on any question shall, at the Desire of one fifth of those Present, be entered on the Journal.

Neither House, during the Session of Congress, shall, without the Consent of the other, adjourn for more than three days, nor to any other Place than that in which the two Houses shall be sitting.

Section 6. The Senators and Representatives shall receive a Compensation for their Services, to be ascertained by law, and paid out of the Treasury of the United States. They shall in all Cases, except Treason, Felony and Breach of the Peace, be privileged from Arrest during their Attendance at the Session of their respective Houses, and in going to and returning from the same; and for any Speech or Debate in either House, they shall not be questioned in any other Place.

No Senator or Representative shall, during the Time for which he was elected, be appointed to any civil Office under the Authority of the United States, which shall have been created, or the Emoluments whereof shall have been increased during such time; and no Person holding any Office under the United States, shall be a Member of either House during his Continuance in Office.

Section 7. All Bills for raising Revenue shall originate in the House of Representatives; but the Senate may propose or concur with Amendments as on other Bills.

Every Bill which shall have passed the House of Representatives and the Senate, shall, before it becomes a Law, be presented to the President of the United States; If he approve he shall sign it, but if not he shall return it, with his Objections to that House in which it shall have originated, who shall enter the Objections at large on their Journal, and proceed to reconsider it. If after such Reconsideration two thirds of that House shall agree to pass the Bill, it shall be sent, together with the Objections, to the other House, by which it shall likewise be reconsidered, and if approved by two thirds of that House, it shall become a Law. But in all such Cases the Votes of both Houses shall be determined by Yeas and Nays, and the Names of the Persons voting for and against the Bill shall be entered on the Journal of each House respectively. If any Bill shall not be returned by the President within ten Days (Sundays excepted) after it shall have been presented to him, the Same shall be a Law, in like Manner as if he had signed it, unless the Congress by their Adjournment prevent its Return, in which Case it shall not be a Law.

Every Order, Resolution, or Vote to which the Concurrence of the Senate and House of Representatives may be necessary (except on a question of Adjournment) shall be presented to the President of the United States, and before the Same shall take Effect, shall be approved by him, or being disapproved by him, shall be repassed by two thirds of the Senate and House of Representatives, according to the Rules and Limitations prescribed in the Case of a Bill.

Section. 8. The Congress shall have Power To lay and collect Taxes, Duties, Imposts and Excises, to pay the Debts and provide for the common Defence and general Welfare of the United States; but all Duties, Imposts and Excises shall be uniform throughout the United States;

To borrow Money on the credit of the United States;

To regulate Commerce with foreign Nations, and among the several States, and with the Indian Tribes;

To establish an uniform Rule of Naturalization, and uniform Laws on the subject of Bankruptcies throughout the United States;

To coin Money, regulate the Value thereof, and of foreign Coin, and fix the Standard of Weights and Measures;

To provide for the Punishment of counterfeiting the Securities and current Coin of the United States;

To establish Post Offices and post Roads;

To promote the Progress of Science and useful Arts, by securing for limited Times to Authors and Inventors the exclusive Right to their respective Writings and Discoveries;

To constitute Tribunals inferior to the supreme Court;

To define and punish Piracies and Felonies committed on the high Seas, and Offenses against the Law of Nations;

To declare War, grant Letters of Marque and Reprisal, and make Rules concerning Captures on land and Water;

To raise and support Armies, but no Appropriation of Money to that Use shall be for a longer Term than two Years;

To provide and maintain a Navy;

To make Rules for the Government and Regulation of the land and naval Forces;

To provide for calling forth the Militia to execute the Laws of the Union, suppress Insurrections and repel Invasions;

To provide for organizing, arming, and disciplining, the Militia, and for governing such Part of them as may be employed in the Service of the United States, reserving to the States respectively, the Appointment of the Officers, and the Authority of training the Militia according to the discipline prescribed by Congress;

To exercise exclusive Legislation in all Cases whatsoever, over such District (not exceeding ten Miles square) as may, by Cession of particular States, and the Acceptance of Congress, become the Seat of the Government of the United States, and to exercise like Authority over all Places purchased by the Consent of the Legislature of the State in which the Same shall be, for the Erection of Forts, Magazines, Arsenals, dock-Yards and other needful Buildings;—And

To make all Laws which shall be necessary and proper for carrying into Execution the foregoing Powers, and all other Powers vested by this Constitution in the Government of the United States, or in any Department or Officer thereof.

Section 9. The Migration or Importation of such Persons as any of the States now existing shall think proper to admit, shall not be prohibited by the Congress prior to the Year one thousand eight hundred and eight, but a Tax or duty may be imposed on such Importation, not exceeding ten dollars for each Person.

The Privilege of the Writ of Habeas Corpus shall not be suspended, unless when in Cases of Rebellion or Invasion the public Safety may require it.

No Bill of Attainder or ex post facto Law shall be passed.

No Capitation, or other direct, Tax shall be laid, unless in Proportion to the Census or Enumeration herein before directed to be taken.

No Tax or Duty shall be laid on Articles exported from any State.

No Preference shall be given by any Regulation of Commerce or Revenue to the Ports of one State over those of another: nor shall Vessels bound to, or from, one State, be obliged to enter, clear, or pay Duties in another.

No Money shall be drawn from the Treasury, but in Consequence of Appropriations made by Law; and a regular Statement and Account of the Receipts and Expenditures of all public Money shall be published from time to time.

No Title of Nobility shall be granted by the United States: And no Person holding any Office of Profit or Trust under them, shall, without the Consent of the Congress, accept of any present, Emolument, Office, or Title, of any kind whatever, from any King, Prince, or foreign State.

Section 10. No State shall enter into any Treaty, Alliance, or Confederation; grant Letters of Marque and Reprisal; coin Money; emit Bills of Credit; make any Thing but gold and silver Coin a Tender in Payment of Debts; pass any Bill of Attainder, ex post facto Law, or Law impairing the Obligation of Contracts, or grant any Title of Nobility;

No State shall, without the Consent of the Congress, lay any Imposts or Duties on Imports or Exports, except what may be absolutely necessary for executing its inspection Laws: and the net Produce of all Duties and Imposts, laid by any State on Imports or Exports, shall be for the Use of the Treasury of the United States; and all such Laws shall be subject to the Revision and Control of the Congress.

No State shall, without the Consent of Congress, lay any Duty of Tonnage, keep Troops, or Ships of War in time of Peace, enter into any Agreement or Compact with another State, or with a foreign Power, or engage in War, unless actually invaded, or in such imminent Danger as will not admit of delay.

Article II.

Section 1. The executive Power shall be vested in a President of the United States of America. He shall hold his Office during the Term of four Years, and, together with the Vice President, chosen for the same Term, be elected, as follows:

Each State shall appoint, in such Manner as the Legislature thereof may direct, a Number of Electors, equal to the whole Number of Senators and Representatives to which the State may be entitled in the Congress: but no Senator or Representative, or Person holding an Office of Trust or Profit under the United States, shall be appointed an Elector.

The Electors shall meet in their respective States, and vote by Ballot for two Persons, of whom one at least shall not be an Inhabitant of the same State with themselves. And they shall make a List of all the Persons voted for, and of the Number of Votes for each; which List they shall sign and certify, and transmit sealed to the Seat of the Government of the United States, directed to the President of the Senate. The President of the Senate shall, in the Presence of the Senate and House of Representatives, open all the Certificates, and the Votes shall then be counted. The Person having the greatest Number of Votes shall be the President, if such Number be a Majority of the whole Number of Electors appointed; and if there be more than one who have such Majority, and have an equal Number of Votes, then the House of Representatives shall immediately chuse by Ballot one of them for President; and if no Person have a Majority, then from the five highest on the List the said House shall in like Manner chuse the President. But in chusing the President, the Votes shall be taken by States, the Representation from each State having one Vote; A quorum for this Purpose shall consist of a Member or Members from two thirds of the States, and a Majority of all the States shall be necessary to a Choice. In every Case, after the Choice of the President, the Person having the greatest Number of Votes of the Electors shall be the Vice President. But if there should remain two or more who have equal Votes, the Senate shall chuse from them by Ballot the Vice President.

The Congress may determine the Time of chusing the Electors, and the Day on which they shall give their Votes; which Day shall be the same throughout the United States.

No Person except a natural born Citizen, or a Citizen of the United States, at the time of the Adoption of this Constitution, shall be eligible to the Office of President; neither shall any person be eligible to that Office who shall not have attained to the Age of thirty five Years, and been fourteen Years a Resident within the United States.

In Case of the Removal of the President from Office, or of his Death, Resignation, or Inability to discharge the Powers and Duties of the said Office, the Same shall devolve on the Vice President, and the Congress may by Law provide for the Case of Removal, Death, Resignation or Inability, both of the President and Vice President, declaring what Officer shall then act as President, and such Officer shall act accordingly, until the Disability be removed, or a President shall be elected.

The President shall, at stated Times, receive for his Services, a Compensation, which shall neither be increased nor diminished during the Period for which he shall have been elected, and he shall not receive within that Period any other Emolument from the United States, or any of them.

Before he enter on the Execution of his Office, he shall take the following Oath or Affirmation:—"I do solemnly swear (or affirm) that I will faithfully execute the Office of President of the United States, and will to the best of my Ability, preserve, protect and defend the Constitution of the United States."

Section 2. The President shall be Commander in Chief of the Army and Navy of the United States, and of the Militia of the several States, when called into the actual Service of the United States; he may require the Opinion, in writing, of the principal Officer in each of the executive Departments, upon any Subject relating to the Duties of their respective Offices, and he shall have Power to grant Reprieves and Pardons for Offenses against the United States, except in Cases of Impeachment.

He shall have Power, by and with the Advice and Consent of the Senate, to make Treaties, provided two thirds of the Senators present concur; and he shall nominate, and by and with the Advice and Consent of the Senate, shall appoint Ambassadors, other public Ministers and Consuls, Judges of the supreme Court, and all other Officers of the United States, whose Appointments are not herein otherwise provided for, and which shall be established by Law: but the Congress may by law vest the Appointment of such inferior Officers, as they think proper, in the President alone, in the Courts of Law, or in the Heads of Departments.

The President shall have Power to fill up all Vacancies that may happen during the Recess of the Senate, by granting Commissions which shall expire at the End of their next Session.

Section 3. He shall from time to time give to the Congress Information of the State of the Union, and recommend to their Consideration such Measures as he shall judge necessary and expedient; he may, on extraordinary Occasions, convene both Houses, or either of them and in Case of Disagreement between them with Respect to the Time of Adjournment, he may adjourn them to such Time as he shall think proper; he shall receive Ambassadors and other public Ministers; he shall take Care that the Laws be faithfully executed, and shall Commission all the Officers of the United States.

Section 4. The President, Vice President and all civil Officers of the United States, shall be removed from Office on Impeachment for, and Conviction of, Treason, Bribery, or other high Crimes and Misdemeanors.

Article III.

Section 1. The judicial Power of the United States, shall be vested in one supreme Court, and in such inferior Courts as the Congress may from time to time ordain and establish. The Judges, both of the supreme and inferior Courts, shall hold their Offices during good Behaviour, and shall at stated Times, receive for their Services, a Compensation, which shall not be diminished during their Continuance in Office.

Section 2. The judicial Power shall extend to all Cases, in Law and Equity, arising under this Constitution, the Laws of the United States, and Treaties made, or which shall be made, under their Authority, —to all Cases affecting Ambassadors, other public Ministers and Consuls; —to all Cases of admiralty and maritime Jurisdiction, —to Controversies to which the United States shall be a Party; —to Controversies between two or more States, —between a State and Citizens of another State; between Citizens of different States,— between Citizens of the same State claiming Lands under Grants of different States, and between a State or the Citizens thereof, and foreign States, Citizens or Subjects.

In all Cases affecting Ambassadors, other public Ministers and Consuls, and those in which a State shall be Party, the supreme Court shall have original Jurisdiction. In all the other Cases before mentioned, the supreme Court shall have appellate Jurisdiction, both as to Law and Fact, with such Exceptions, and under such Regulations as the Congress shall make.

The Trial of all Crimes, except in Cases of Impeachment; shall be by Jury, and such Trial shall be held in the State where the said Crimes shall have been committed but when not committed within any State, the Trial shall be at such Place or Places as the Congress may by Law have directed.

Section 3. Treason against the United States, shall consist only in levying War against them, or in adhering to their Enemies, giving them Aid and Comfort. No Person shall be convicted of Treason unless on the Testimony of two Witnesses to the same overt Act, or on Confession in open Court.

The Congress shall have Power to declare the Punishment of Treason, but no Attainder of Treason shall work Corruption of Blood, or Forfeiture except during the Life of the Person attainted.

Article IV.

Section 1. Full Faith and Credit shall be given in each State to the public Acts, Records, and judicial Proceedings of every other State; And the Congress may by general Laws prescribe the Manner in which such Acts, Records and Proceedings shall be proved, and the Effect thereof.

Section 2. The Citizens of each State shall be entitled to all Privileges and Immunities of Citizens in the several States.

A Person charged in any State with Treason, Felony, or other Crime, who shall flee from Justice, and be found in another State, shall on Demand of the executive Authority of the State from which he fled, be delivered up, to be removed to the State having Jurisdiction of the Crime.

No Person held to Service or Labour in one State, under the Laws thereof, escaping into another, shall, in Consequence of any Law or Regulation therein, be discharged from such Service or Labour, but shall be delivered up on Claim of the party to whom such Service or Labour may be due.

Section 3. New States may be admitted by the Congress into this Union; but no new State shall be formed or erected within the Jurisdiction of any other State; nor any State be formed by the Junction of two or more States, or Parts of States, without the Consent of the Legislatures of the States concerned as well as of the Congress.

The Congress shall have power to dispose of and make all needful Rules and Regulations respecting the Territory or other Property belonging to the United States; and nothing in this Constitution shall be construed as to Prejudice any Claims of the United States, or of any particular State.

Section 4. The United States shall guarantee to every State in this Union a Republican Form of Government, and shall protect each of them against Invasion; and on Application of the Legislature, or of the Executive (when the Legislature cannot be convened) against domestic Violence.

Article V.

The Congress, whenever two thirds of both houses shall deem it necessary, shall propose Amendments to this Constitution, or, on the Application of the Legislatures of two thirds of the several States, shall call a Convention for proposing Amendments, which in either Case, shall be valid to all Intents and Purposes, as Part of this Constitution, when ratified by the Legislatures of three fourths of the several States, or by Conventions in three fourths thereof, as the one or the other Mode of Ratification may be proposed by the Congress; Provided that no Amendment which may be made prior to the Year One thousand eight hundred and eight shall in any Manner affect the first and fourth Clauses in the Ninth Section of the first Article; and that no State, without its Consent, shall be deprived of its equal Suffrage in the Senate.

Article VI.

All Debts contracted and Engagements entered into, before the Adoption of this Constitution, shall be as valid against the United States under this Constitution, as under the Confederation.

This Constitution, and the Laws of the United States which shall be made in Pursuance thereof; and all Treaties made, or which shall be made, under the Authority of the United States, shall be the supreme Law of the Land; and the Judges in every State shall be bound thereby, any Thing in the Constitution or Laws of any State to the Contrary notwithstanding.

The Senators and Representatives before mentioned, and the Members of the several State Legislatures, and all executive and judicial Officers, both of the United States and of the several States, shall be bound by Oath or Affirmation, to support this Constitution; but no religious Test shall ever be required as a Qualification to any Office or public Trust under the United States.

Article VII.

The Ratification of the Conventions of nine States, shall be sufficient for the Establishment of this Constitution between the States so ratifying the Same.

Done in Convention by the Unanimous Consent of the States present the Seventeenth Day of September in the Year of our Lord one thousand seven hundred and Eighty seven and of the Independence of the United States of America the Twelfth, In Witness whereof We have hereunto subscribed our Names,

G.⁰ Washington—Presd.t and deputy from Virginia

New Hampshire John Langdon, Nicholas Gilman

Massachusetts Nathaniel Gorham, Rufus King

Connecticut Wm. Saml. Johnson, Roger Sherman

New York Alexander Hamilton

New Jersey Wil: Livingston, David Brearley, Wm. Paterson, Jona: Dayton

Pennsylvania B Franklin, Thomas Mifflin, Robt Morris, Geo. Clymer, Thos. FitzSimons, Jared Ingersoll, James Wilson, Gouv Morris

Delaware Geo: Read, Gunning Bedford jun, John Dickinson, Richard Bassett, Jaco: Broom

Maryland James McHenry, Dan of St. Thos. Jenifer, Danl Carroll

Virginia John Blair, James Madison Jr.

North Carolina Wm. Blount, Richd. Dobbs Spaight, Hu Williamson

South Carolina J. Rutledge, Charles Cotesworth Pinckney, Charles Pinckney, Pierce Butler

Georgia William Few, Abr Baldwin

Attest William Jackson, Secretary

The Bill of Rights (Amendments I-X)
Passed by Congress September 25, 1789. Ratified December 15, 1791.

Amendment I
Congress shall make no law respecting an establishment of religion, or prohibiting the free exercise thereof; or abridging the freedom of speech, or of the press; or the right of the people peaceably to assemble, and to petition the Government for a redress of grievances.

Amendment II
A well regulated Militia, being necessary to the security of a free State, the right of the people to keep and bear Arms, shall not be infringed.

Amendment III
No Soldier shall, in time of peace be quartered in any house, without the consent of the Owner, nor in time of war, but in a manner to be prescribed by law.

Amendment IV

The right of the people to be secure in their persons, houses, papers, and effects, against unreasonable searches and seizures, shall not be violated, and no Warrants shall issue, but upon probable cause, supported by Oath or affirmation, and particularly describing the place to be searched, and the persons or things to be seized.

Amendment V

No person shall be held to answer for a capital, or otherwise infamous crime, unless on a presentment or indictment of a Grand Jury, except in cases arising in the land or naval forces, or in the Militia, when in actual service in time of War or public danger; nor shall any person be subject for the same offence to be twice put in jeopardy of life or limb; nor shall be compelled in any criminal case to be a witness against himself, nor be deprived of life, liberty, or property, without due process of law; nor shall private property be taken for public use, without just compensation.

Amendment VI

In all criminal prosecutions, the accused shall enjoy the right to a speedy and public trial, by an impartial jury of the State and district wherein the crime shall have been committed, which district shall have been previously ascertained by law, and to be informed of the nature and cause of the accusation; to be confronted with the witnesses against him; to have compulsory process for obtaining witnesses in his favor, and to have the Assistance of Counsel for his defence.

Amendment VII

In Suits at common law, where the value in controversy shall exceed twenty dollars, the right of trial by jury shall be preserved, and no fact tried by a jury, shall be otherwise re-examined in any Court of the United States, than according to the rules of the common law.

Amendment VIII

Excessive bail shall not be required, nor excessive fines imposed, nor cruel and unusual punishments inflicted.

Amendment IX

The enumeration in the Constitution, of certain rights, shall not be construed to deny or disparage others retained by the people.

Amendment X

The powers not delegated to the United States by the Constitution, nor prohibited by it to the States, are reserved to the States respectively, or to the people.

Amendment XI
Passed by Congress March 4, 1794. Ratified February 7, 1795.

The Judicial power of the United States shall not be construed to extend to any suit in law or equity, commenced or prosecuted against one of the United States by Citizens of another State, or by Citizens or Subjects of any Foreign State.

Amendment XII
Passed by Congress December 9, 1803. Ratified June 15, 1804.

The Electors shall meet in their respective states and vote by ballot for President and Vice-President, one of whom, at least, shall not be an inhabitant of the same state with themselves; they shall name in their ballots the person voted for as President, and in distinct ballots the person voted for as Vice-President, and they shall make distinct lists of all persons voted for as President, and of all persons voted for as Vice-President, and of the number of votes for each, which lists they shall sign and certify, and transmit sealed to the seat of the government of the United States, directed to the President of the Senate;—the President of the Senate shall, in the presence of the Senate and House of Representatives, open all the certificates and the votes shall then be counted;—The person having the greatest number of votes for President, shall be the President, if such number be a majority of the whole number of Electors appointed; and if no person have such majority, then from the persons having the highest numbers not exceeding three on the list of those voted for as President, the House of Representatives shall choose immediately, by ballot, the President. But in choosing the President, the votes shall be taken by states, the representation from each state having one vote; a quorum for this purpose shall consist of a member or members from two-thirds of the states, and a majority of all the states shall be necessary to a choice. And if the House of Representatives shall not choose a President whenever the right of choice shall devolve upon them, before the fourth day of March next following, then the Vice-President shall act as President, as in case of the death or other constitutional disability of the President. The person having the greatest number of votes as Vice-President, shall be the Vice-President, if such number be a majority of the whole number of Electors appointed, and if no person have a majority, then from the two highest numbers on the list, the Senate shall choose the Vice-President; a quorum for the purpose shall consist of two-thirds of the whole number of Senators, and a majority of the whole number shall be necessary to a choice. But no person constitutionally ineligible to the office of President shall be eligible to that of Vice-President of the United States.

Amendment XIII

Passed by Congress January 31, 1865. Ratified December 6, 1865.

Section 1. Neither slavery nor involuntary servitude, except as a punishment for crime whereof the party shall have been duly convicted, shall exist within the United States, or any place subject to their jurisdiction.

Section 2. Congress shall have power to enforce this article by appropriate legislation.

Amendment XIV

Passed by Congress June 13, 1866. Ratified July 9, 1868.

Section 1. All persons born or naturalized in the United States, and subject to the jurisdiction thereof, are citizens of the United States and of the State wherein they reside. No State shall make or enforce any law which shall abridge the privileges or immunities of citizens of the United States; nor shall any State deprive any person of life, liberty, or property, without due process of law; nor deny to any person within its jurisdiction the equal protection of the laws.

Section 2. Representatives shall be apportioned among the several States according to their respective numbers, counting the whole number of persons in each State, excluding Indians not taxed. But when the right to vote at any election for the choice of electors for President and Vice-President of the United States, Representatives in Congress, the Executive and Judicial officers of a State, or the members of the Legislature thereof, is denied to any of the male inhabitants of such State, being twenty-one years of age, and citizens of the United States, or in any way abridged, except for participation in rebellion, or other crime, the basis of representation therein shall be reduced in the proportion which the number of such male citizens shall bear to the whole number of male citizens twenty-one years of age in such State.

Section 3. No person shall be a Senator or Representative in Congress, or elector of President and Vice-President, or hold any office, civil or military, under the United States, or under any State, who, having previously taken an oath, as a member of Congress, or as an officer of the United States, or as a member of any State legislature, or as an executive or judicial officer of any State, to support the Constitution of the United States, shall have engaged in insurrection or rebellion against the same, or given aid or comfort to the enemies thereof. But Congress may by a vote of two-thirds of each House, remove such disability.

Section 4. The validity of the public debt of the United States, authorized by law, including debts incurred for payment of pensions and bounties for services in suppressing insurrection or rebellion, shall not be questioned. But neither the United States nor any State shall assume or pay any debt or obligation incurred in aid of insurrection or rebellion against the United States, or any claim for the loss or emancipation of any slave; but all such debts, obligations and claims shall be held illegal and void.

Section 5. The Congress shall have the power to enforce, by appropriate legislation, the provisions of this article.

Amendment XV

Passed by Congress February 26, 1869. Ratified February 3, 1870.

Section 1. The right of citizens of the United States to vote shall not be denied or abridged by the United States or by any State on account of race, color, or previous condition of servitude.

Section 2. The Congress shall have the power to enforce this article by appropriate legislation.

Amendment XVI

Passed by Congress July 2, 1909. Ratified February 3, 1913.

The Congress shall have power to lay and collect taxes on incomes, from whatever source derived, without apportionment among the several States, and without regard to any census or enumeration.

Amendment XVII

Passed by Congress May 13, 1912. Ratified April 8, 1913.

The Senate of the United States shall be composed of two Senators from each State, elected by the people thereof, for six years; and each Senator shall have one vote. The electors in each State shall have the qualifications requisite for electors of the most numerous branch of the State legislature.

When vacancies happen in the representation of any State in the Senate, the executive authority of such State shall issue writs of election to fill such vacancies: *Provided,* That the legislature of any State may empower the executive thereof to make temporary appointments until the people fill the vacancies by election as the legislature may direct.

This amendment shall not be so construed as to affect the election or term of any Senator chosen before it becomes valid as part of the Constitution.

Amendment XVIII

Passed by Congress December 18, 1917. Ratified January 16, 1919. Repealed by Amendment XXI.

Section 1. After one year from the ratification of this article the manufacture, sale, or transportation of intoxicating liquors within, the importation thereof into, or the exportation thereof from the United States and all territory subject to the jurisdiction thereof for beverage purposes is hereby prohibited.

Section 2. The Congress and the several States shall have concurrent power to enforce this article by appropriate legislation.

Section 3. This article shall be inoperative unless it shall have been ratified as an amendment to the Constitution by the legislatures of the several States, as provided in the Constitution, within seven years from the date of the submission hereof to the States by the Congress.

Amendment XIX
Passed by Congress June 4, 1919. Ratified August 18, 1920.

The right of citizens of the United States to vote shall not be denied or abridged by the United States or by any State on account of sex.

Congress shall have power to enforce this article by appropriate legislation.

Amendment XX
Passed by Congress March 2, 1932. Ratified January 23, 1933.

Section 1. The terms of the President and the Vice President shall end at noon on the 20th day of January, and the terms of Senators and Representatives at noon on the 3d day of January, of the years in which such terms would have ended if this article had not been ratified; and the terms of their successors shall then begin.

Section 2. The Congress shall assemble at least once in every year, and such meeting shall begin at noon on the 3d day of January, unless they shall by law appoint a different day.

Section 3. If, at the time fixed for the beginning of the term of the President, the President elect shall have died, the Vice President elect shall become President. If a President shall not have been chosen before the time fixed for the beginning of his term, or if the President elect shall have failed to qualify, then the Vice President elect shall act as President until a President shall have qualified; and the Congress may by law provide for the case wherein neither a President elect nor a Vice President shall have qualified, declaring who shall then act as President, or the manner in which one who is to act shall be selected, and such person shall act accordingly until a President or Vice President shall have qualified.

Section 4. The Congress may by law provide for the case of the death of any of the persons from whom the House of Representatives may choose a President whenever the right of choice shall have devolved upon them, and for the case of the death of any of the persons from whom the Senate may choose a Vice President whenever the right of choice shall have devolved upon them.

Section 5. Sections 1 and 2 shall take effect on the 15th day of October following the ratification of this article.

Section 6. This article shall be inoperative unless it shall have been ratified as an amendment to the Constitution by the legislatures of three-fourths of the several States within seven years from the date of its submission.

Amendment XXI
Passed by Congress February 20, 1933. Ratified December 5, 1933.

Section 1. The eighteenth article of amendment to the Constitution of the United States is hereby repealed.

Section 2. The transportation or importation into any State, Territory, or Possession of the United States for delivery or use therein of intoxicating liquors, in violation of the laws thereof, is hereby prohibited.

Section 3. This article shall be inoperative unless it shall have been ratified as an amendment to the Constitution by conventions in the several States, as provided in the Constitution, within seven years from the date of the submission hereof to the States by the Congress.

Amendment XXII
Passed by Congress March 21, 1947. Ratified February 27, 1951.

Section 1. No person shall be elected to the office of the President more than twice, and no person who has held the office of President, or acted as President, for more than two years of a term to which some other person was elected President shall be elected to the office of President more than once. But this Article shall not apply to any person holding the office of President when this Article was proposed by Congress, and shall not prevent any person who may be holding the office of President, or acting as President, during the term within which this Article becomes operative from holding the office of President or acting as President during the remainder of such term.

Section 2. This article shall be inoperative unless it shall have been ratified as an amendment to the Constitution by the legislatures of three-fourths of the several States within seven years from the date of its submission to the States by the Congress.

Amendment XXIII
Passed by Congress June 16, 1960. Ratified March 29, 1961.

Section 1. The District constituting the seat of Government of the United States shall appoint in such manner as Congress may direct:

A number of electors of President and Vice President equal to the whole number of Senators and Representatives in Congress to which the District would be entitled if it were a State, but in no event more than the least populous State; they shall be in addition to those appointed by the States, but they shall be considered, for the purposes of the election of President and Vice President, to be electors appointed by a State; and they shall meet in the District and perform such duties as provided by the twelfth article of amendment.

Section 2. The Congress shall have power to enforce this article by appropriate legislation.

Amendment XXIV

Passed by Congress August 27, 1962. Ratified January 23, 1964.

Section 1. The right of citizens of the United States to vote in any primary or other election for President or Vice President, for electors for President or Vice President, or for Senator or Representative in Congress, shall not be denied or abridged by the United States or any State by reason of failure to pay poll tax or other tax.

Section 2. The Congress shall have power to enforce this article by appropriate legislation.

Amendment XXV

Passed by Congress July 6, 1965. Ratified February 10, 1967.

Section 1. In case of the removal of the President from office or of his death or resignation, the Vice President shall become President.

Section 2. Whenever there is a vacancy in the office of the Vice President, the President shall nominate a Vice President who shall take office upon confirmation by a majority vote of both Houses of Congress.

Section 3. Whenever the President transmits to the President pro tempore of the Senate and the Speaker of the House of Representatives his written declaration that he is unable to discharge the powers and duties of his office, and until he transmits to them a written declaration to the contrary, such powers and duties shall be discharged by the Vice President as Acting President.

Section 4. Whenever the Vice President and a majority of either the principal officers of the executive departments or of such other body as Congress may by law provide, transmit to the President pro tempore of the Senate and the Speaker of the House of Representatives their written declaration that the President is unable to discharge the powers and duties of his office, the Vice President shall immediately assume the powers and duties of the office as Acting President.

Thereafter, when the President transmits to the President pro tempore of the Senate and the Speaker of the House of Representatives his written declaration that no inability exists, he shall resume the powers and duties of his office unless the Vice President and a majority of either the principal officers of the executive departments or of such other body as Congress may by law provide, transmit within four days to the President pro tempore of the Senate and the Speaker of the House of Representatives their written declaration that the President is unable to discharge the powers and duties of his office. Thereupon Congress shall decide the issue, assembling within forty-eight hours for that purpose if not in session. If the Congress, within twenty-one days after receipt of the latter written declaration, or, if Congress is not in session, within twenty-one days after Congress is required to assemble, determines by two-thirds vote of both Houses that the President is unable to discharge the powers and duties of his office, the Vice President shall continue to discharge the same as Acting President; otherwise, the President shall resume the powers and duties of his office.

Amendment XXVI
Passed by Congress March 23, 1971. Ratified July 1, 1971.

Section 1. The right of citizens of the United States, who are eighteen years of age or older, to vote shall not be denied or abridged by the United States or by any State on account of age.

Section 2. The Congress shall have power to enforce this article by appropriate legislation.

Amendment XXVII
Originally proposed September 25, 1789. Ratified May 7, 1992.

No law, varying the compensation for the services of the Senators and Representatives, shall take effect, until an election of representatives shall have intervened.

Twelve Tables of Roman Law (excerpt)
(c. 451 BC)

If he (plaintiff) summon him (defendant) into court, he shall go. If he does not go, (plaintiff) shall call witnesses. Then only he shall take him by force. If he refuses or flees, he (plaintiff) shall lay hands on him. If disease or age is an impediment, he shall grant him a team (of oxen). He shall not spread with cushions the covered carriage if he does not wish to.

Whoever is in need of evidence, he shall go on every third day to call out loud before the doorway of the witness.

A dreadfully deformed child shall be killed.

Our ancestors saw fit that females, by reason of levity of disposition, shall remain in guardianship, even when they have attained their majority.

A spendthrift is forbidden to exercise administration over his own goods.

If any person has sung or composed against another person a song such as was causing slander or insult . . . he shall be clubbed to death.

If a person has maimed another's limb, let there be retaliation in kind, unless he agrees to make compensation with him.

Whoever is convicted of speaking false witness shall be flung from the Tarpeian Rock.

No person shall hold meetings in the City at night.

The penalty shall be capital punishment for a judge or arbiter legally appointed who has been found guilty of receiving a bribe for giving a decision.

Putting to death . . . of any man who has not been convicted, whosoever he might be, is forbidden.

Marriage shall not take place between a patrician and a plebeian.

Whatever the People has last ordained shall be held as binding by law.

Magna Carta (excerpt) *(1215)*

Preamble

John, by the grace of God, king of England, lord of Ireland, duke of Normandy and Aquitaine, and count of Anjou, to the archbishop, bishops, abbots, earls, barons, justiciaries, foresters, sheriffs, stewards, servants, and to all his bailiffs and liege subjects, greetings. Know that, having regard to God and for the salvation of our soul, and those of all our ancestors and heirs, and unto the honor of God and the advancement of his holy Church and for the rectifying of our realm, we have granted as underwritten by advice of our venerable fathers, Stephen, archbishop of Canterbury, primate of all England and cardinal of the holy Roman Church, [and various named archbishops and earls], our liegemen.

1. In the first place we have granted to God, and by this our present charter confirmed for us and our heirs forever that the English Church shall be free, and shall have her rights entire, and her liberties inviolate; and we will that it be thus observed; which is apparent from this that the freedom of elections, which is reckoned most important and very essential to the English Church, we, of our pure and unconstrained will, did grant, and did by our charter confirm and did obtain the ratification of the same from our lord, Pope Innocent III, before the quarrel arose between us and our barons: and this we will observe, and our will is that it be observed in good faith by our heirs forever. We have also granted to all freemen of our kingdom, for us and our heirs forever, all the underwritten liberties, to be had and held by them and their heirs, of us and our heirs forever. . . .

9. Neither we nor our bailiffs will seize any land or rent for any debt, as long as the chattels of the debtor are sufficient to repay the debt; nor shall the sureties of the debtor be distrained

so long as the principal debtor is able to satisfy the debt; and if the principal debtor shall fail to pay the debt, having nothing wherewith to pay it, then the sureties shall answer for the debt; and let them have the lands and rents of the debtor, if they desire them, until they are indemnified for the debt which they have paid for him, unless the principal debtor can show proof that he is discharged thereof as against the said sureties. . . .

12. No scutage [monetary payments to replace military service] nor aid [tax] shall be imposed on our kingdom, unless by common counsel of our kingdom, except for ransoming our person, for making our eldest son a knight, and for once marrying our eldest daughter; and for these there shall not be levied more than a reasonable aid. In like manner it shall be done concerning aids from the city of London.

13. And the city of London shall have all its ancient liberties and free customs, as well by land as by water; furthermore, we decree and grant that all other cities, boroughs, towns, and ports shall have all their liberties and free customs.

14. And for obtaining the common counsel of the kingdom anent the assessing of an aid (except in the three cases aforesaid) or of a scutage, we will cause to be summoned the archbishops, bishops, abbots, earls, and greater barons, severally by our letters; and we will moreover cause to be summoned generally, through our sheriffs and bailiffs, and others who hold of us in chief, for a fixed date, namely, after the expiry of at least forty days, and at a fixed place; and in all letters of such summons we will specify the reason of the summons. And when the summons has thus been made, the business shall proceed on the day appointed, according to the counsel of such as are present, although not all who were summoned have come. . . .

20. A freeman shall not be amerced [fined or punished] for a slight offense, except in accordance with the degree of the offense; and for a grave offense he shall be amerced in accordance with the gravity of the offense, yet saving always his "contentment"; and a merchant in the same way, saving his "merchandise"; and a villein shall be amerced in the same way, saving his "wainage" if they have fallen into our mercy: and none of the aforesaid amercements shall be imposed except by the oath of honest men of the neighborhood.

21. Earls and barons shall not be amerced except through their peers, and only in accordance with the degree of the offense. . . .

28. No constable or other bailiff of ours shall take corn or other provisions from anyone without immediately tendering money therefor, unless he can have postponement thereof by permission of the seller.

29. No constable shall compel any knight to give money in lieu of castle-guard, when he is willing to perform it in his own person, or (if he himself cannot do it from any reasonable cause) then by another responsible man. Further, if we have led or sent him upon military service, he shall be relieved from guard in proportion to the time during which he has been on service because of us.

30. No sheriff or bailiff of ours, or other person, shall take the horses or carts of any freeman for transport duty, against the will of the said freeman.

31. Neither we nor our bailiffs shall take, for our castles or for any other work of ours, wood which is not ours, against the will of the owner of that wood.

32. We will not retain beyond one year and one day, the lands of those who have been convicted of felony, and the lands shall thereafter be handed over to the lords of the fiefs. . . .

35. Let there be one measure of wine throughout our whole realm; and one measure of ale; and one measure of corn, to wit, "the London quarter"; and one width of cloth (whether dyed, or russet, or "halberget"), to wit, two ells within the selvedges; of weights also let it be as of measures. . . .

38. No bailiff for the future shall, upon his own unsupported complaint, put anyone to his "law" without credible witnesses brought for this purpose. . . .

40. To no one will we sell, to no one will we refuse or delay, right or justice.

41. All merchants shall have safe and secure exit from England, and entry to England, with the right to tarry there and to move about as well by land as by water, for buying and selling by the ancient and right customs, quit from all evil tolls, except (in time of war) such merchants as are of the land at war with us. And if such are found in our land at the beginning of the war, they shall be detained, without injury to their bodies or goods, until information be received by us, or by our chief justiciar, how the merchants of our land found in the land at war with us are treated; and if our men are safe there, the others shall be safe in our land.

The White Cliffs of Dover, England

42. It shall be lawful in future for anyone (excepting always those imprisoned or outlawed in accordance with the law of the kingdom, and natives of any country at war with us, and merchants, who shall be treated as if above provided) to leave our kingdom and to return, safe and secure by land and water, except for a short period in time of war, on grounds of public policy—reserving always the allegiance due to us. . . .

45. We will appoint as justices, constables, sheriffs, or bailiffs only such as know the law of the realm and mean to observe it well. . . .

54. No one shall be arrested or imprisoned upon the appeal of a woman, for the death of any other than her husband. . . .

61. Since, moreover, for God and the amendment of our kingdom and for the better allaying of the quarrel that has arisen between us and our barons, we have granted all these

concessions, desirous that they should enjoy them in complete and firm endurance forever, we give and grant to them the underwritten security, namely, that the barons choose five and twenty barons of the kingdom, whomsoever they will, who shall be bound with all their might, to observe and hold, and cause to be observed, the peace and liberties we have granted and confirmed to them by this our present Charter, so that if we, or our justiciar, or our bailiffs or any one of our officers, shall in anything be at fault towards anyone, or shall have broken any one of the articles of this peace or of this security, and the offense be notified to four barons of the foresaid five and twenty, the said four barons shall repair to us (or our justiciar, if we are out of the realm) and, laying the transgression before us, petition to have that transgression redressed without delay. And if we shall not have corrected the transgression (or, in the event of our being out of the realm, if our justiciar shall not have corrected it) within forty days, reckoning from the time it has been intimated to us (or to our justiciar, if we should be out of the realm), the four barons aforesaid shall refer that matter to the rest of the five and twenty barons, and those five and twenty barons shall, together with the community of the whole realm, distrain and distress us in all possible ways, namely, by seizing our castles, lands, possessions, and in any other way they can, until redress has been obtained as they deem fit, saving harmless our own person, and the persons of our queen and children; and when redress has been obtained, they shall resume their old relations towards us.

62. And all the will, hatreds, and bitterness that have arisen between us and our men, clergy and lay, from the date of the quarrel, we have completely remitted and pardoned to everyone. Moreover, all trespasses occasioned by the said quarrel, from Easter in the sixteenth year of our reign till the restoration of peace, we have fully remitted to all, both clergy and laymen, and completely forgiven, as far as pertains to us. And on this head, we have caused to be made for them letters testimonial patent of the lord Stephen, archbishop of Canterbury, of the lord Henry, archbishop of Dublin, of the bishops aforesaid, and of Master Pandulf as touching this security and the concessions aforesaid.

63. Wherefore we will and firmly order that the English Church be free, and that the men in our kingdom have and hold all the aforesaid liberties, rights, and concessions, well and peaceably, freely and quietly, fully and wholly, for themselves and their heirs, of us and our heirs, in all respects and in all places forever, as is aforesaid. An oath, moreover, has been taken, as well on our part as on the part of the barons, that all these conditions aforesaid shall be kept in good faith and without evil intent.

Given under our hand—the above named and many others being witnesses—in the meadow which is called Runnymede, between Windsor and Staines, on the fifteenth day of June, in the seventeenth year of our reign.

On the Divine Right of Kings (excerpt)
James I of England (1609)

King James presented this speech to Parliament in 1609.

King James I

The state of monarchy is the supremest thing upon earth. . . . Kings are justly called gods, for that they exercise a manner or resemblance of divine power upon earth. For if you will consider the attributes to God, you shall see how they agree in the person of a king. God has power to create, or destroy, make, or unmake at his pleasure, to give life, or send death, to judge all, and to be judged nor accountable to none: to raise low things, and to make high things low at his pleasure, and to God are both soul and body due. And the like power have Kings; they make and unmake their subjects: they have power of raising, and casting down: of life, and of death: judges over all their subjects, and in all causes, and yet accountable to none but God only.

Now in these our times we are to distinguish between the state of kings in their first original, and between the state of kings and monarchs, that do at this time govern in civil kingdoms. . . . In the first original of kings, whereof some had their beginning by conquest, and some by election of the people, their wills at that time served for law; Yet how soon kingdoms began to be settled in civility and policy, then did kings set down their minds by laws. . . . And I am sure to go to my grave with that reputation and comfort, that never king was in all his time more careful to have his laws duly observed, and himself to govern thereafter, than I.

I conclude then this point touching the power of kings, with this axiom of divinity, that as to dispute what God may do, is blasphemy. . . so is it sedition in subjects, to dispute what a king may do in the height of his power: But just kings will ever be willing to declare what they will do, if they will not incur the curse of God. I will not be content that my power be disputed upon: but I shall ever be willing to make the reason appear of all my doings, and rule my actions according to my laws. . . . Therefore all kings that are not tyrants, or perjured, will be glad to bound themselves within the limits of their laws; and they that persuade them the contrary, are vipers, and pests, both against them and the Commonwealth.

English Bill of Rights (excerpt) *(1689)*

When the Catholic King James II fled from England, Parliament declared that he had abdicated and offered the throne to William and Mary. The next year, the new monarchs signed a Bill of Rights, guaranteeing certain protections to individuals and insuring that a Catholic could not assume the throne.

[. . . Parliament hereby declares:]

That the pretended power of suspending the laws or the execution of laws by regal authority without consent of Parliament is illegal;

That the pretended power of dispensing with laws or the execution of laws by regal authority, as it hath been assumed and exercised of late, is illegal;

That the commission for erecting the late Court of Commissioners for Ecclesiastical Causes, and all other commissions and courts of like nature, are illegal and pernicious;

William and Mary of England

That levying money for or to the use of the Crown by pretence of prerogative, without grant of Parliament, for longer time, or in other manner than the same is or shall be granted, is illegal;

That it is the right of the subjects to petition the king, and all commitments and prosecutions for such petitioning are illegal;

That the raising or keeping a standing army within the kingdom in time of peace, unless it be with consent of Parliament, is against law;

That the subjects which are Protestants may have arms for their defence suitable to their conditions and as allowed by law;

That election of members of Parliament ought to be free;

That the freedom of speech and debates or proceedings in Parliament ought not to be impeached or questioned in any court or place out of Parliament;

That excessive bail ought not to be required, nor excessive fines imposed, nor cruel and unusual punishments inflicted;

That jurors ought to be duly impanelled and returned, and jurors which pass upon men in trials for high treason ought to be freeholders;

That all grants and promises of fines and forfeitures of particular persons before conviction are illegal and void;

And that for redress of all grievances, and for the amending, strengthening and preserving of the laws, Parliaments ought to be held frequently.

. . .

And whereas it hath been found by experience that it is inconsistent with the safety and welfare of this Protestant kingdom to be governed by a popish prince, or by any king or queen marrying a papist, the said Lords Spiritual and Temporal and Commons do further pray that it may be enacted, that all and every person and persons that is, are or shall be reconciled to or shall hold communion with the see or Church of Rome, or shall profess the popish religion, or shall marry a papist, shall be excluded and be for ever incapable to inherit, possess or enjoy the crown and government of this realm and Ireland and the dominions thereunto belonging or any part of the same, or to have, use or exercise any regal power, authority or jurisdiction within the same. . . .

Two Treatises of Government (excerpt)
John Locke (1690)

CHAP. IX. Of the Ends of Political Society and Government.

Sec. 123. If man in the state of nature be so free, as has been said; if he be absolute lord of his own person and possessions, equal to the greatest, and subject to no body, why will he part with his freedom? why will he give up this empire, and subject himself to the dominion and controul of any other power? To which it is obvious to answer, that though in the state of nature he hath such a right, yet the enjoyment of it is very uncertain, and constantly exposed to the invasion of others: for all being kings as much as he, every man his equal, and the greater part no strict observers of equity and justice, the enjoyment of the property he has in this state is very unsafe, very unsecure. This makes him willing to quit a condition, which, however free, is full of fears and continual dangers: and it is not without reason, that he seeks out, and is willing to join in society with others, who are already united, or have a mind to unite, for the mutual preservation of their lives, liberties and estates, which I call by the general name, property.

Sec. 124. The great and chief end, therefore, of men's uniting into commonwealths, and putting themselves under government, is the preservation of their property. To which in the state of nature there are many things wanting. First, There wants an established, settled, known law, received and allowed by common consent to be the standard of right and wrong, and the common measure to decide all controversies between them: for though the law of nature be plain and intelligible to all rational creatures; yet men being biased by their interest, as well as ignorant for want of study of it, are not apt to allow of it as a law binding to them in the application of it to their particular cases.

Sec. 125. Secondly, In the state of nature there wants a known and indifferent judge, with authority to determine all differences according to the established law: for every one in that state being both judge and executioner of the law of nature, men being partial to themselves, passion and revenge is very apt to carry them too far, and with too much heat, in their own cases; as well as negligence, and unconcernedness, to make them too remiss in other men's.

Sec. 126. Thirdly, In the state of nature there often wants power to back and support the sentence when right, and to give it due execution. They who by any injustice offended, will seldom fail, where they are able, by force to make good their injustice; such resistance many times makes the punishment dangerous, and frequently destructive, to those who attempt it.

Sec. 127. Thus mankind, notwithstanding all the privileges of the state of nature, being but in an ill condition, while they remain in it, are quickly driven into society. Hence it comes to pass, that we seldom find any number of men live any time together in this state. The inconveniencies that they are therein exposed to, by the irregular and uncertain exercise of the power every man has of punishing the transgressions of others, make them take sanctuary under the established laws of government, and therein seek the preservation of their property. It is this makes them so willingly give up every one his single power of punishing, to be exercised by such alone, as shall be appointed to it amongst them; and by such rules as the community, or those authorized by them to that purpose, shall agree on. And in this we have the original right and rise of both the legislative and executive power, as well as of the governments and societies themselves.

John Locke

Sec. 128. For in the state of nature, to omit the liberty he has of innocent delights, a man has two powers. The first is to do whatsoever he thinks fit for the preservation of himself, and others within the permission of the law of nature: by which law, common to them all, he and all the rest of mankind are one community, make up one society, distinct from all other creatures. And were it not for the corruption and vitiousness of degenerate men, there would be no need of any other; no necessity that men should separate from this great and natural community, and by positive agreements combine into smaller and divided associations. The other power a man has in the state of nature, is the power to punish the crimes committed against that law. Both these he gives up, when he joins in a private, if I may so call it, or particular politic society, and incorporates into any commonwealth, separate from the rest of mankind.

Sec. 129. The first power, viz. of doing whatsoever he thought for the preservation of himself, and the rest of mankind, he gives up to be regulated by laws made by the society, so far forth as the preservation of himself, and the rest of that society shall require; which laws of the society in many things confine the liberty he had by the law of nature.

Sec. 130. Secondly, The power of punishing he wholly gives up, and engages his natural force, (which he might before employ in the execution of the law of nature, by his own single authority, as he thought fit) to assist the executive power of the society, as the law thereof shall require: for being now in a new state, wherein he is to enjoy many conveniencies, from the labour, assistance, and society of others in the same community, as well as protection from its whole strength; he is to part also with as much of his natural liberty, in providing for himself, as the good, prosperity, and safety of the society shall require; which is not only necessary, but just, since the other members of the society do the like.

Sec. 131.   But though men, when they enter into society, give up the equality, liberty, and executive power they had in the state of nature, into the hands of the society, to be so far disposed of by the legislative, as the good of the society shall require; yet it being only with an intention in every one the better to preserve himself, his liberty and property; (for no rational creature can be supposed to change his condition with an intention to be worse) the power of the society, or legislative constituted by them, can never be supposed to extend farther, than the common good; but is obliged to secure every one's property, by providing against those three defects above mentioned, that made the state of nature so unsafe and uneasy. And so whoever has the legislative or supreme power of any commonwealth, is bound to govern by established standing laws, promulgated and known to the people, and not by extemporary decrees; by indifferent and upright judges, who are to decide controversies by those laws; and to employ the force of the community at home, only in the execution of such laws, or abroad to prevent or redress foreign injuries, and secure the community from inroads and invasion. And all this to be directed to no other end, but the peace, safety, and public good of the people.

Preamble of the
Frame of Government of Pennsylvania
William Penn (1682)

The English Quaker William Penn oversaw the establishment of the colony of Pennsylvania. Penn wrote the original frame or structure of government for the colony in 1682. The details of his government system were later changed, and the colony always was subject to the provisions of a royal charter. In this opening section of the Frame of Government, Penn sets forth his understanding of the nature and purpose of government.

When the great and wise *God* had made the world, of all his creatures it pleased him to choose man his deputy to rule it; and to fit him for so great a charge and trust, he did not only qualify him with skill and power but with integrity to use them justly. This native goodness was equally his honor and his happiness; and whilst he stood here, all went well; there was no need of coercive or compulsive means, the precept of divine love and truth, in his bosom, was the guide and keeper of his innocency. But lust prevailing against duty made a lamentable breach upon it; and the law, that before had no power over him, took place upon him, and his disobedient posterity, that such as would not live comformable to the holy law within should fall under the reproof and correction of the just law without in a judicial administration.

This the Apostle [Paul] teaches in divers of his epistles: "The law," says he, "was added because of transgressions." In another place, "Knowing that the law was not made for the righteous man; but for the disobedient and ungodly, for sinners, for unholy and profane, for murderers, for whoremongers, for them that defile themselves with mankind, and for mansteaters, for liars, for perjured persons," etc.; but this is not all, he opens and carries the matter of government a little further: "Let every soul be subject to the higher powers; for there is no power but of *God.* The powers that be are ordained of *God:* whosoever therefore resisteth the power, resisteth the ordinance of *God.* For rulers are not a terror to good works, but to evil:

William Penn

wilt thou then not be afraid of the power? Do that which is good, and thou shalt have praise of the same." "He is the minister of *God* to thee for good." "Wherefore ye must needs be subject, not only for wrath, but for conscience' sake."

This settles the divine right of government beyond exception, and that for two ends: first, to terrify evildoers; secondly, to cherish those that do well; which gives government a life beyond corruption and makes it as durable in the world, as good men shall be. So that government seems to me a part of religion itself, a thing sacred in its institution and end. For, if it does not directly remove the cause, it crushes the effects of evil and is, as such (though a lower, yet), an emanation of the same Divine Power that is both author and object of pure religion; the difference lying here, that the one is more free and mental, the other more corporal and compulsive in its operations; but that is only to evildoers; government itself being otherwise as capable of kindness, goodness, and charity, as a more private society. They weakly err that think there is no other use of government than correction, which is the coarsest part of it: daily experience tells us that the care and regulation of many other affairs, more soft, and daily necessary, make up much of the greatest part of government; and which must have followed the peopling of the world, had Adam never fell, and will continue among men, on earth, under the highest attainments they may arrive at, by the coming of the blessed *Second Adam*, the *Lord* from heaven. Thus much of government in general, as to its rise and end.

For particular *frames* and *models*, it will become me to say little; and comparatively I will say nothing. My reasons are:

First. That the age is too nice and difficult for it; there being nothing the wits of men are more busy and divided upon. It is true, they seem to agree to the end, to wit, happiness; but, in the means, they differ, as to divine, so to this human felicity; and the cause is much the same, not always want of light and knowledge, but want of using them rightly. Men side with their passions against their reason, and their sinister interests have so strong a bias upon their minds that they lean to them against the good of the things they know.

Secondly. I do not find a model in the world, that time, place, and some singular emergencies have not necessarily altered; nor is it easy to frame a civil government that shall serve all places alike.

Thirdly. I know what is said by the several admirers of *monarchy, aristocracy,* and *democracy,* which are the rule of one, a few, and many, and are the three common ideas of government, when men discourse on the subject.

But I choose to solve the controversy with this small distinction, and it belongs to all three: *Any government is free to the people under it* (whatever be the frame) *where the laws rule, and the people are a party to those laws,* and more than this is tyranny, oligarchy, or confusion.

But, lastly, when all is said, there is hardly one frame of government in the world so ill designed by its first founders that, in good hands, would not do well enough; and story tells us, the best, in ill ones, can do nothing that is great or good; witness the *Jewish* and *Roman states.* Governments, like clocks, go from the motion men give them, and as governments are made and moved by men, so by them they are ruined too. Wherefore governments rather depend upon men than men upon governments. Let men be good, and the government cannot be bad; if it be ill, they will cure it. But, if men be bad, let the government be ever so good, they will endeavor to warp and spoil it to their turn.

I know some say, "Let us have good laws, and no matter for the men that execute them"; but let them consider that, though good laws do well, good men do better, for good laws may want good men and be abolished or evaded by ill men; but good men will never want good laws nor suffer ill ones. It is true, good laws have some awe upon ill ministers, but that is where they have not power to escape or abolish them, and the people are generally wise and good, but a loose and depraved people (which is the question) love laws and an administration like themselves. That, therefore, which makes a good constitution, must keep it, viz.: men of wisdom and virtue, qualities that, because they descend not with worldly inheritances, must be carefully propagated by a virtuous education of youth; for which after ages will owe more to the care and prudence of founders, and the successive magistracy, than to their parents, for their private patrimonies.

These considerations of the weight of government, and the nice and various opinions about it, made it uneasy to me to think of publishing the ensuing frame and conditional laws, forseeing both the censures they will meet with from men of differing humors and engagements and the occasion they may give of discourse beyond my design.

But, next to the power of necessity (which is a solicitor that will take no denial), this induced me to a compliance: that we have (with reverence to God, and good conscience to men), to the best of our skill, contrived and composed the *frame* and *laws* of this government, to the great end of all government, viz.: *To support power in reverence with the people, and to secure the people from the abuse of power*; that they may be free by their just obedience, and the magistrates honorable, for their just administration; for liberty without obedience is confusion, and obedience without liberty is slavery. To carry this evenness is partly owing to the constitution and partly to the magistracy; where either of these fail, government will be subject to convulsions; but, where both are wanting, it must be totally subverted; then where both meet, the government is like to endure. Which I humbly pray and hope *God* will please to make the lot of this of *Pennsylvania*. Amen.

Thoughts on Government
John Adams (1776)

John Adams wrote this treatise in the spring of 1776 as he and many other Americans contemplated the possibility of a new government for the thirteen British colonies. It was written as a response to a request from a fellow member of the Continental Congress for an outline of his ideas on the subject.

My dear Sir,

If I was equal to the task of forming a plan for the government of a colony, I should be flattered with your request, and very happy to comply with it; because, as the divine science of politics is the science of social happiness, and the blessings of society depend entirely on the constitutions of government, which are generally institutions that last for many generations, there can be no employment more agreeable to a benevolent mind than a research after the best.

Pope flattered tyrants too much when he said,

For forms of government let fools contest,
That which is best administered is best.

Nothing can be more fallacious than this. But poets read history to collect flowers, not fruits; they attend to fanciful images, not the effects of social institutions. Nothing is more certain, from the history of nations and nature of man, than that some forms of government are better fitted for being well administered than others.

We ought to consider what is the end of government, before we determine which is the best form. Upon this point all speculative politicians will agree, that the happiness of society is the end of government, as all divines and moral philosophers will agree that the happiness of the individual is the end of man. From this principle it will follow, that the form of government which communicates ease, comfort, security, or, in one word, happiness, to the greatest number of persons, and in the greatest degree, is the best.

All sober inquirers after truth, ancient and modern, pagan and Christian, have declared that the happiness of man, as well as his dignity, consists in virtue. Confucius, Zoroaster, Socrates, Mahomet, not to mention authorities really sacred, have agreed in this.

If there is a form of government, then, whose principle and foundation is virtue, will not every sober man acknowledge it better calculated to promote the general happiness than any other form?

Fear is the foundation of most governments; but it is so sordid and brutal a passion, and renders men in whose breasts it predominates so stupid and miserable, that Americans will not be likely to approve of any political institution which is founded on it.

Honor is truly sacred, but holds a lower rank in the scale of moral excellence than virtue. Indeed, the former is but a part of the latter, and consequently has not equal pretensions to support a frame of government productive of human happiness. The

foundation of every government is some principle or passion in the minds of the people. The noblest principles and most generous affections in our nature, then, have the fairest chance to support the noblest and most generous models of government.

A man must be indifferent to the sneers of modern Englishmen, to mention in their company the names of Sidney, Harrington, Locke, Milton, Nedham, Neville, Burnet, and Hoadly. No small fortitude is necessary to confess that one has read them. The wretched condition of this country, however, for ten or fifteen years past, has frequently reminded me of their principles and reasonings. They will convince any candid mind, that there is no good government but what is republican. That the only valuable part of the British constitution is so; because the very definition of a republic is "an empire of laws, and not of men." That, as a republic is the best of

John Adams

governments, so that particular arrangement of the powers of society, or, in other words, that form of government which is best contrived to secure an impartial and exact execution of the laws, is the best of republics.

Of republics there is an inexhaustible variety, because the possible combinations of the powers of society are capable of innumerable variations.

As good government is an empire of laws, how shall your laws be made? In a large society, inhabiting an extensive country, it is impossible that the whole should assemble to make laws. The first necessary step, then, is to depute power from the many to a few of the most wise and good. But by what rules shall you choose your representatives? Agree upon the number and qualifications of persons who shall have the benefit of choosing, or annex this privilege to the inhabitants of a certain extent of ground.

The principle difficulty lies, and the greatest care should be employed in constituting this representative assembly. It should be in miniature an exact portrait of the people at large. It should think, feel, reason and act like them. That it may be the interest of this assembly to do strict justice at all times, it should be an equal representation, or, in other words, equal interests among the people should have equal interests in it. Great care should be taken to effect this, and to prevent unfair, partial, and corrupt elections. Such regulations, however, may be better made in times of greater tranquility than the present; and they will spring up themselves naturally, when all the powers of government come to be in the hands of the people's friends. At present, it will be safest to proceed in all established modes, to which the people have been familiarized by habit.

A representation of the people in one assembly being obtained, a question arises, whether all the powers of government, legislative, executive, and judicial, shall be left in this body? I think a people cannot be long free, nor ever happy, whose government is in one assembly. My reasons for this opinion are as follow:—

1. A single assembly is liable to all the vices, follies, and frailties of an individual; subject to fits of humor, starts of passion, flights of enthusiasm, partialities, or prejudice, and consequently productive of hasty results and absurd judgments. And all these errors ought to be corrected and defects supplied by some controlling power.

2. A single assembly is apt to be avaricious, and in time will not scruple to exempt itself from burdens, which it will lay, without compunction, on its constituents.

3. A single assembly is apt to grow ambitious, and after a time will not hesitate to vote itself perpetual. This was one fault of the Long Parliament; but more remarkably of Holland, whose assembly first voted themselves from annual to septennial, then for life, and after a course of years, that all vacancies happening by death or otherwise, should be filled by themselves, without any application to constituents at all.

4. A representative assembly, although extremely well qualified, and absolutely necessary, as a branch of the legislative, is unfit to exercise the executive power, for want of two essential properties, secrecy and dispatch.

5. A representative assembly is still less qualified for the judicial power, because it is too numerous, too slow, and too little skilled in the laws.

6. Because a single assembly, possessed of all the powers of government, would make arbitrary laws for their own interest, execute all laws arbitrarily for their own interest, and adjudge all controversies in their own favor.

But shall the whole power of legislation rest in one assembly? Most of the foregoing reasons apply equally to prove that the legislative power ought to be more complex; to which we may add, that if the legislative power is wholly in one assembly, and the executive in another, or in a single person, these two powers will oppose and encroach upon each other, until the contest shall end in war, and the whole power, legislative and executive, be usurped by the strongest.

The judicial power, in such case, could not mediate, or hold the balance between the two contending powers, because the legislative would undermine it. And this shows the necessity, too, of giving the executive power a negative upon the legislative, otherwise this will be continually encroaching upon that.

To avoid these dangers, let a distinct assembly be constituted, as a mediator between the two extreme branches of the legislature, that which represents the people, and that which is vested with the executive power.

Let the representative assembly then elect by ballot, from among themselves or their constituents, or both, a distinct assembly, which, for the sake of perspicuity, we will call a council. It may consist of any number you please, say twenty or thirty, and should have a free and independent exercise of its judgment, and consequently a negative voice in the legislature.

These two bodies, thus constituted, and made integral parts of the legislature, let them unite, and by joint ballot choose a governor, who, after being stripped of most of those badges of domination, called prerogatives, should have a free and independent exercise of his judgment, and be made also an integral part of the legislature. This, I know, is liable to objections; and, if you please, you may make him only president of the council, as in Connecticut. But as the governor is to be invested with the executive power, with consent of council, I think he ought to have a negative upon the legislative. If he is annually elective, as he ought to be, he will always have so much reverence and affection for the people, their representatives and counselors, that, although you give him an independent exercise of his judgment, he will seldom use it in opposition to the two houses, except in cases the public utility of which would be conspicuous; and some such cases would happen.

In the present exigency of American affairs, when, by an act of Parliament, we are put out of the royal protection, and consequently discharged from our allegiance, and it has become necessary to assume government for our immediate security, the governor, lieutenant-governor, secretary, treasurer, commissary, attorney-general, should be chosen by joint ballot of both houses. And these and all other elections, especially of representatives and counselors, should be annual, there not being in the whole circle of the sciences a maxim more infallible than this, "where annual elections end, there slavery begins."

These great men, in this respect, should be, once a year,

Like bubbles on the sea of matter borne,
They rise, they break, and to that sea return.

This will teach them the great political virtues of humility, patience, and moderation, without which every man in power becomes a ravenous beast of prey.

This mode of constituting the great offices of state will answer very well for the present; but if by experiment it should be found inconvenient, the legislature may, at its leisure, devise other methods of creating them, by elections of the people at large, as in Connecticut, or it may enlarge the term for which they shall be chosen to seven years, or three years, or for life, or make any other alterations which the society shall find productive of its ease, its safety, its freedom, or, in one word, its happiness.

A rotation of all offices, as well as of representatives and counselors, has many advocates, and is contended for with many plausible arguments. It would be attended, no doubt, with many advantages; and if the society has a sufficient number of suitable characters to supply the great number of vacancies which would be made by such a rotation, I can see no objection to it. These persons may be allowed to serve for three years, and then be excluded three years, or for any longer or shorter term.

Any seven or nine of the legislative council may be made a quorum, for doing business as a privy council, to advise the governor in the exercise of the executive branch of power, and in all acts of state.

The governor should have the command of the militia and of all your armies. The power of pardons should be with the governor and council.

Judges, justices, and all other officers, civil and military, should be nominated and appointed by the governor, with the advice and consent of council, unless you choose to have a government more popular; if you do, all officers, civil and military, may be chosen by joint ballot of both houses; or, in order to preserve the independence and importance of each house, by ballot of one house, concurred in by the other. Sheriffs should be chosen by the freeholders of counties; so should registers of deeds and clerks of counties.

All officers should have commissions, under the hand of the governor and seal of the colony.

The dignity and stability of government in all its branches, the morals of the people, and every blessing of society depend so much upon an upright and skillful administration of justice, that the judicial power ought to be distinct from both the legislative and executive, and independent upon both, that so it may be a check upon both, as both should be checks upon that. The judges, therefore, should be always men of learning and experience in the laws, of exemplary morals, great patience, calmness, coolness, and attention. Their minds should not be distracted with jarring interests; they should not be dependent upon any man, or body of men. To these ends, they should hold estates for life in their offices; or, in other words, their commissions should be during good behavior, and their salaries ascertained and established by law. For misbehavior, the grand inquest of the colony, the house of representatives, should impeach them before the governor and council, where they should have time and opportunity to make their defense; but, if convicted, should be removed from their offices, and subjected to such other punishment as shall be proper.

A militia law, requiring all men, or with very few exceptions besides cases of conscience, to be provided with arms and ammunition, to be trained at certain seasons; and requiring counties, towns, or other small districts, to be provided with public stocks of ammunition and entrenching utensils, and with some settled plans for transporting provisions after the militia, when marched to defend their country against sudden invasions; and requiring certain districts to be provided with field-pieces, companies of matrosses, and perhaps some regiments of light-horse, is always a wise institution, and, in the present circumstances of our country, indispensable.

Laws for liberal education of youth, especially of the lower class of people, are so extremely wise and useful, that, to a humane and generous mind, no expense for this purpose would be thought extravagant.

The very mention of sumptuary laws will excite a smile. Whether our countrymen have wisdom and virtue enough to submit to them, I know not; but the happiness of the people might be greatly promoted by them, and a revenue saved sufficient to carry on this war forever. Frugality is a great revenue, besides curing us of vanities, levities, and fopperies, which are real antidotes to all great, manly, and warlike virtues.

But must not all commissions run in the name of a king? No. Why may they not as well run thus, "The colony of --- to A.B. greeting," and be tested by the governor?

Why may not writs, instead of running in the name of the king, run thus, "The colony of --- to the sheriff," &c., and be tested by the chief justice?

Why may not indictments conclude, "against the peace of the colony of --- and the dignity of the same?"

A constitution founded on these principles introduces knowledge among the people, and inspires them with a conscious dignity becoming freemen; a general emulation takes place, which causes good humor, sociability, good manners, and good morals to be general. That elevation of sentiment inspired by such a government, makes the common people brave and enterprising. That ambition which is inspired by it makes them sober, industrious, and frugal. You will find among them some elegance, perhaps, but more solidity; a little pleasure, but a great deal of business; some politeness, but more civility. If you compare such a country with the regions of domination, whether monarchical or aristocratical, you will fancy yourself in Arcadia or Elysium.

If the colonies should assume governments separately, they should be left entirely to their own choice of the forms; and if a continental constitution should be formed, it should be a congress, containing a fair and adequate representation of the colonies, and its authority should sacredly be confined to those cases, namely, war, trade, disputes between colony and colony, the post-office, and the unappropriated lands of the crown, as they used to be called.

These colonies, under such forms of government, and in such a union, would be unconquerable by all the monarchies of Europe.

You and I, my dear friend, have been sent into life at a time when the greatest lawgivers of antiquity would have wished to live. How few of the human race have ever enjoyed an opportunity of making an election of government, more than of air, soil, or climate, for themselves or their children! When, before the present epocha, had three millions of people full power and a fair opportunity to form and establish the wisest and happiest government that human wisdom can contrive? I hope you will avail yourself and your country of that extensive learning and indefatigable industry which you possess, to assist her in the formation of the happiest governments and the best character of a great people. For myself, I must beg you to keep my name out of sight; for this feeble attempt, if it should be known to be mine, would oblige me to apply to myself those lines of the immortal John Milton, in one of his sonnets:—

I did but prompt the age to quit their clogs
By the known rules of ancient liberty,
When straight a barbarous noise environs me
Of owls and cuckoos, asses, apes, and dogs.

The Federalist Number 2
John Jay (1787)

John Jay

**Concerning Dangers from
Foreign Force and Influence
October 31, 1787**

To the People of the State of New York:

When the people of America reflect that they are now called upon to decide a question, which, in its consequences, must prove one of the most important that ever engaged their attention, the propriety of their taking a very comprehensive, as well as a very serious, view of it, will be evident.

Nothing is more certain than the indispensable necessity of government, and it is equally undeniable, that whenever and however it is instituted, the people must cede to it some of their natural rights in order to vest it with requisite powers. It is well worthy of consideration therefore, whether it would conduce more to the interest of the people of America that they should, to all general purposes, be one nation, under one federal government, or that they should divide themselves into separate confederacies, and give to the head of each the same kind of powers which they are advised to place in one national government.

It has until lately been a received and uncontradicted opinion that the prosperity of the people of America depended on their continuing firmly united, and the wishes, prayers, and efforts of our best and wisest citizens have been constantly directed to that object. But politicians now appear, who insist that this opinion is erroneous, and that instead of looking for safety and happiness in union, we ought to seek it in a division of the States into distinct confederacies or sovereignties. However extraordinary this new doctrine may appear, it nevertheless has its advocates; and certain characters who were much opposed to it formerly, are at present of the number. Whatever may be the arguments or inducements which have wrought this change in the sentiments and declarations of these gentlemen, it certainly would not be wise in the people at large to adopt these new political tenets without being fully convinced that they are founded in truth and sound policy.

It has often given me pleasure to observe that independent America was not composed of detached and distant territories, but that one connected, fertile, widespreading country was the portion of our western sons of liberty. Providence has in a particular manner blessed it with a variety of soils and productions, and watered it with innumerable streams, for the delight and accommodation of its inhabitants. A succession of navigable waters forms a kind of chain round its borders, as if to bind it together; while the most noble rivers in the world, running at convenient distances, present them with highways for the easy communication of friendly aids, and the mutual transportation and exchange of their various commodities.

With equal pleasure I have as often taken notice that Providence has been pleased to give this one connected country to one united people—a people descended from the same ancestors, speaking the same language, professing the same religion, attached to the same principles of government, very similar in their manners and customs, and who, by their joint counsels, arms, and efforts, fighting side by side throughout a long and bloody war, have nobly established general liberty and independence.

This country and this people seem to have been made for each other, and it appears as if it was the design of Providence, that an inheritance so proper and convenient for a band of brethren, united to each other by the strongest ties, should never be split into a number of unsocial, jealous, and alien sovereignties.

Similar sentiments have hitherto prevailed among all orders and denominations of men among us. To all general purposes we have uniformly been one people, each individual citizen everywhere enjoying the same national rights, privileges, and protection. As a nation we have made peace and war; as a nation we have vanquished our common enemies; as a nation we have formed alliances, and made treaties, and entered into various compacts and conventions with foreign states.

A strong sense of the value and blessings of union induced the people, at a very early period, to institute a federal government to preserve and perpetuate it. They formed it almost as soon as they had a political existence; nay, at a time when their habitations were in flames, when many of their citizens were bleeding, and when the progress of hostility and desolation left little room for those calm and mature inquiries and reflections which must ever precede the formation of a wise and well-balanced government for a free people. It is not to be wondered at, that a government instituted in times so inauspicious, should on experiment be found greatly deficient and inadequate to the purpose it was intended to answer.

This intelligent people perceived and regretted these defects. Still continuing no less attached to union than enamored of liberty, they observed the danger which immediately threatened the former and more remotely the latter; and being pursuaded that ample security for both could only be found in a national government more wisely framed, they as with one voice, convened the late convention at Philadelphia, to take that important subject under consideration.

This convention, composed of men who possessed the confidence of the people, and many of whom had become highly distinguished by their patriotism, virtue and wisdom, in times which tried the minds and hearts of men, undertook the arduous task. In the mild season of peace, with minds unoccupied by other subjects, they passed many months in cool, uninterrupted, and daily consultation; and finally, without having been awed by power, or influenced by any passions except love for their country, they presented and recommended to the people the plan produced by their joint and very unanimous councils.

Admit, for so is the fact, that this plan is only *recommended*, not imposed, yet let it be remembered that it is neither recommended to *blind* approbation, nor to *blind* reprobation; but to that sedate and candid consideration which the magnitude and importance of the subject demand, and which it certainly ought to receive. But this (as was remarked in the foregoing number of this paper) is more to be wished than expected, that it may be so considered and examined. Experience on a former occasion teaches us not to be too sanguine in such hopes. It is not yet forgotten that well-grounded apprehensions of imminent danger induced the people of America to form the memorable Congress of 1774. That body recommended certain measures to their constituents, and the event proved their wisdom; yet it is fresh in our memories how soon the press began to teem with pamphlets and weekly papers against those very measures. Not only many of the officers of government, who obeyed the dictates of personal interest, but others, from a mistaken estimate of consequences, or the undue influence of former attachments, or whose ambition aimed at objects which did not correspond with the public good, were indefatigable in their efforts to pursuade the people to reject the advice of that patriotic Congress. Many, indeed, were deceived and deluded, but the great majority of the people reasoned and decided judiciously; and happy they are in reflecting that they did so.

They considered that the Congress was composed of many wise and experienced men. That, being convened from different parts of the country, they brought with them and communicated to each other a variety of useful information. That, in the course of the time they passed together in inquiring into and discussing the true interests of their country, they must have acquired very accurate knowledge on that head. That they were individually interested in the public liberty and prosperity, and therefore that it was not less their inclination than their duty to recommend only such measures as, after the most mature deliberation, they really thought prudent and advisable.

These and similar considerations then induced the people to rely greatly on the judgment and integrity of the Congress; and they took their advice, notwithstanding the various arts and endeavors used to deter them from it. But if the people at large had reason to confide in the men of that Congress, few of whom had been fully tried or generally known, still greater reason have they now to respect the judgment and advice of the convention, for it is well known that some of the most distinguished members of that Congress, who have been since tried and justly approved for patriotism and abilities, and who have grown old in acquiring political information, were also members of this convention, and carried into it their accumulated knowledge and experience.

It is worthy of remark that not only the first, but every succeeding Congress, as well as the late convention, have invariably joined with the people in thinking that the prosperity of America depended on its Union. To preserve and perpetuate it was the great object of the people in forming that convention, and it is also the great object of the plan which the convention has advised them to adopt. With what propriety, therefore, or for what good purposes, are attempts at this particular period made by some men to depreciate the importance of the Union? Or why is it suggested that three or four confederacies would be better than one? I am persuaded in my own mind that the people have always thought right on this subject, and that their universal and uniform attachment to the cause of the Union rests on great and weighty reasons, which I shall endeavor to develop and explain in some ensuing papers. They who promote the idea of substituting a number of distinct confederacies in the room of the plan of the convention, seem clearly to foresee that the rejection of it would put the continuance of the Union in the utmost jeopardy. That certainly would be the case, and I sincerely wish that it may be as clearly foreseen by every good citizen, that whenever the dissolution of the Union arrives, America will have reason to exclaim, in the words of the poet: "Farewell! A Long Farewell to All My Greatness."

Publius

Speech by Patrick Henry Opposing Ratification of the Constitution (excerpt) (1788)

. . . I rose yesterday to ask a question which arose in my own mind. When I asked that question, I thought the meaning of my interrogation was obvious. The fate of this question and of America may depend on this. Have they said, We, the states? Have they made a proposal of a compact between states? If they had, this would be a confederation. It is otherwise most clearly a consolidated government. The question turns, sir, on that poor little thing—the expression, We, the people, instead of the states, of America. I need not take much pains to show that the principles of this system are extremely pernicious, impolitic, and dangerous.

Is this a monarchy, like England—a compact between prince and people, with checks on the former to secure the liberty of the latter? Is this a confederacy, like Holland—an association of a number of independent states, each of which retains its individual sovereignty? It is not a democracy, wherein the people retain all their rights securely. Had these principles been adhered to, we should not have been brought to this alarming transition, from a confederacy to a consolidated government. We have no detail of these great considerations, which, in my opinion, ought to have abounded before we should recur to a government of this kind.

Here is a resolution as radical as that which separated us from Great Britain. It is radical in this transition; our rights and privileges are endangered, and the sovereignty of the states will be relinquished: and cannot we plainly see that this is actually the case? The rights of conscience, trial by jury, liberty of the press, all your immunities and franchises, all pretensions to human rights and privileges, are rendered insecure, if not lost, by this change, so loudly talked of by some, and inconsiderately by others. Is this tame relinquishment of rights worthy of freemen? Is it worthy of that manly fortitude that ought to characterize republicans? It is said eight states have adopted this plan. I declare that if twelve states and a half had adopted it, I would, with manly firmness, and in spite of an erring world, reject it. You are not to inquire how your trade may be increased, nor how you are to become a great and powerful people, but how your liberties can be secured; for liberty ought to be the direct end of your government.

. . . Is it necessary for your liberty that you should abandon those great rights by the adoption of this system? Is the relinquishment of the trial by jury and the liberty of the press necessary for your liberty? Will the abandonment of your most sacred rights tend to the security of your liberty? Liberty, the greatest of all earthly blessing—give us that precious jewel, and you may take every thing else! But I am fearful I have lived long enough to become an old-fashioned fellow. Perhaps an invincible attachment to the dearest rights of man may, in these refined, enlightened days, be deemed old-fashioned; if so, I am contented to be so. I say, the time has been when every pulse of my heart beat for American liberty, and which, I believe, had a counterpart in the breast of every true American; but suspicions have gone forth—suspicions of my integrity—publicly reported that my professions are not real.

Twenty-three years ago was I supposed a traitor to my country? I was then said to be the bane of sedition, because I supported the rights of my country. I may be thought suspicious when I say our privileges and rights are in danger. But, sir, a number of the people of this country are weak enough to think these things are too true. I am happy to find that the gentleman on the other side declares they are groundless. But, sir, suspicion is a virtue as long as its object is the preservation of the public good, and as long as it stays within proper bounds: should it fall on me, I am contented: conscious rectitude is a powerful consolation. I trust there are many who think my professions for the public good to be real. Let your suspicion look to both sides. There are many on the other side, who possibly may have been persuaded to the necessity of these measures, which I conceive to be dangerous to your liberty. Guard with jealous attention the public liberty. Suspect every one who approaches that jewel. Unfortunately, nothing will preserve it but downright force. Whenever you give up that force, you are inevitably ruined.

I am answered by gentlemen, that, though I might speak of terrors, yet the fact was, that we were surrounded by none of the dangers I apprehended. I conceive this new government to be one of those dangers: it has produced those horrors which distress many of our best citizens. We are come hither to preserve the poor commonwealth of Virginia, if it can be possibly done: something must be done to preserve your liberty and mine. The Confederation, this same despised government, merits, in my opinion, the highest encomium: it carried us through a long and dangerous war; it rendered us victorious in that bloody conflict with a powerful nation; it has secured us a territory greater than any European monarch possesses: and shall a government which has been thus strong and vigorous, be accused of imbecility, and abandoned for want of energy? Consider what you are about to do before you part with the government. Take longer time in reckoning things; revolutions like this have happened in almost every country in Europe; similar examples are to be found in ancient Greece and ancient Rome—instances of the people losing their liberty by their own carelessness and the ambition of a few. We are cautioned by the honorable gentleman, who presides, against faction and turbulence. I acknowledge that licentiousness is dangerous, and that it ought to be provided against: I acknowledge, also, the new form of government may effectually prevent it: yet there is another thing it will as effectually do—it will oppress and ruin the people.

There are sufficient guards placed against sedition and licentiousness; for, when power is given to this government to suppress these, or for any other purpose, the language it assumes is clear, express, and unequivocal; but when this Constitution speaks of privileges, there is an ambiguity, sir, a fatal ambiguity—an ambiguity which is very astonishing. In the clause under consideration, there is the strangest language that I can conceive. I mean, when it says that there shall not be more representatives than one for every thirty thousand. Now, sir, how easy is it to evade this privilege! "The number shall not exceed one for every thirty thousand." This may be satisfied by one representative from each state. Let our numbers be ever so great, this immense continent may, by this artful expression, be reduced to have but thirteen representatives. I confess this construction is not natural; but the ambiguity of the expression lays a good ground for a quarrel. Why was it not clearly and unequivocally expressed, that they should be entitled to have one for every thirty thousand? This would have obviated all disputes; and was this difficult to be done? What is the inference? When population increases, and a state shall send representatives in this proportion, Congress may remand them, because the right of having one for every thirty thousand is not clearly expressed. This possibility of reducing the number to one for each state approximates to probability by that other expression—"but each state shall at least have one representative." Now, is it not clear that, from the first expression, the number might be reduced so much that some states should have no representatives at all, were it not for the insertion of this last expression? And as this is the only restriction upon them, we may fairly conclude that they may restrain the number to one from each state. . . .

My great objection to this government is, that it does not leave us the means of defending our rights, or of waging war against tyrants. It is urged by some gentlemen, that this new plan will bring us an acquisition of strength—an army, and the militia of the states. This is an idea extremely ridiculous: gentlemen cannot be earnest. This acquisition will trample on our fallen liberty. Let my beloved Americans guard against that fatal lethargy that has pervaded the universe. Have we the means of resisting disciplined armies, when our only defence, the militia, is put into the hands of Congress? The honorable gentleman said that great danger would ensue if the Convention rose without adopting this system. I ask, Where is that danger? I see none. Other gentlemen have told us, within these walls, that the union is gone, or that the union will be gone. Is not this trifling with the judgment of their fellow-citizens? Till they tell us the grounds of their fears, I will consider them as imaginary. I rose to make inquiry where those dangers were; they could make no answer: I believe I never shall have that answer. Is there a disposition in the people of this country to revolt against the dominion of laws? Has there been a single tumult in Virginia? Have not the people of Virginia, when laboring under the severest pressure of accumulated distresses, manifested the most cordial acquiescence in the execution of the laws? What could be more awful than their unanimous acquiescence under general distresses? Is there any revolution in Virginia? Whither is the spirit of America gone? Whither is the genius of America fled? It was but yesterday, when our enemies marched in triumph through our country. Yet the people of this country could not be appalled by their pompous armaments. . . . Where is the peril, now, compared to that? Some minds are agitated by foreign alarms. Happily for us, there is no real danger from Europe; that country is engaged in more arduous business: from that quarter there is no cause of fear: you may sleep in safety forever for them. . . .

Consider our situation, sir: go to the poor man, and ask him what he does. He will inform you that he enjoys the fruits of his labor, under his own fig-tree, with his wife and children around him, in peace and security. Go to every other member of society,—you will find the same tranquil ease and content; you will find no alarms or disturbances. Why, then, tell us of danger, to terrify us into an adoption of this new form of government? And yet who knows the dangers that this new system may produce? They are out of the sight of the common people: they cannot foresee latent consequences. I dread the operation of it on the middling and lower classes of people: it is for them I fear the adoption of this system. . . .

In this scheme of energetic government, the people will find two sets of tax-gatherers—the state and the federal sheriffs. This, it seems to me, will produce such dreadful oppression as the people cannot possibly bear. The federal sheriff may commit what oppression, make what distresses, he pleases, and ruin you with impunity; for how are you to tie his hands? Have you any sufficiently decided means of preventing him from sucking your blood by speculations, commissions, and fees? Thus thousands of your people will be most shamefully robbed: our state sheriffs, those unfeeling blood-suckers have, under the watchful eye of our legislature, committed the most horrid and barbarous ravages on our people. It has required the most constant vigilance of the legislature to keep them from totally ruining the people; a repeated succession of laws has been made to suppress their iniquitous speculations and cruel extortions; and as often has their nefarious ingenuity devised methods of evading the force of those laws: in the struggle they have generally triumphed over the legislature. . . .

Your President may easily become king. Your Senate is so imperfectly constructed that your dearest rights may be sacrificed by what may be a small minority; and a very small minority may continue forever unchangeably this government, although horridly defective. Where are your checks in this government? Your strongholds will be in the hands of your enemies. It is on a supposition that your American governors shall be honest, that all the good qualities of this government are founded; but its defective and imperfect construction puts it in their power to perpetrate the worst of mischiefs, should they be bad men; and, sir, would not all the world, from the eastern to the western hemisphere, blame our distracted folly in resting our rights upon the contingency of our rulers being good or bad? Show me that age and country where the rights and liberties of the people were placed on the sole chance of their rulers being good men, without a consequent loss of liberty! I say that the loss of that dearest privilege has ever followed, with absolute certainty, every such mad attempt.

If your American chief be a man of ambition and abilities, how easy is it for him to render himself absolute! The army is in his hands, and if he be a man of address, it will be attached to him, and it will be the subject of long meditation with him to seize the first auspicious moment to accomplish his design; and, sir, will the American spirit solely relieve you when this happens? I would rather infinitely—and I am sure most of this Convention are of the same opinion—have a king, lords, and commons, than a government so replete with such insupportable evils. If we make a king, we may prescribe the rules by which he shall rule his people, and interpose such checks as shall prevent him from infringing them; but the President, in the field, at the head of his army, can prescribe the terms on which he shall reign master, so far that it will puzzle any American ever to get his neck from under the galling yoke. I cannot with patience think of this idea. . . .

This, sir, is my great objection to the Constitution, that there is no true responsibility—and that the preservation of our liberty depends on the single chance of men being virtuous enough to make laws to punish themselves. . . .

Exchange of Letters between the Danbury (Connecticut) Baptist Association and President Thomas Jefferson *(1801-1802)*

The Danbury Baptist Association wrote to President Thomas Jefferson during his first year in office. The organization hoped to obtain his endorsement of their belief that they should not be discriminated against by the Connecticut state government, even though the Congregationalist Church was the established church in the state. In his reply, Jefferson used the phrase "wall of separation" to describe his belief in the separation of church and state. Here are the Association's letter and Jefferson's reply.

The Danbury (Connecticut) Baptist Association to President Thomas Jefferson, October 7, 1801.

Sir,

Among the many millions in America and Europe who rejoice in your Election to office; we embrace the first opportunity which we have enjoyed in our collective capacity, since your Inauguration, to express our great satisfaction, in your appointment to the chief Magistracy in the United States; And though our mode of expression may be less courtly and pompous than what many others clothe their addresses with, we beg you, Sir, to believe that none are more sincere.

Our Sentiments are uniformly on the side of Religious Liberty—That Religion is at all times and places a matter between God and individuals—That no man ought to suffer in name, person, or effects on account of his religious Opinions—That the legitimate Power of civil government extends no further than to punish the man who works *ill to his neighbor*: But Sir our constitution of government is not specific. Our ancient charter together with the Laws made coincident therewith, were adopted on the Basis of our government, at the time of our revolution; and such had been our Laws & usages, and such still are; that Religion is considered as the first object of Legislation; and therefore what religious privileges we enjoy (as a minor part of the State) we enjoy as favors granted, and not as inalienable rights: and these favors we receive at the expense of such degrading acknowledgements, as are inconsistent with the rights of freemen. It is not to be wondered at therefore; if those, who seek after power & gain under the pretense of *government & Religion* should reproach their fellow men—should reproach their chief Magistrate, as an enemy of religion, Law and good order because he will not, dare not assume the prerogative of Jehovah and make Laws to govern the Kingdom of Christ.

Sir, we are sensible that the President of the United States, is not the national legislator, and also sensible that the national government cannot destroy the Laws of each State; but our hopes are strong that the sentiments of our beloved President, which have had such genial affect already, like the radiant beams of the Sun, will shine and prevail through all these States and all the world till Hierarchy and Tyranny be destroyed from the Earth. Sir, when we reflect on your past services, and see a glow of philanthropy and good will shining forth in a course of more than thirty years we have reason to believe that America's God has raised you up to fill the chair of State out of that good will which he bears to the Millions which you preside over. May God strengthen you for the arduous task which providence & the voice of the people have called you to sustain and support you in your Administration against all the predetermined opposition of those who wish to rise to wealth & importance on the poverty and subjection of the people.

And may the Lord preserve you safe from every evil and bring you at last to his Heavenly Kingdom through Jesus Christ our Glorious Mediator.

Signed in behalf of the Association, The Committee:
    Nehemiah Dodge, Ephram Robbins, Stephen S. Nelson

Jefferson's Reply

To messers. Nehemiah Dodge, Ephraim Robbins, & Stephen S. Nelson, a committee of the Danbury Baptist Association in the state of Connecticut.

Gentlemen,
    The affectionate sentiments of esteem and approbation which you are so good as to express towards me, on behalf of the Danbury Baptist Association, give me the highest satisfaction. My duties dictate a faithful and zealous pursuit of the interests of my constituents, & in proportion as they are persuaded of my fidelity to those duties, the discharge of them becomes more and more pleasing.

    Believing with you that religion is a matter which lies solely between Man & his God, that he owes account to none other for his faith or his worship, that the legitimate powers of government reach actions only, & not opinions, I contemplate with sovereign reverence that act of the whole American people which declared that their legislature should "make no law respecting an establishment of religion, or prohibiting the free exercise thereof," thus building a wall of separation between Church & State. Adhering to this expression of the supreme will of the nation in behalf of the rights of conscience, I shall see with sincere satisfaction the progress of those sentiments which tend to restore to man all his natural rights, convinced he has no natural right in opposition to his social duties.

    I reciprocate your kind prayers for the protection & blessing of the common father and creator of man, and tender you for yourselves & your religious association, assurances of my high respect & esteem.

Th Jefferson
Jan. 1. 1802.

McCulloch v. Maryland (excerpt) (1819)

This decision of the U.S. Supreme Court was significant for at least two reasons. (1) It broadened the scope of the "necessary and proper" clause of the Constitution by confirming the authority of the Federal government to create a national bank, even though the Constitution did not specifically give Congress this power. (2) The decision confirmed the authority of the Federal government over the state governments. The State of Maryland had attempted to tax a branch of the Bank of the United States, which had been chartered by Congress.

Chief Justice [John] Marshall delivered the opinion of the Court.

. . . The first question made in the cause is, has Congress power to incorporate a bank? . . .

The power now contested was exercised by the first Congress elected under the present constitution. The bill for incorporating the bank of the United States did not steal upon an unsuspecting legislature, and pass unobserved. Its principle was completely understood, and was opposed with equal zeal and ability. After being resisted, first in the fair and open field of debate, and afterwards in the executive cabinet, with as much persevering talent as any measure has ever experienced, and being supported by arguments which convinced minds as pure and as intelligent as this country can boast, it became a law. The original act was permitted to expire; but a short experience of the embarrassments to which the refusal to revive it exposed the government, convinced those who were most prejudiced against the measure of its necessity, and induced the passage of the present law. It would require no ordinary share of intrepidity to assert that a measure adopted under these circumstances was a bold and plain usurpation, to which the constitution gave no countenance. . . .

This government is acknowledged by all to be one of enumerated powers. The principle, that it can exercise only the powers granted to it, [is] now universally admitted. But the question respecting the extent of the powers actually granted, is perpetually arising, and will probably continue to arise, as long as our system shall exist. . . .

Statue of John Marshall in Washington, D.C.

Among the enumerated powers, we do not find that of establishing a bank or creating a corporation. But there is no phrase in the instrument which, like the articles of confederation, excludes incidental or implied powers; and which requires that everything granted shall be expressly and minutely described. Even the 10th amendment, which was framed for the purpose of quieting the excessive jealousies which had been excited, omits the word "expressly," and declares only that the powers "not delegated to the United States, nor prohibited to the States, are reserved to the States or to the people"; thus leaving the question, whether the particular power which may become the subject of contest has been delegated to the one government, or prohibited to the other, to depend on a fair construction of the whole instrument. The men who drew and adopted this amendment had experienced the embarrassments resulting from the insertion of this word in the articles of confederation, and probably omitted it to avoid those embarrassments. A constitution, to contain an accurate detail of all the subdivisions of which its great powers will admit, and of all the means by which they may be carried into execution, would partake of the prolixity of a legal code, and could scarcely be embraced by the human mind. It would probably never be understood by the public. Its nature, therefore, requires, that only its great outlines should be marked, its important objects designated, and the minor ingredients which compose those objects be deduced from the nature of the objects themselves. That this idea was entertained by the framers of the American constitution, is not only to be inferred from the nature of the instrument, but from the language. Why else were some of the limitations, found in the ninth section of the 1st article, introduced? It is also, in some degree, warranted by their having omitted to use any restrictive term which might prevent its receiving a fair and just interpretation. In considering this question, then, we must never forget that it is a constitution we are expounding.

Although, among the enumerated powers of government, we do not find the word "bank," or "incorporation," we find the great powers to lay and collect taxes; to borrow money; to regulate commerce; to declare and conduct a war; and to raise and support armies and navies. The sword and the purse, all the external relations, and no inconsiderable portion of the industry of the nation, are entrusted to its government. . . . [I]t may with great reason be contended, that a government, entrusted with such ample powers, on the due execution of which the happiness and prosperity of the nation so vitally depends, must also be entrusted with ample means for their execution. The power being given, it is the interest of the nation to facilitate its execution. . . .

The government which has a right to do an act, and has imposed on it the duty of performing that act, must, according to the dictates of reason, be allowed to select the means. . . . But the constitution of the United States has not left the right of Congress to employ the necessary means, for the execution of the powers conferred on the government, to general reasoning. To its enumeration of powers is added that of making "all laws which shall be necessary and proper for carrying into execution the foregoing powers, and all other powers vested by this constitution, in the government of the United States, or in any department thereof." The counsel for the State of Maryland have urged various arguments, to prove that this clause, though in terms a grant of power, is not so in effect; but is really restrictive of the general right, which might otherwise be implied, of selecting means for executing the enumerated powers. . . .

Almost all compositions contain words, which, taken in their rigorous sense, would convey a meaning different from that which is obviously intended. It is essential to just construction, that many words which import something excessive should be understood in a more mitigated sense—in that sense which common usage justifies. The word "necessary" is of this description. It has not a fixed character peculiar to itself. It admits of all degrees of comparison; and is often connected with other words, which increase or diminish the impression the mind receives of the urgency it imports. A thing may be necessary, very necessary, absolutely or indispensably necessary. To no mind would the same idea be conveyed by these several phrases. This comment on the word is well illustrated by the passage cited at the bar, from the 20th section of the 1st article of the constitution. It is, we think, impossible to compare the sentence which prohibits a State from laying "imposts, or duties on imports or exports, except what may be absolutely necessary for executing its inspection laws," with that which authorizes Congress "to make all laws which shall be necessary and proper for carrying into execution" the powers of the general government, without feeling a conviction that the convention understood itself to change materially the meaning of the word "necessary," by prefixing the word "absolutely." This word, then, like others, is used in various senses; and, in its construction, the subject, the context, the intention of the person using them, are all to be taken into view.

Let this be done in the case under consideration. The subject is the execution of those great powers on which the welfare of a nation essentially depends. It must have been the intention of those who gave these powers, to insure, as far as human prudence could insure, their beneficial execution. This could not be done by confiding the choice of means to such narrow limits as not to leave it in the power of Congress to adopt any which might be appropriate, and which were conducive to the end. This provision is made in a constitution intended to endure for ages to come, and, consequently, to be adapted to the various crises of human affairs. To have prescribed the means by which government should, in all future time, execute its powers, would have been to change, entirely, the character of the instrument, and give it the properties of a legal code. It would have been an unwise attempt to provide, by immutable rules, for exigencies which, if foreseen at all, must have been seen dimly, and which can be best provided for as they occur. To have declared that the best means shall not be used, but those alone without which the power given would be nugatory, would have been to deprive the legislature of the capacity to avail itself of experience, to exercise its reason, and to accommodate its legislation to circumstances. If we apply this principle of construction to any of the powers of the government, we shall find it so pernicious in its operation that we shall be compelled to discard it. . . .

The result of the most careful and attentive consideration bestowed upon this clause is, that if it does not enlarge, it cannot be construed to restrain the powers of Congress, or to impair the rights of the legislature to exercise its best judgment in the selection of measures to carry into execution the constitutional powers of the government. If no other motive for its insertion can be suggested, a sufficient one is found in the desire to remove all doubts respecting the right to legislate on that vast mass of incidental powers which must be involved in the constitution, if that instrument be not a splendid bauble.

We admit, as all must admit, that the powers of the government are limited, and that its limits are not to be transcended. But we think the sound construction of the constitution must allow to the national legislature that discretion, with respect to the means by which the powers it confers are to be carried into execution, which will enable that body to perform the high duties assigned to it, in the manner most beneficial to the people. Let the end be legitimate, let it be within the scope of the constitution, and all means which are appropriate, which are plainly adapted to that end, which are not prohibited, but consist with the letter and spirit of the constitution, are constitutional. . . .

Should Congress, in the execution of its powers, adopt measures which are prohibited by the constitution; or should Congress, under the pretext of executing its powers, pass laws for the accomplishment of objects not entrusted to the government; it would become the painful duty of this tribunal, should a case requiring such a decision come before it, to say that such an act was not the law of the land. But where the law is not prohibited, and is really calculated to effect any of the objects entrusted to the government, to undertake here to inquire into the degree of its necessity, would be to pass the line which circumscribes the judicial department, and to tread on legislative ground. This court disclaims all pretensions to such a power. . . .

After the most deliberate consideration, it is the unanimous and decided opinion of this Court, that the act to incorporate the Bank of the United States is a law made in pursuance of the constitution, and is a part of the supreme law of the land. . . .

It being the opinion of the Court, that the act incorporating the bank is constitutional; and that the power of establishing a branch in the State of Maryland might be properly exercised by the bank itself, we proceed to inquire—

2. Whether the State of Maryland may, without violating the constitution, tax that branch?

That the power of taxation is one of vital importance; that it is retained by the States; that it is not abridged by the grant of a similar power to the government of the Union; that it is to be concurrently exercised by the two governments: are truths which have never been denied. But, such is the paramount character of the constitution, that its capacity to withdraw any subject from the action of even this power, is admitted. The States are expressly forbidden to lay any duties on imports or exports, except what may be absolutely necessary for executing their inspection laws. If the obligation of this prohibition must be conceded, the same paramount character would seem to restrain, as it certainly may restrain, a State from such other exercise of this power; as is in its nature incompatible with, and repugnant to, the constitutional laws of the Union. . . .

On this ground the counsel for the bank place its claim to be exempted from the power of a State to tax its operations. There is no express provision for the case, but the claim has been sustained on a principle which so entirely pervades the constitution, is so intermixed with the materials which compose it, so interwoven with its web, so blended with its texture, as to be incapable of being separated from it, without rending it into shreds. . . .

The argument on the part of the State of Maryland is, not that the States may directly resist a law of Congress, but that they may exercise their acknowledged powers upon it, and that the constitution leaves them this right in the confidence that they will not abuse it.

Before we proceed to examine this argument, and to subject it to the test of the constitution, we must be permitted to bestow a few considerations on the nature and extent of this original right of taxation, which is acknowledged to remain with the States. It is admitted that the power of taxing the people and their property is essential to the very existence of government, and may be legitimately exercised on the objects to which it is applicable, to the utmost extent to which the government may choose to carry it. The only security against the abuse of this power, is found in the structure of the government itself. In imposing a tax the legislature acts upon its constituents. . . .

The sovereignty of a State extends to everything which exists by its own authority, or is so introduced by its permission; but does it extend to those means which are employed by Congress to carry into execution powers conferred on that body by the people of the United States? We think it demonstrable that it does not. Those powers are not given by the people of a single State. They are given by the people of the United States, to a government whose laws, made in pursuance of the constitution, are declared to be supreme. Consequently, the people of a single State cannot confer a sovereignty which will extend over them.

If we measure the power of taxation residing in a State, by the extent of sovereignty which the people of a single State possess, and can confer on its government, we have an intelligible standard, applicable to every case to which the power may be applied. We have a principle which leaves the power of taxing the people and property of a State unimpaired; which leaves to a State the command of all its resources, and which places beyond its reach, all those powers which are conferred by the people of the United States on the government of the Union, and all those means which are given for the purpose of carrying those powers into execution. We have a principle which is safe for the States, and safe for the Union. We are relieved, as we ought to be, from clashing sovereignty; from interfering powers; from a repugnancy between a right in one government to pull down what there is an acknowledged right in another to build up; from the incompatibility of a right in one government to destroy what there is a right in another to preserve. We are not driven to the perplexing inquiry, so unfit for the judicial department, what degree of taxation is the legitimate use, and what degree may amount to the abuse of the power. The attempt to use it on the means employed by the government of the Union, in pursuance of the constitution, is itself an abuse, because it is the usurpation of a power which the people of a single State cannot give. . . .

That the power to tax involves the power to destroy; that the power to destroy may defeat and render useless the power to create; that there is a plain repugnance, in conferring on one government a power to control the constitutional measures of another, which other, with respect to those very measures, is declared to be supreme over that which exerts the control, are propositions not to be denied. But all inconsistencies are to be reconciled by the magic of the word CONFIDENCE. Taxation, it is said, does not necessarily and unavoidably destroy. To carry it to the excess of destruction would be an abuse, to presume which, would banish that confidence which is essential to all government. . . .

If we apply the principle for which the State of Maryland contends, to the constitution generally, we shall find it capable of changing totally the character of that instrument. We shall find it capable of arresting all the measures of the government, and of prostrating it at the foot of the States. The American people have declared their constitution, and the laws made in pursuance thereof, to be supreme; but this principle would transfer the supremacy, in fact, to the States.

If the States may tax one instrument, employed by the government in the execution of its powers, they may tax any and every other instrument. They may tax the mail; they may tax the mint; they may tax patent rights; they may tax the papers of the custom-house; they may tax judicial process; they may tax all the means employed by the government, to an excess which would defeat all the ends of government. This was not intended by the American people. They did not design to make their government dependent on the States. . . .

The Court has bestowed on this subject its most deliberate consideration. The result is a conviction that the States have no power, by taxation or otherwise, to retard, impede, burden, or in any manner control, the operations of the constitutional laws enacted by Congress to carry into execution the powers vested in the general government. This is, we think, the unavoidable consequence of that supremacy which the constitution has declared.

We are unanimously of opinion, that the law passed by the legislature of Maryland, imposing a tax on the Bank of the United States, is unconstitutional and void.

This opinion does not deprive the States of any resources which they originally possessed. It does not extend to a tax paid by the real property of the bank, in common with the other real property within the State, nor to a tax imposed on the interest which the citizens of Maryland may hold in this institution, in common with other property of the same description throughout the State. But this is a tax on the operations of the bank, and is, consequently, a tax on the operation of an instrument employed by the government of the Union to carry its powers into execution. Such a tax must be unconstitutional.

Wesberry v. Sanders (excerpt) (1964)

For many years, Federal courts did not want to become involved in what they called "political questions" regarding state legislatures and Congress. This principle was set aside in Baker v. Carr *(1962), in which the U.S. Supreme Court ruled that the Tennessee state legislature was required to reapportion its seats in keeping with population changes so as to make the legislative districts as nearly equal in population as possible. The state legislature had not redrawn its districts in some sixty years, and the state's growing urban areas were grossly underrepresented in the legislature. The principle used in that decision and confirmed in* Wesberry *was "one man, one vote"; that is, the value of one person's vote should be as nearly equal as possible to every other person's vote. A failure by a state to do this prevented citizens from receiving equal protection under the law and thus was a violation of the U.S. Constitution. This made malapportionment a Constitutional issue and not simply a political question. Two years later, the Court applied the same principle in* Wesberry v. Sanders, *which dealt with Congressional districts in Georgia that had not been reapportioned in thirty years.*

Mr. Justice [Hugo] Black delivered the opinion of the Court.

Appellants are citizens and qualified voters of Fulton County, Georgia, and as such are entitled to vote in congressional elections in Georgia's Fifth Congressional District. That district, one of ten created by a 1931 Georgia statute, includes Fulton, DeKalb, and Rockdale Counties and has a population according to the 1960 census of 823,680. The average population of the ten districts is 394,312, less than half that of the Fifth. One district, the Ninth, has only 272,154 people, less than one-third as many as the Fifth. Since there is only one Congressman for each district, this inequality of population means that the Fifth District's Congressman has to represent from two to three times as many people as do Congressmen from some of the other Georgia districts.

Claiming that these population disparities deprived them and voters similarly situated of a right under the Federal Constitution to have their

Justice Hugo Black

votes for Congressmen given the same weight as the votes of other Georgians, the appellants brought this action . . . asking that the Georgia statute be declared invalid and that the appellees, the Governor and Secretary of State of Georgia, be enjoined from conducting elections under it. The complaint alleged that appellants were deprived of the full benefit of their right to vote, in violation of (1) Art. I, 2, of the Constitution of the United States, which provides that "The House of Representatives shall be composed of Members chosen every second Year by the People of the several States . . ."; (2) the Due Process, Equal Protection, and Privileges and Immunities Clauses of the Fourteenth Amendment; and (3) that part of Section 2 of the Fourteenth Amendment which provides that "Representatives shall be apportioned among the several States according to their respective numbers . . . ."

The case was heard by a three-judge District Court, which found unanimously, from facts not disputed, that:

> It is clear by any standard . . . that the population of the Fifth District is grossly out of balance with that of the other nine congressional districts of Georgia and in fact, so much so that the removal of DeKalb and Rockdale Counties from the District, leaving only Fulton with a population of 556,326, would leave it exceeding the average by slightly more than forty per cent.

Notwithstanding these findings, a majority of the [District] Court dismissed the complaint, citing as their guide Mr. Justice Frankfurter's minority opinion in *Colegrove v. Green,* an opinion stating that challenges to apportionment of congressional districts raised only "political" questions, which were not justiciable. . . . We noted probable jurisdiction [and thus agreed to hear the case. We believe] that in debasing the weight of appellants' votes the State has abridged the right to vote for members of Congress guaranteed them by the United States Constitution, that the District Court should have entered a declaratory judgment to that effect, and that it was therefore error to dismiss this suit. The question of what relief should be given we leave for further consideration and decision by the District Court in light of existing circumstances.

Baker v. Carr considered a challenge to a 1901 Tennessee statute providing for apportionment of State Representatives and Senators under the State's constitution, which called for apportionment among counties or districts "according to the number of qualified voters in each." The complaint there charged that the State's constitutional command to apportion on the basis of the number of qualified voters had not been followed in the 1901 statute and that the districts were so discriminatorily disparate in number of qualified voters that the plaintiffs and persons similarly situated were, "by virtue of the debasement of their votes," denied the equal protection of the laws guaranteed them by the Fourteenth Amendment. The cause there of the alleged "debasement" of votes for state legislators— districts containing widely varying numbers of people—was precisely that which was alleged to debase votes for Congressmen in *Colegrove v. Green* and in the present case. The

Court in *Baker* pointed out that the opinion of Mr. Justice Frankfurter in *Colegrove*, upon the reasoning of which the majority below leaned heavily in dismissing "for want of equity," was approved by only three of the seven Justices sitting. After full consideration of *Colegrove*, the Court in *Baker* held (1) that the District Court had jurisdiction of the subject matter; (2) that the qualified Tennessee voters there had standing to sue; and (3) that the plaintiffs had stated a justiciable cause of action on which relief could be granted.

The reasons which led to these conclusions in *Baker* are equally persuasive here. . . . [N]othing in the language of [Article I of the Constitution] gives support to a construction that would immunize state congressional apportionment laws which debase a citizen's right to vote from the power of courts to protect the constitutional rights of individuals from legislative destruction. . . . The right to vote is too important in our free society to be stripped of judicial protection by such an interpretation of Article I. This dismissal can no more be justified on the ground of "want of equity" than on the ground of "nonjusticiability." We therefore hold that the District Court erred in dismissing the complaint.

This brings us to the merits. We agree with the District Court that the 1931 Georgia apportionment grossly discriminates against voters in the Fifth Congressional District. A single Congressman represents from two to three times as many Fifth District voters as are represented by each of the Congressmen from the other Georgia congressional districts. The apportionment statute thus contracts the value of some votes and expands that of others. If the Federal Constitution intends that when qualified voters elect members of Congress each vote be given as much weight as any other vote, then this statute cannot stand.

We hold that, construed in its historical context, the command of Art. I, 2, that Representatives be chosen "by the People of the several States" means that as nearly as is practicable one man's vote in a congressional election is to be worth as much as another's. This rule is followed automatically, of course, when Representatives are chosen as a group on a statewide basis, as was a widespread practice in the first 50 years of our Nation's history. It would be extraordinary to suggest that in such statewide elections the votes of inhabitants of some parts of a State, for example, Georgia's thinly populated Ninth District, could be weighted at two or three times the value of the votes of people living in more populous parts of the State, for example, the Fifth District around Atlanta. We do not believe that the Framers of the Constitution intended to permit the same vote-diluting discrimination to be accomplished through the device of districts containing widely varied numbers of inhabitants. To say that a vote is worth more in one district than in another would not only run counter to our fundamental ideas of democratic government, it would cast aside the principle of a House of Representatives elected "by the People," a principle tenaciously fought for and established at the Constitutional Convention. The history of the Constitution, particularly that part of it relating to the adoption of Art. I, 2, reveals that those who framed the Constitution meant that, no matter what the mechanics of an election, whether statewide or by districts, it was population which was to be the basis of the House of Representatives. . . .

[Here follows a review of the debates in the Constitutional Convention regarding the election of members to the U.S. Congress.]

The debates at the Convention make at least one fact abundantly clear: that when the delegates agreed that the House should represent "people" they intended that in allocating Congressmen the number assigned to each State should be determined solely by the number of the State's inhabitants. The Constitution embodied Edmund Randolph's proposal for a periodic census to ensure "fair representation of the people," an idea endorsed by Mason as assuring that "numbers of inhabitants" should always be the measure of representation in the House of Representatives. . . .

It would defeat the principle solemnly embodied in the Great Compromise—equal representation in the House for equal numbers of people—for us to hold that, within the States, legislatures may draw the lines of congressional districts in such a way as to give some voters a greater voice in choosing a Congressman than others. The House of Representatives, the Convention agreed, was to represent the people as individuals, and on a basis of complete equality for each voter. The delegates were quite aware of what Madison called the "vicious representation" in Great Britain whereby "rotten boroughs" with few inhabitants were represented in Parliament on or almost on a par with cities of greater population. Wilson urged that people must be represented as individuals, so that America would escape the evils of the English system under which one man could send two members to Parliament to represent the borough of Old Sarum while London's million people sent but four. . . .

While it may not be possible to draw congressional districts with mathematical precision, that is no excuse for ignoring our Constitution's plain objective of making equal representation for equal numbers of people the fundamental goal for the House of Representatives. That is the high standard of justice and common sense which the Founders set for us.

United States Supreme Court Building, Washington, D.C.

Tonkin Gulf Resolution *(August 7, 1964)*

Joint Resolution

To promote the maintenance of international peace and security in Southeast Asia.

Whereas naval units of the communist regime in Vietnam, in violation of the principles of the Charter of the United Nations and of international law, have deliberately and repeatedly attacked United States naval vessels lawfully present in international waters, and have thereby created a serious threat to international peace; and

Whereas these attacks are part of a deliberate and systematic campaign of aggression that the communist regime in North Vietnam has been waging against its neighbors and the nations joined with them in the collective defense of their freedom; and

Whereas the United States is assisting the peoples of Southeast Asia to protect their freedom and has no territorial, military or political ambitions in that area, but desires only that these peoples should be left in peace to work out their own destinies in their own way: Now, therefore, be it

Resolved by the Senate and House of Representatives of the United States of America in Congress assembled, That the Congress approves and supports the determination of the President, as Commander in Chief, to take all necessary measures to repel any armed attack against the forces of the United States and to prevent further aggression.

Section 2. The United States regards as vital to its national interest and to world peace the maintenance of international peace and security in southeast Asia. Consonant with the Constitution of the United States and the Charter of the United Nations and in accordance with its obligations under the Southeast Asia Collective Defense Treaty, the United States is, therefore, prepared, as the President determines, to take all necessary steps, including the use of armed force, to assist any member or protocol state of the Southeast Asia Collective Defense Treaty requesting assistance in defense of its freedom.

Section 3. This resolution shall expire when the President shall determine that the peace and security of the area is reasonably assured by international conditions created by action of the United Nations or otherwise, except that it may be terminated earlier by concurrent resolution of the Congress.

White House Meeting with President Lyndon B. Johnson on the Situation in Vietnam, 1968

Joint Resolution to Authorize the Use of United States Armed Forces Against Iraq
(October 10, 2002)

Whereas in 1990 in response to Iraq's war of aggression against and illegal occupation of Kuwait, the United States forged a coalition of nations to liberate Kuwait and its people in order to defend the national security of the United States and enforce United Nations Security Council resolutions relating to Iraq;

Whereas after the liberation of Kuwait in 1991, Iraq entered into a United Nations sponsored cease-fire agreement pursuant to which Iraq unequivocally agreed, among other things, to eliminate its nuclear, biological, and chemical weapons programs and the means to deliver and develop them, and to end its support for international terrorism;

Whereas the efforts of international weapons inspectors, United States intelligence agencies, and Iraqi defectors led to the discovery that Iraq had large stockpiles of chemical weapons and a large scale biological weapons program, and that Iraq had an advanced nuclear weapons development program that was much closer to producing a nuclear weapon than intelligence reporting had previously indicated;

Whereas Iraq, in direct and flagrant violation of the cease-fire, attempted to thwart the efforts of weapons inspectors to identify and destroy Iraq's weapons of mass destruction stockpiles and development capabilities, which finally resulted in the withdrawal of inspectors from Iraq on October 31, 1998;

Whereas in 1998 Congress concluded that Iraq's continuing weapons of mass destruction programs threatened vital United States interests and international peace and security, declared Iraq to be in "material and unacceptable breach of its international obligations" and urged the President "to take appropriate action, in accordance with the Constitution and relevant laws of the United States, to bring Iraq into compliance with its international obligations" (Public Law 105-235);

Whereas Iraq both poses a continuing threat to the national security of the United States and international peace and security in the Persian Gulf region and remains in material and unacceptable breach of its international obligations by, among other things, continuing to possess and develop a significant chemical and biological weapons capability, actively seeking a nuclear weapons capability, and supporting and harboring terrorist organizations;

Whereas Iraq persists in violating resolutions of the United Nations Security Council by continuing to engage in brutal repression of its civilian population thereby threatening international peace and security in the region, by refusing to release, repatriate, or account for non-Iraqi citizens wrongfully detained by Iraq, including an American serviceman, and by failing to return property wrongfully seized by Iraq from Kuwait;

Whereas the current Iraqi regime has demonstrated its capability and willingness to use weapons of mass destruction against other nations and its own people;

Whereas the current Iraqi regime has demonstrated its continuing hostility toward, and willingness to attack, the United States, including by attempting in 1993 to assassinate former President Bush and by firing on many thousands of occasions on United States and Coalition Armed Forces engaged in enforcing the resolutions of the United Nations Security Council;

Whereas members of al Qaida, an organization bearing responsibility for attacks on the United States, its citizens, and interests, including the attacks that occurred on September 11, 2001, are known to be in Iraq;

Whereas Iraq continues to aid and harbor other international terrorist organizations, including organizations that threaten the lives and safety of American citizens;

Whereas the attacks on the United States of September 11, 2001, underscored the gravity of the threat posed by the acquisition of weapons of mass destruction by international terrorist organizations;

Whereas Iraq's demonstrated capability and willingness to use weapons of mass destruction, the risk that the current Iraqi regime will either employ those weapons to launch a surprise attack against the United States or its Armed Forces or provide them to international terrorists who would do so, and the extreme magnitude of harm that would result to the United States and its citizens from such an attack, combine to justify action by the United States to defend itself;

U.S. Soldier Clearing a Suspected al Qaida Prison Camp in Iraq, 2007

Whereas United Nations Security Council Resolution 678 authorizes the use of all necessary means to enforce United Nations Security Council Resolution 660 and subsequent relevant resolutions and to compel Iraq to cease certain activities that threaten international peace and security, including the development of weapons of mass destruction and refusal or obstruction of United Nations weapons inspections in violation of United Nations Security Council Resolution 687, repression of its civilian population in violation of United Nations Security Council Resolution 688, and threatening its neighbors or United Nations operations in Iraq in violation of United Nations Security Council Resolution 949;

Whereas Congress in the Authorization for Use of Military Force Against Iraq Resolution (Public Law 102-1) has authorized the President "to use United States Armed Forces pursuant to United Nations Security Council Resolution 678 (1990) in order to achieve implementation of Security Council Resolutions 660, 661, 662, 664, 665, 666, 667, 669, 670, 674, and 677";

Whereas in December 1991, Congress expressed its sense that it "supports the use of all necessary means to achieve the goals of United Nations Security Council Resolution 687 as being consistent with the Authorization of Use of Military Force Against Iraq Resolution (Public Law 102-1)," that Iraq's repression of its civilian population violates United Nations Security Council Resolution 688 and "constitutes a continuing threat to the peace, security, and stability of the Persian Gulf region," and that Congress, "supports the use of all necessary means to achieve the goals of United Nations Security Council Resolution 688";

Whereas the Iraq Liberation Act (Public Law 105-338) expressed the sense of Congress that it should be the policy of the United States to support efforts to remove from power the current Iraqi regime and promote the emergence of a democratic government to replace that regime;

Whereas on September 12, 2002, President Bush committed the United States to "work with the United Nations Security Council to meet our common challenge" posed by Iraq and to "work for the necessary resolutions," while also making clear that "the Security Council resolutions will be enforced, and the just demands of peace and security will be met, or action will be unavoidable";

Whereas the United States is determined to prosecute the war on terrorism and Iraq's ongoing support for international terrorist groups combined with its development of weapons of mass destruction in direct violation of its obligations under the 1991 cease-fire and other United Nations Security Council resolutions make clear that it is in the national security interests of the United States and in furtherance of the war on terrorism that all relevant United Nations Security Council resolutions be enforced, including through the use of force if necessary;

Whereas Congress has taken steps to pursue vigorously the war on terrorism through the provision of authorities and funding requested by the President to take the necessary actions against international terrorists and terrorist organizations, including those nations, organizations or persons who planned, authorized, committed or aided the terrorist attacks that occurred on September 11, 2001, or harbored such persons or organizations;

Whereas the President and Congress are determined to continue to take all appropriate actions against international terrorists and terrorist organizations, including those nations, organizations or persons who planned, authorized, committed or aided the terrorist attacks that occurred on September 11, 2001, or harbored such persons or organizations;

Whereas the President has authority under the Constitution to take action in order to deter and prevent acts of international terrorism against the United States, as Congress recognized in the joint resolution on Authorization for Use of Military Force (Public Law 107-40); and

Whereas it is in the national security of the United States to restore international peace and security to the Persian Gulf region;

Now, therefore, be it resolved by the Senate and House of Representatives of the United States of America in Congress assembled,

SEC. 1. SHORT TITLE.

This joint resolution may be cited as the "Authorization for the Use of Military Force Against Iraq."

SEC. 2. SUPPORT FOR UNITED STATES DIPLOMATIC EFFORTS.

The Congress of the United States supports the efforts by the President to—

(a) strictly enforce through the United Nations Security Council all relevant Security Council resolutions applicable to Iraq and encourages him in those efforts; and

(b) obtain prompt and decisive action by the Security Council to ensure that Iraq abandons its strategy of delay, evasion and noncompliance and promptly and strictly complies with all relevant Security Council resolutions.

SEC. 3. AUTHORIZATION FOR USE OF UNITED STATES ARMED FORCES.

(a) AUTHORIZATION. The President is authorized to use the Armed Forces of the United States as he determines to be necessary and appropriate in order to

(1) defend the national security of the United States against the continuing threat posed by Iraq; and

(2) enforce all relevant United Nations Security Council Resolutions regarding Iraq.

(b) PRESIDENTIAL DETERMINATION.

In connection with the exercise of the authority granted in subsection (a) to use force the President shall, prior to such exercise or as soon thereafter as may be feasible, but no later than 48 hours after exercising such authority, make available to the Speaker of the House of Representatives and the President Pro Tempore of the Senate his determination that

(1) reliance by the United States on further diplomatic or other peaceful means alone either (A) will not adequately protect the national security of the United States against the continuing threat posed by Iraq or (B) is not likely to lead to enforcement of all relevant United Nations Security Council resolutions regarding Iraq, and

(2) acting pursuant to this resolution is consistent with the United States and other countries continuing to take the necessary actions against international terrorists and terrorist organizations, including those nations, organizations or persons who planned, authorized, committed or aided the terrorists attacks that occurred on September 11, 2001.

(c) WAR POWERS RESOLUTION REQUIREMENTS. —

(1) SPECIFIC STATUTORY AUTHORIZATION.—Consistent with section 8(a)(1) of the War Powers Resolution, the Congress declares that this section is intended to constitute specific statutory authorization within the meaning of section 5(b) of the War Powers Resolution.

(2) APPLICABILITY OF OTHER REQUIREMENTS.—Nothing in this resolution supersedes any requirement of the War Powers Resolution.

SEC. 4. REPORTS TO CONGRESS

(a) The President shall, at least once every 60 days, submit to the Congress a report on matters relevant to this joint resolution, including actions taken pursuant to the exercise of authority granted in Section 2 and the status of planning for efforts that are expected to be required after such actions are completed, including those actions described in section 7 of Public Law 105-338 (the Iraq Liberation Act of 1998).

(b) To the extent that the submission of any report described in subsection (a) coincides with the submission of any other report on matters relevant to this joint resolution otherwise required to be submitted to Congress pursuant to the reporting requirements of Public Law 93-148 (the War Powers Resolution), all such reports may be submitted as a single consolidated report to the Congress.

(c) To the extent that the information required by section 3 of Public Law 102-1 is included in the report required by this section, such report shall be considered as meeting the requirements of Section 3 of Public Law 102-1.

U.S. Troops in Iraq, 2003

2004 State of the Union Address
George W. Bush

Delivered January 20, 2004

Mr. Speaker, Vice President Cheney, Members of Congress, distinguished guests, and fellow citizens:

America this evening is a nation called to great responsibilities. And we are rising to meet them.

As we gather tonight, hundreds of thousands of American servicemen and women are deployed across the world in the war on terror. By bringing hope to the oppressed, and delivering justice to the violent, they are making America more secure.

Each day, law enforcement personnel and intelligence officers are tracking terrorist threats; analysts are examining airline passenger lists; the men and women of our new Homeland Security Department are patrolling our coasts and borders. And their vigilance is protecting America.

President George W. Bush

Americans are proving once again to be the hardest working people in the world. The American economy is growing stronger. The tax relief you passed is working.

Tonight, Members of Congress can take pride in the great works of compassion and reform that skeptics had thought impossible. You're raising the standards for our public schools; and you're giving our senior citizens prescription drug coverage under Medicare.

We have faced serious challenges together, and now we face a choice. We can go forward with confidence and resolve, or we can turn back to the dangerous illusion that terrorists are not plotting and outlaw regimes are no threat to us. We can press on with economic growth, and reforms in education and Medicare, or we can turn back to old policies and old divisions.

We've not come all this way—through tragedy, and trial, and war—only to falter and leave our work unfinished. Americans are rising to the tasks of history, and they expect the same from us. In their efforts, their enterprise, and their character, the American people are showing that the state of our Union is confident and strong.

Our greatest responsibility is the active defense of the American people. Twenty-eight months have passed since September the 11th, 2001—over two years without an attack on American soil—and it is tempting to believe that the danger is behind us. That hope is understandable, comforting—and false. The killing has continued in Bali, Jakarta, Casablanca, Riyadh, Mombassa, Jerusalem, Istanbul, and Baghdad. The terrorists continue to plot against America and the civilized world. And by our will and courage, this danger will be defeated.

Inside the United States, where the war began, we must continue to give our homeland security and law enforcement personnel every tool they need to defend us. And one of those essential tools is the PATRIOT Act, which allows Federal law enforcement to better share information, to track terrorists, to disrupt their cells, and to seize their assets. For years, we have used similar provisions to catch embezzlers and drug traffickers. If these methods are good for hunting criminals, they are even more important for hunting terrorists. Key provisions of the PATRIOT Act are set to expire next year. The terrorist threat will not expire on that schedule. Our law enforcement needs this vital legislation to protect our citizens. You need to renew the PATRIOT Act.

America is on the offensive against the terrorists who started this war. Last March, Khalid Shaikh Mohammed, a mastermind of September the 11th, awoke to find himself in the custody of U.S. and Pakistani authorities. Last August the 11th brought the capture of the terrorist Hambali, who was a key player in the attack in Indonesia that killed over 200 people. We're tracking al-Qaida around the world, and nearly two-thirds of their known leaders have now been captured or killed. Thousands of very skilled and determined military personnel are on the manhunt, going after the remaining killers who hide in cities and caves, and, one by one, we will bring these terrorists to justice.

As part of the offensive against terror, we are also confronting the regimes that harbor and support terrorists, and could supply them with nuclear, chemical, or biological weapons. The United States and our allies are determined: We refuse to live in the shadow of this ultimate danger.

The first to see our determination were the Taliban, who made Afghanistan the primary training base of al-Qaida killers. As of this month, that country has a new constitution, guaranteeing free elections and full participation by women. Businesses are opening, health care centers are being established, and the boys and girls of Afghanistan are back in school. With the help from the new Afghan Army, our coalition is leading aggressive raids against surviving members of the Taliban and al-Qaida. The men and women of Afghanistan are building a nation that is free, and proud, and fighting terror—and America is honored to be their friend.

Since we last met in this chamber, combat forces of the United States, Great Britain, Australia, Poland, and other countries enforced the demands of the United Nations, ended the rule of Saddam Hussein, and the people of Iraq are free. Having broken the Baathist regime, we face a remnant of violent Saddam supporters. Men who ran away from our troops in battle are now dispersed and attack from the shadows.

These killers, joined by foreign terrorists, are a serious, continuing danger. Yet we're making progress against them. The once all-powerful ruler of Iraq was found in a hole, and now sits in a prison cell. Of the top 55 officials of the former regime, we have captured or killed 45. Our forces are on the offensive, leading over 1,600 patrols a day, and conducting an average of 180 raids a week. We are dealing with these thugs in Iraq, just as surely as we dealt with Saddam Hussein's evil regime.

The work of building a new Iraq is hard, and it is right. And America has always been willing to do what it takes for what is right. Last January, Iraq's only law was the whim of one brutal man. Today our coalition is working with the Iraqi Governing Council to draft a basic law, with a bill of rights. We're working with Iraqis and the United Nations to prepare for a transition to full Iraqi sovereignty by the end of June. As democracy takes hold in Iraq, the enemies of freedom will do all in their power to spread violence and fear. They are trying to shake the will of our country and our friends, but the United States of America will never be intimidated by thugs and assassins. The killers will fail, and the Iraqi people will live in freedom.

Month by month, Iraqis are assuming more responsibility for their own security and their own future. And tonight we are honored to welcome one of Iraq's most respected leaders: the current President of the Iraqi Governing Council, Adnan Pachachi. Sir, America stands with you and the Iraqi people as you build a free and peaceful nation.

Because of American leadership and resolve, the world is changing for the better. Last month, the leader of Libya voluntarily pledged to disclose and dismantle all of his regime's weapons of mass destruction programs, including a uranium enrichment project for nuclear weapons. Colonel Qadhafi correctly judged that his country would be better off, and far more secure, without weapons of mass murder. Nine months of intense negotiations involving the United States and Great Britain succeeded with Libya, while 12 years of diplomacy with Iraq did not. And one reason is clear: For diplomacy to be effective, words must be credible—and no one can now doubt the word of America.

Different threats require different strategies. Along with nations in the region, we are insisting that North Korea eliminate its nuclear program. America and the international community are demanding that Iran meet its commitments and not develop nuclear weapons. America is committed to keeping the world's most dangerous weapons out of the hands of the most dangerous regimes.

When I came to this rostrum on September 20th, 2001, I brought the police shield of a fallen officer, my reminder of lives that ended, and a task that does not end. I gave to you and to all Americans my complete commitment to securing our country and defeating our enemies. And this pledge, given by one, has been kept by many. You in the Congress have provided the resources for our defense, and cast the difficult votes of war and peace. Our closest allies have been unwavering. America's intelligence personnel and diplomats have been skilled and tireless.

And the men and women of the American military—they have taken the hardest duty. We've seen their skill and their courage in armored charges, and midnight raids, and lonely hours on faithful watch. We have seen the joy when they return, and felt the sorrow when one is lost. I've had the honor of meeting our servicemen and women at many posts, from the deck of a carrier in the Pacific, to a mess hall in Baghdad. Many of our troops are listening tonight. And I want you and your families to know: America is proud of you. And my Administration, and this Congress, will give you the resources you need to fight and win the war on terror.

I know that some people question if America is really in a war at all. They view terrorism more as a crime, a problem to be solved mainly with law enforcement and indictments. After the World Trade Center was first attacked in 1993, some of the guilty were indicted and tried and convicted, and sent to prison. But the matter was not settled. The terrorists were still training and plotting in other nations, and drawing up more ambitious plans. After the chaos and carnage of September the 11th, it is not enough to serve our enemies with legal papers. The terrorists and their supporters declared war on the United States, and war is what they got.

Some in this chamber, and in our country, did not support the liberation of Iraq. Objections to war often come from principled motives. But let us be candid about the consequences of leaving Saddam Hussein in power. We're seeking all the facts. Already the Kay Report identified dozens of weapons of mass destruction-related program activities and significant amounts of equipment that Iraq concealed from the United Nations. Had we failed to act, the dictator's weapons of mass destruction programs would continue to this day. Had we failed to act, Security Council resolutions on Iraq would have been revealed as empty threats, weakening the United Nations and encouraging defiance by dictators around the world. Iraq's torture chambers would still be filled with victims—terrified and innocent. The killing fields of Iraq, where hundreds of thousands of men, women, and children vanished into the sands, would still be known only to the killers. For all who love freedom and peace, the world without Saddam Hussein's regime is a better and safer place!

Some critics have said our duties in Iraq must be internationalized. This particular criticism is hard to explain to our partners in Britain, Australia, Japan, South Korea, the Philippines, Thailand, Italy, Spain, Poland, Denmark, Hungary, Bulgaria, Ukraine, Romania, the Netherlands, Norway, El Salvador, and the 17 other countries that have committed troops to Iraq. As we debate at home, we must never ignore the vital contributions of our international partners, or dismiss their sacrifices. From the beginning, America has sought international support for our operations in Afghanistan and Iraq, and we have gained much support. There is a difference, however, between leading a coalition of many nations, and submitting to the objections of a few. America will never seek a permission slip to defend the security of our country.

We also hear doubts that democracy is a realistic goal for the greater Middle East, where freedom is rare. Yet it is mistaken, and condescending, to assume that whole cultures and great religions are incompatible with liberty and self-government. I believe that God has planted in every human heart the desire to live in freedom. And even when that desire is crushed by tyranny for decades, it will rise again.

As long as the Middle East remains a place of tyranny, despair, and anger, it will continue to produce men and movements that threaten the safety of America and our friends. So America is pursuing a forward strategy of freedom in the greater Middle East. We will challenge the enemies of reform, confront the allies of terror, and expect a higher standard from our friend [sic]. To cut through the barriers of hateful propaganda, the Voice of America and other broadcast services are expanding their programming in Arabic and Persian—and soon, a new television service will begin providing reliable news and information across the region. I will send you a proposal to double the budget of the National Endowment for Democracy, and to focus its new work on the development of free elections and free markets, free press, and free labor unions in the Middle East. And above all, we will finish the historic work of democracy in Afghanistan and Iraq, so those nations can light the way for others, and help transform a troubled part of the world.

America is a Nation with a mission, and that mission comes from our most basic beliefs. We have no desire to dominate, no ambitions of empire. Our aim is a democratic peace—a peace founded upon the dignity and rights of every man and woman. America acts in this cause with friends and allies at our side, yet we understand our special calling: This great Republic will lead the cause of freedom.

In these last three years, adversity has also revealed the fundamental strengths of the American economy. We have come through recession, and terrorist attack, and corporate scandals, and the uncertainties of war. And because you acted to stimulate our economy with tax relief, this economy is strong, and growing stronger.

You have doubled the child tax credit from 500 to a thousand dollars, reduced the marriage penalty, begun to phase out the death tax, reduced taxes on capital gains and stock dividends, cut taxes on small businesses, and you have lowered taxes for every American who pays income taxes.

Americans took those dollars and put them to work, driving this economy forward. The pace of economic growth in the third quarter of 2003 was the fastest in nearly 20 years. New home construction: the highest in almost 20 years. Home ownership rates: the highest ever. Manufacturing activity is increasing. Inflation is low. Interest rates are low. Exports are growing. Productivity is high. And jobs are on the rise.

These numbers confirm that the American people are using their money far better than government would have, and you were right to return it.

America's growing economy is also a changing economy. As technology transforms the way almost every job is done, America becomes more productive, and workers need new skills. Much of our job growth will be found in high-skilled fields like health care and biotechnology. So we must respond by helping more Americans gain the skills to find good jobs in our new economy.

All skills begin with the basics of reading and math, which are supposed to be learned in the early grades of our schools. Yet for too long, for too many children, those skills were never mastered. By passing the No Child Left Behind Act, you have made the expectation of literacy the law of our country. We are providing more funding for our schools—a 36 percent increase since 2001. We're requiring higher standards. We are regularly testing every child on the fundamentals. We are reporting results to parents, and making sure they have better options when schools are not performing. We are making progress toward excellence for every child in America.

But the status quo always has defenders. Some want to undermine the No Child Left Behind Act by weakening standards and accountability. Yet the results we require are really a matter of common sense: We expect third graders to read and do math at the third grade level—and that's not asking too much. Testing is the only way to identify and help students who are falling behind.

This Nation will not go back to the days of simply shuffling children along from grade to grade without them learning the basics. I refuse to give up on any child, and the No Child Left Behind Act is opening the door of opportunity to all of America's children.

At the same time, we must ensure that older students and adults can gain the skills they need to find work now. Many of the fastest-growing occupations require strong math and science preparation, and training beyond the high school level. So tonight I propose a series of measures called Jobs for the 21st Century. This program will provide extra help to middle and high school students who fall behind in reading and math, expand Advanced Placement programs in low-income schools, invite math and science professionals from the private sector to teach part-time in our high schools. I propose larger Pell Grants for students who prepare for college with demanding courses in high school. I propose increasing our support for America's fine community colleges. I do so, so they can train workers for industries that are creating the most new jobs. By all these actions, we will help more and more Americans to join in the growing prosperity of our country.

Job training is important, and so is job creation. We must continue to pursue an aggressive, pro-growth economic agenda.

Congress has some unfinished business on the issue of taxes. The tax reductions you passed are set to expire. Unless you act—unless you act—unless you act, the unfair tax on marriage will go back up. Unless you act, millions of families will be charged 300 dollars more in Federal taxes for every child. Unless you act, small businesses will pay higher taxes. Unless you act, the death tax will eventually come back to life. Unless you act, Americans face a tax increase. What Congress has given, the Congress should not take away: For the sake of job growth, the tax cuts you passed should be permanent.

Our agenda for jobs and growth must help small business owners and employees with relief from needless federal regulation, and protect them from junk and frivolous lawsuits.

Consumers and businesses need reliable supplies of energy to make our economy run, so I urge you to pass legislation to modernize our electricity system, promote conservation, and make America less dependent on foreign sources of energy.

My administration is promoting free and fair trade to open up new markets for America's entrepreneurs and manufacturers and farmers—to create jobs for American workers. Younger workers should have the opportunity to build a nest egg by saving part of their Social Security taxes in a personal retirement account. We should make the Social Security system a source of ownership for the American people. And we should limit the burden of government on this economy by acting as good stewards of taxpayers' dollars.

In two weeks, I will send you a budget that funds the war, protects the homeland, and meets important domestic needs, while limiting the growth in discretionary spending to less than 4 percent. This will require that Congress focus on priorities, cut wasteful spending, and be wise with the people's money. By doing so, we can cut the deficit in half over the next five years.

Tonight, I also ask you to reform our immigration laws so they reflect our values and benefit our economy. I propose a new temporary worker program to match willing foreign workers with willing employers when no Americans can be found to fill the job. This reform will be good for our economy because employers will find needed workers in an honest and orderly system. A temporary worker program will help protect our homeland, allowing Border Patrol and law enforcement to focus on true threats to our national security.

I oppose amnesty, because it would encourage further illegal immigration, and unfairly reward those who break our laws. My temporary worker program will preserve the citizenship path for those who respect the law, while bringing millions of hardworking men and women out from the shadows of American life.

Our nation's health care system, like our economy, is also in a time of change. Amazing medical technologies are improving and saving lives. This dramatic progress has brought its own challenge, in the rising costs of medical care and health insurance. Members of Congress, we must work together to help control those costs and extend the benefits of modern medicine throughout our country.

Meeting these goals requires bipartisan effort, and two months ago you showed the way. By strengthening Medicare and adding a prescription drug benefit, you kept a basic commitment to our seniors: You are giving them the modern medicine they deserve.

Starting this year, under the law you passed, seniors can choose to receive a drug discount card, saving them 10 to 25 percent off the retail price of most prescription drugs—and millions of low-income seniors can get an additional $600 to buy medicine. Beginning next year, seniors will have new coverage for preventive screenings against diabetes and heart disease, and seniors just entering Medicare can receive wellness exams.

In January of 2006, seniors can get prescription drug coverage under Medicare. For a monthly premium of about $35, most seniors who do not have that coverage today can expect to see their drug bills cut roughly in half. Under this reform, senior citizens will be able to keep their Medicare just as it is, or they can choose a Medicare plan that fits them best—just as you, as members of Congress, can choose an insurance plan that meets your needs. And starting this year, millions of Americans will be able to save money tax-free for their medical expenses in a health savings account.

I signed this measure proudly, and any attempt to limit the choices of our seniors, or to take away their prescription drug coverage under Medicare, will meet my veto.

On the critical issue of health care, our goal is to ensure that Americans can choose and afford private health care coverage that best fits their individual needs. To make insurance more affordable, Congress must act to address rapidly rising health care costs. Small businesses should be able to band together and negotiate for lower insurance rates, so they can cover more workers with health insurance. I urge you to pass association health plans. I ask you to give lower-income Americans a refundable tax credit that would allow millions to buy their own basic health insurance.

By computerizing health records, we can avoid dangerous medical mistakes, reduce costs, and improve care. To protect the doctor-patient relationship, and keep good doctors doing good work, we must eliminate wasteful and frivolous medical lawsuits. And tonight I propose that individuals who buy catastrophic health care coverage, as part of our new health savings accounts, be allowed to deduct 100 percent of the premiums from their taxes.

A government-run health care system is the wrong prescription.

By keeping costs under control, expanding access, and helping more Americans afford coverage, we will preserve the system of private medicine that makes America's health care the best in the world.

We are living in a time of great change—in our world, in our economy, in science and medicine. Yet some things endure—courage and compassion, reverence and integrity, respect for differences of faith and race. The values we try to live by never change. And they are instilled in us by fundamental institutions, such as families and schools and religious congregations. These institutions, these unseen pillars of civilization, must remain strong in America, and we will defend them. We must stand with our families to help them raise healthy, responsible children. When it comes to helping children make right choices, there is work for all of us to do.

One of the worst decisions our children can make is to gamble their lives and futures on drugs. Our government is helping parents confront this problem with aggressive education, treatment, and law enforcement. Drug use in high school has declined by 11 percent over the last two years. Four hundred thousand fewer young people are using illegal drugs than in the year 2001. In my budget, I proposed new funding to continue our aggressive, community-based strategy to reduce demand for illegal drugs. Drug testing in our schools has proven to be an effective part of this effort. So tonight I proposed an additional $23 millions [sic] for schools that want to use drug testing as a tool to save children's lives. The aim here is not to punish children, but to send them this message: We love you, and we don't want to lose you.

To help children make right choices, they need good examples. Athletics play such an important role in our society, but, unfortunately, some in professional sports are not setting much of an example. The use of performance-enhancing drugs like steroids in baseball, football, and other sports is dangerous, and it sends the wrong message—that there are shortcuts to accomplishment, and that performance is more important than character. So tonight I call on team owners, union representatives, coaches, and players to take the lead, to send the right signal, to get tough, and to get rid of steroids now.

To encourage right choices, we must be willing to confront the dangers young people face even when they're difficult to talk about. Each year, about 3 million teenagers contract sexually-transmitted diseases that can harm them, or kill them, or prevent them from ever becoming parents. In my budget, I propose a grassroots campaign to help inform families about these medical risks. We will double federal funding for abstinence programs, so schools can teach this fact of life: Abstinence for young people is the only certain way to avoid sexually-transmitted diseases.

Decisions children now make can affect their health and character for the rest of their lives. All of us—parents and schools and government—must work together to counter the negative influence of the culture, and to send the right messages to our children.

A strong America must also value the institution of marriage. I believe we should respect individuals as we take a principled stand for one of the most fundamental, enduring institutions of our civilization. Congress has already taken a stand on this issue by passing the Defense of Marriage Act, signed in 1996 by President Clinton. That statute protects marriage under federal law as a union of a man and a woman, and declares that one state may not redefine marriage for other states. Activist judges, however, have begun redefining marriage by court order, without regard for the will of the people and their elected representatives. On an issue of such great consequence, the people's voice must be heard. If judges insist on forcing their arbitrary will upon the people, the only alternative left to the people would be the constitutional process. Our nation must defend the sanctity of marriage.

The outcome of this debate is important, and so is the way we conduct it. The same moral tradition that defines marriage also teaches that each individual has dignity and value in God's sight.

It's also important to strengthen our communities by unleashing the compassion of America's religious institutions. Religious charities of every creed are doing some of the most vital work in our country—mentoring children, feeding the hungry, taking the hand of the lonely. Yet government has often denied social service grants and contracts to these groups, just because they have a cross or a Star of David or a crescent on the wall. By executive order, I have opened billions of dollars in grant money to competition that includes faith-based charities. Tonight I ask you to codify this into law, so people of faith can know that the law will never discriminate against them again.

In the past, we've worked together to bring mentors to children of prisoners, and provide treatment for the addicted, and help for the homeless. Tonight I ask you to consider another group of Americans in need of help. This year, some 600,000 inmates will be released from prison back into society. We know from long experience that if they can't find work, or a home, or help, they are much more likely to commit crime and return to prison. So tonight, I propose a four-year, 300 million dollar prisoner re-entry initiative to expand job training and placement services, to provide transitional housing, and to help newly released prisoners get mentoring, including from faith-based groups. America is the land of second chance, and when the gates of the prison open, the path ahead should lead to a better life.

For all Americans, the last three years have brought tests we did not ask for, and achievements shared by all. By our actions, we have shown what kind of nation we are. In grief, we have found the grace to go on. In challenge, we rediscovered the courage and daring of a free people. In victory, we have shown the noble aims and good heart of America. And having come this far, we sense that we live in a time set apart.

I've been witness to the character of the people of America, who have shown calm in times of danger, compassion for one another, and toughness for the long haul. All of us have been partners in a great enterprise. And even some of the youngest understand that we are living in historic times. Last month a girl in Lincoln, Rhode Island, sent me a letter. It began, "Dear George W. Bush. If there's anything you know, I, Ashley Pearson, age 10, can do to help anyone, please send me a letter and tell me what I can do to save our country." She added this P.S.: "If you can send a letter to the troops, please put, 'Ashley Pearson believes in you.'"

Tonight, Ashley, your message to our troops has just been conveyed. And, yes, you have some duties yourself. Study hard in school, listen to your mom or dad, help someone in need, and when you and your friends see a man or woman in uniform, say, "thank you." And, Ashley, while you do your part, all of us here in this great chamber will do our best to keep you and the rest of America safe and free.

My fellow citizens, we now move forward, with confidence and faith. Our nation is strong and steadfast. The cause we serve is right, because it is the cause of all mankind. The momentum of freedom in our world is unmistakable—and it is not carried forward by our power alone. We can trust in that greater power who guides the unfolding of the years. And in all that is to come, we can know that His purposes are just and true.

May God continue to bless America.

South Dakota 2006 Law Regarding Abortion

AN ACT

ENTITLED, An Act to establish certain legislative findings, to reinstate the prohibition against certain acts causing the termination of an unborn human life and to prescribe a penalty therefor.

BE IT ENACTED BY THE LEGISLATURE OF THE STATE OF SOUTH DAKOTA:

Section 1. The Legislature finds that the State of South Dakota has a compelling and paramount interest in the preservation and protection of all human life and finds that the guarantee of due process of law under the South Dakota Bill of Rights applies equally to born and unborn human beings.

Section 2. The Legislature finds that the life of a human being begins when the ovum is fertilized by male sperm. The Legislature finds that the explosion of knowledge derived from new recombinant DNA technologies over the past twenty-five years has reinforced the validity of the finding of this scientific fact.

Section 3. The Legislature finds that, based upon the evidence derived from thirty years of legalized abortions in this country, the interests of pregnant mothers protected under the South Dakota Bill of Rights have been adversely affected as abortions terminate the constitutionally protected fundamental interest of the pregnant mother in her relationship

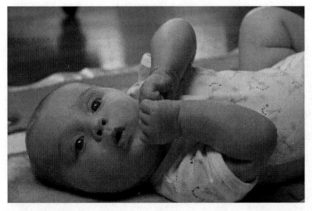

with her child and abortions are performed without a truly informed or voluntary consent or knowing waiver of the woman's rights and interests. The Legislature finds that the state has a duty to protect the pregnant mother's fundamental interest in her relationship with her unborn child.

Section 4. The Legislature finds that abortion procedures impose significant risks to the health and life of the pregnant mother, including subjecting women to significant risk of severe depression, suicidal ideation, suicide, attempted suicide, post traumatic stress disorders, adverse impact in the lives of women, physical injury, and a greater risk of death than risks associated with carrying the unborn child to full term and childbirth.

Section 5. The Legislature finds that a pregnant mother, together with the unborn human child, each possess a natural and inalienable right to life under the South Dakota Bill of Rights.

Section 6. That chapter 22-17 be amended by adding thereto a NEW SECTION to read as follows:

No person may knowingly administer to, prescribe for, or procure for, or sell to any pregnant woman any medicine, drug, or other substance with the specific intent of causing or abetting the termination of the life of an unborn human being unless it is necessary to preserve the life of the pregnant woman, or if there is a serious risk of substantial and irreversible impairment of a major bodily function of the pregnant woman. No person may knowingly use or employ any instrument or procedure upon a pregnant woman with the specific intent of causing or abetting the termination of the life of an unborn human being unless it is necessary to preserve the life of the pregnant woman, or if there is a serious risk of substantial and irreversible impairment of a major bodily function of the pregnant woman.

Any violation of this section is a Class 5 felony.

Section 7. That chapter 22-17 be amended by adding thereto a NEW SECTION to read as follows:

Nothing in section 6 of this Act may be construed to prohibit the sale, use, prescription, or administration of a contraceptive measure, drug or chemical, if it is administered prior to the time when a pregnancy could be determined through conventional medical testing and if the contraceptive measure is sold, used, prescribed, or administered in accordance with manufacturer instructions.

Section 8. That chapter 22-17 be amended by adding thereto a NEW SECTION to read as follows:

No licensed physician who performs a medical procedure designed or intended to prevent the death of a pregnant mother or a serious risk of substantial and irreversible impairment of a major bodily function of the pregnant woman is guilty of violating section 6 of this Act. However, the physician shall make reasonable medical efforts under the circumstances to preserve both the life of the mother and the life of her unborn child in a manner consistent with conventional medical practice.

Medical treatment provided to the mother by a licensed physician which results in the accidental or unintentional injury or death of the unborn child is not a violation of this statute.

Nothing in this Act may be construed to subject the pregnant mother upon whom any abortion is performed or attempted to any criminal conviction and penalty.

Section 9. That chapter 22-17 be amended by adding thereto a NEW SECTION to read as follows:

Terms used in this Act mean:

(1) "Pregnant," the human female reproductive condition, of having a living unborn human being within her body throughout the entire embryonic and fetal ages of the unborn child from fertilization to full gestation and child birth;

(2) "Unborn human being," an individual living member of the species homo sapiens throughout the entire embryonic and fetal ages of the unborn child from fertilization to full gestation and childbirth;

(3) "Serious risk of the substantial and irreversible impairment of a major bodily function," any medically diagnosed condition that so complicates the pregnancy of the woman as to directly or indirectly cause the substantial and irreversible physical impairment of the pregnant woman;

(4) "Fertilization," that point in time when a male human sperm penetrates the zona pellucida of a female human ovum.

Section 10. That § 34-23A-2 be repealed.

Section 11. That § 34-23A-3 be repealed.

Section 12. That § 34-23A-4 be repealed.

Section 13. That § 34-23A-5 be repealed.

Section 14. If any provision of this Act is found to be unconstitutional, the provision is severable; and the other provisions of this Act remain effective.

Section 15. Nothing in this Act may be construed to repeal, by implication or otherwise, any provision not explicitly repealed.

Section 16. If any provision of this Act is ever temporarily or permanently restrained or enjoined by judicial order, the provisions of chapters 34-23A and 22-17 shall be enforced. However, if such temporary or permanent restraining order or injunction is subsequently stayed or dissolved, or otherwise ceases to have effect, all provisions of this Act that are not restrained shall have full force and effect.

"The U.S. Supreme Court"
from *Democracy in America*
Alexis de Tocqueville (1835)

Alexis de Tocqueville was a French attorney who visited the United States in 1831. His book Democracy in America *(two volumes, published in 1835 and 1840) is a brilliant analysis of American life and government. Much of what he wrote is still relevant today. Here are some of his comments on the Supreme Court, which at the time had seven members.*

When we have examined in detail the organization of the Supreme Court and the entire prerogatives which it exercises, we shall readily admit that a more imposing judicial power was never constituted by any people. The Supreme Court is placed higher than any other known tribunal, both by the nature of its rights and the class of justiciable parties which it controls.

In all the civilized countries of Europe the government has always shown the greatest reluctance to allow the cases in which it was itself interested to be decided by the ordinary course of justice. This repugnance is naturally greater as the government is more absolute; and, on the other hand, the privileges of the courts of justice are extended with the increasing liberties of the people; but no European nation has yet held that all judicial controversies, without regard to their origin, can be left to the judges of common law.

In America this theory has been actually put in practice; and the Supreme Court of the United States is the sole tribunal of the nation. Its power extends to all cases arising under laws and treaties made by the national authorities, to all cases of admiralty and maritime jurisdiction, and, in general, to all points that affect the law of nations. It may even be affirmed that, although its constitution is essentially judicial, its prerogatives are almost entirely political. Its sole object is to enforce the execution of the laws of the Union; and the Union regulates only the relations of the government with the citizens, and of the nation with foreign powers; the relations of citizens among themselves are almost all regulated by the sovereignty of the states.

A second and still greater cause of the preponderance of this court may be adduced. In the nations of Europe the courts of justice are called upon to try only the controversies of private individuals, but the Supreme Court of the United States summons sovereign powers to its bar. When the clerk of the court advances on the steps of the tribunal and simply says: "The State of New York versus The State of Ohio," it is impossible not to feel that the court which he addresses is no ordinary body; and when it is recollected that one of these parties represents one million, and the other two millions of men, one is struck by the responsibility of the seven judges, whose decision is about to satisfy or to disappoint so large a number of their fellow citizens.

The peace, the prosperity, and the very existence of the Union are vested in the hands of the seven Federal judges. Without them the Constitution would be a dead letter: the executive appeals to them for assistance against the encroachments of the legislative power, the legislature demands their protection against the assaults of the executive; they defend the Union from the disobedience of the states, the states from the exaggerated claims of the Union, the public interest against private interests, and the conservative spirit of stability against the fickleness of the democracy. Their power is enormous, but it is the power of public opinion. They are all-powerful as long as the people respect the law; but they would be impotent against popular neglect or contempt of the law. The force of public opinion is the most intractable of agents, because its exact limits cannot be defined; and it is not less dangerous to exceed than to remain below the boundary prescribed.

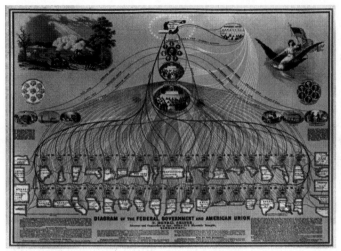
Diagram of the Federal Government, c. 1862

Not only must the Federal judges be good citizens, and men of that information and integrity which are indispensable to all magistrates, but they must be statesmen, wise to discern the signs of the times, not afraid to brave the obstacles that can be subdued, nor slow to turn away from the current when it threatens to sweep them off, and the supremacy of the Union and the obedience due to the laws along with them.

The President, who exercises a limited power, may err without causing great mischief in the state. Congress may decide amiss without destroying the Union, because the electoral body in which the Congress originates may cause it to retract its decision by changing its members. But if the Supreme Court is ever composed of imprudent or bad men, the Union may be plunged into anarchy or civil war.

Used by permission of the American Studies Collection of Hypertext Historic Documents maintained by the University of Virginia:
http://xroads.virginia.edu/~HYPER/DETOC/colophon.html

"On a Visit to the Senate When He Was Twelve" from *The Education of Henry Adams* Henry Adams (1907)

Henry Adams was the great-grandson of John Adams and the grandson of John Quincy Adams. His family was prominent in Massachusetts and American government and politics for well over a century. The Education of Henry Adams was his autobiography. It was completed in 1905 but only published after his death in 1918. Adams had a skeptical perspective about many things, including religion; but he also shared some wise insights. The following is his recollection of being taken by his father (a prominent figure in his own right) onto the floor of the U.S. Senate in 1850 when Henry was twelve years old. The book is written in the third person.

His father took him to the Capitol and on the floor of the Senate, which then, and long afterwards, until the era of tourists, was freely open to visitors. The old Senate Chamber resembled a pleasant political club. Standing behind the Vice-President's chair, which is now the Chief Justice's, the boy was presented to some of the men whose names were great in their day, and as familiar to him as his own. Clay and Webster and Calhoun were there still, but with them a Free Soil candidate for the Vice-Presidency [Henry Adams' father, Charles Francis Adams] had little to do; what struck boys most was their type. Senators were a species; they all wore an air, as they wore a blue dress coat or brass buttons; they were Roman.

The type of Senator in 1850 was rather charming at its best, and the Senate, when in good temper, was an agreeable body, numbering only some sixty members, and affecting the airs of courtesy. Its vice was not so much a vice of manners or temper as of attitude. The statesman of all periods was apt to be pompous,

Old Senate Chamber
This chamber was used by the Senate from 1819-1859.
It was occupied by the Supreme Court from 1860 until 1935.
The chamber was then used as a meeting room until 1976
when it was restored to its mid-nineteenth century appearance.

but even pomposity was less offensive than familiarity—on the platform as in the pulpit— and Southern pomposity, when not arrogant, was genial and sympathetic, almost quaint and childlike in its simple-mindedness; quite a different thing from the Websterian or Conklinian pomposity of the North.

The boy felt at ease there, more at home than he had ever felt in Boston State House, though his acquaintance with the codfish in the House of Representatives went back beyond distinct recollection. Senators spoke kindly to him, and seemed to feel so, for they had known his family socially; and, in spite of slavery, even J. Q. Adams in his later years, after he ceased to stand in the way of rivals, had few personal enemies. Decidedly the Senate, pro-slavery though it were, seemed a friendly world.

Used by permission of the American Studies Collection of Hypertext Historic Documents maintained by the University of Virginia: http://xroads.virginia.edu/~HYPER/hadams/ha_home.html

U.S. Senate Chamber

"The House of Representatives"
from *Congressional Government*
Woodrow Wilson (1885)

Woodrow Wilson is the only President to have earned a Ph.D. His degree was in political science, and his dissertation was published in 1885 as Congressional Government. *Wilson showed little patience with what he saw as business as usual in Congress, especially with the committee system.*

Like a vast picture thronged with figures of equal prominence and crowded with elaborate and obtrusive details, Congress is hard to see satisfactorily and appreciatively at a single view and from a single stand-point. Its complicated forms and diversified structure confuse the vision, and conceal the system which underlies its composition. It is too complex to be understood without an effort, without a careful and systematic process of analysis. Consequently, very few people do understand it, and its doors are practically shut against the comprehension of the public at large. If Congress had a few authoritative leaders whose figures were very distinct and very conspicuous to the eye of the world, and who could represent and stand for the national legislature in the thoughts of that very numerous, and withal very respectable, class of persons who must think specifically and in concrete forms when they think at all, those persons who can make something out of men but very little out of intangible generalizations, it would be quite within the region of possibilities for the majority of serious confusion of thought. I suppose that almost everybody who just now gives any heed to the policy of Great Britain, with regard even to the reform of the franchise and other like strictly legislative questions, thinks of Mr. Gladstone and his colleagues rather than of the House of Commons, whose servants they are. The question is not, What will Parliament do? but, What will Mr. Gladstone do? And there is even less doubt that it is easier and more natural to look upon the legislative designs of Germany as locked up behind

Democratic Members of the House of Representatives Visit Governor Woodrow Wilson in Sea Girt, New Jersey, 1912

Bismarck's heavy brows than to think of them as dependent upon the determinations of the Reichstag, although as a matter of fact its consent is indispensable even to the plans of the imperious and domineering Chancellor.

But there is no great minister or ministry to represent the will and being of Congress in the common thought. The Speaker of the House of Representatives stands as near to the leadership as any one; but his will does not run as a formative and imperative power in legislation much beyond the appointment of the committees who are to lead the House and do its work for it, and it is, therefore, not entirely satisfactory to the public mind to trace all legislation to him. He may have a controlling hand in starting it; but he sits too still in his chair, and is too evidently not on the floor of the body over which he presides, to make it seem probable to the ordinary judgment that he has much immediate concern in legislation after it is once set afoot. Everybody knows that he is a staunch and avowed partisan, and that he likes to make smooth, whenever he can, the legislative paths of his party; but it does not seem likely that all important measures originate with him, or that he is the author of every distinct policy. And in fact he is not. He is a great party chief, but the hedging circumstances of his official position as presiding officer prevent his performing the part of active leadership. He appoints the leaders of the House, but he is not himself its leader.

The leaders of the House are the chairmen of the principal Standing Committees. Indeed, to be exactly accurate, the House has as many Standing Committees as there are leading classes of legislation, and in the consideration of every topic of business the House is guided by a special leader in the person of the chairman of the Standing Committee, charged with the superintendence of measures of the particular class to which that topic belongs. It is this multiplicity of leaders, this many-headed leadership, which makes the organization of the House too complex to afford uninformed people and unskilled observers any easy clue to its methods of rule. For the chairmen of the Standing Committees do not constitute a cooperative body like a ministry. They do not consult and concur in the adoption of homogeneous and mutually helpful measures; there is no thought of acting in concert. Each Committee goes its own way at its own pace. It is impossible to discover any unity or method in the disconnected and therefore unsystematic, confused, and desultory action of the House, or any common purpose in the measures which its Committees from time to time recommend.

And it is not only to the unanalytic thought of the common observer who looks at the House from the outside of its doings seem helter-skelter, and without comprehendible rule; it is not at once easy to understand them when they are scrutinized in their daily headway through open session by one who is inside the House. The newly-elected member, entering its doors for the first time, and with no more knowledge of its rules and customs than the more intelligent of his constituents possess, always experiences great difficulty in adjusting his preconceived ideas of congressional life to the strange and unlooked-for conditions by which he finds himself surrounded after he has been sworn in and has become a part of the great legislative machine. Indeed there are generally many things connected with his career in Washington to disgust and dispirit, if not to aggrieve, the new member. In the first place, his local reputation does not follow him to the federal capital. Possibly the members from his own State know him, and receive him into full fellowship; but no one else knows him, except as an adherent of this or that party, or as a new-comer from this or that State. He finds his station insignificant, and his identity indistinct. But this social humiliation which he experiences in circles in which to be a congressman does not of itself confer distinction, because it is only to be one among many, is probably not to be compared with the chagrin and disappointment which come in company with the inevitable discovery that he is equally without weight or title to consideration in the House itself. No man, when chosen to the membership of a body possessing great powers and exalted prerogatives, likes to find his activity repressed, and himself suppressed, by imperative rules and precedents which seem to have been framed for the deliberate purpose of making usefulness unattainable by individual members. Yet such the new member finds the rules and precedents have grown, not out of set purpose to curtail the privileges of new members as such, but out of the plain necessities of business; it remains the fact that he suffers under their curb, and it is not until "custom hath made it in him a property of easiness" that he submits to them with anything like good grace.

Not all new members suffer alike, of course, under this trying discipline; because it is not every new member that comes to his seat with serious purposes of honest, earnest, and duteous work. There are numerous tricks and subterfuges, soon learned and easily used, by means of which the most idle and self-indulgent members may readily make such show of exemplary diligence as will quite satisfy, if it does not positively delight, constituents in Buncombe. But the number of congressmen who deliberately court uselessness and counterfeit well-doing is probably small. The great majority doubtless have a keen enough sense of their duty and a sufficiently unhesitating desire to do it; and it may safely be taken for granted that the zeal of new members is generally hot and insistent. If it be not hot to begin with, it is like to become so by reason of friction with the rules, because such men must inevitably be chafed by the bonds of restraint drawn about them by the inexorable observances of the House.

Often the new member goes to Washington as the representative of a particular line of policy, having been elected, it may be, as an advocate of free trade, or as a champion of protection; and it is naturally his first care upon entering on his duties to seek immediate opportunity for the expression of his views and immediate means of giving them definite shape and thrusting them upon the attention of Congress. His disappointment is, therefore, very keen when he finds both opportunity and means denied to him. He can introduce his bill; but that is all he can do, and he must do that at a particular time and in a particular manner. This he is likely to learn through rude experience, if he be not cautious to inquire beforehand the details of practice. He is likely to make a rash start, upon the supposition that Congress observes the ordinary rules of parliamentary practice to which he has become accustomed in the debating clubs familiar to his youth, and in the mass-meetings known to his later experience. His bill is doubtless ready for presentation early in the session, and some day, taking advantage of a pause in the proceedings, when there seems to be no business before the House, he rises to read it and move its adoption. But he finds getting the floor an arduous and precarious undertaking. There are certain to be others who want it as well as he; and his indignation is stirred by the fact that the Speaker does not so much as turn towards him, though he must have heard his call, but recognizes some one else readily and as a matter of course. If he be obstreperous and persistent in his cries of "Mr. Speaker," he may get that great functionary's attention for a moment,—only to be told, however, that he is out of order, and that his bill can be introduced at that stage only by unanimous consent: immediately there are mechanically-uttered but emphatic exclamations of objection, and he is forced to sit down confused and disgusted. He has, without knowing it, obtruded himself and the way of the "regular order of business," and been run over in consequence, without being quite clear as to how the accident occurred.

Moved by the pain and discomfiture of this first experience to respect, if not to fear, the rules, the new member casts about, by study or inquiry, to find out, if possible, the nature and occasion of his privileges. He learns that his only safe day is Monday. On that day the roll of the States is called, and members may introduce bills as their States are reached in the call. So on Monday he essays another bout with the rules, confident this time of being on their safe side,—but mayhap indiscreetly and unluckily over-confident. For if he supposes, as he naturally will, that after his bill has been sent up to be read by the clerk he may say a few words in its behalf, and in that belief sets out upon his long-considered remarks, he will be knocked down by the rules as surely as he was on the first occasion when he gained the floor for a brief moment. The rap of Mr. Speaker's gavel is sharp, immediate and peremptory. He is curtly informed that no debate is in order; the bill can only be referred to the appropriate Committee.

This is, indeed, disheartening; it is his first lesson on committee government, and the master's rod smarts; but the sooner he learns the prerogatives and powers of the Standing Committees the sooner will he penetrate the mysteries of the rules and avoid the pain of further contact with their thorny side. The privileges of the Standing Committees are the beginning and the end of the rules. Both the House of Representatives and the Senate conduct their business by what may figuratively, but not inaccurately, be called an odd device of disintegration. The House virtually both deliberates and legislates in small sections. Time would fail it to discuss all the bills brought in, for they every session number thousands; and it is to be doubted whether, even if time allowed, the ordinary processes of debate and amendment would suffice to sift the chaff from the wheat in the bushels of bills every week piled upon the clerk's desk. Accordingly, no futile attempt is made to do anything of the kind. The work is parceled out, most of it to the forty-seven Standing Committees which constitute the regular organization of the House, some of it to select committees appointed for special and temporary purposes. Each of the almost numberless bills that come pouring in on Mondays is "read a first and second time,"—simply perfunctorily read, that is, by its title, by the clerk, and passed by silent assent through its first formal courses, for the purpose of bringing it to the proper stage for commitment,—and referred without debate to the appropriate Standing Committee. Practically, no bill escapes commitment—save, of course, bills introduced by committees, and a few which may now and then be crowed through under a suspension of rules, granted by a two-thirds vote—though the exact disposition to be made of a bill is not always determined easily and as a matter of course. Besides the great Committee of Ways and Means and the equally great Committee on Appropriations, there are Standing Committees on Banking and Currency, on Claims, on Commerce, on the Public Lands, on Post-Offices and Post-Roads, on the Judiciary, on Public Expenditures, on Manufactures, on Agriculture, on Military Affairs, on Naval Affairs, on Mines and Mining, on Education and Labor, on Patents, and on a score of other branches of legislative concern; but careful and differential as is the topical division of the subjects of legislation which is represented in the titles of these Committees, it is not always evident to which Committee each particular bill should go. Many bills affect subjects which may be regarded as lying as properly within the jurisdiction of one as of another of the Committees; for no hard and fast lines separate the various classes of business which the Committees are commissioned to take in charge. Their jurisdictions overlap at many points, and it must frequently happen that bills are read which cover just this common ground. Over the commitment of such bills sharp and interesting skirmishes often take place. There is active competition for them, the ordinary, quiet routine of matter-of-course reference being interrupted by rival motion seeking to give very different directions to the disposition to be made of them. To which Committee should a bill "to fix and establish the maximum rates of fares of the Union Pacific and central Pacific Railroads" be sent,—to the Committee on Commerce or to the Committee on the Pacific Railroads? Should a bill which prohibits the mailing of certain classes of letters and circulars go to the Committee on Post-Offices and Post-Roads, because it relates to the mails, or to the Committee on the Judiciary, because it proposes to make any transgression of its prohibition a crime? What is the proper disposition of any bill which thus seems to lie within two distinct committee jurisdictions?

The fate of bills committed is generally not uncertain. As a rule, a bill committed is a bill doomed. When it goes from the clerk's desk to a committee-room it crosses a parliamentary bridge of sighs to dim dungeons of silence whence it will never return. The means and time of its death are unknown, but its friends never see it again. Of course no Standing Committee is privileged to take upon itself the full powers of the House it represents, and formally and decisively reject a bill referred to it; its disapproval, if it disapproves, must be reported to the House in the form of a recommendation that the bill "do not pass." But it is easy, and therefore common, to let the session pass without making any report at all upon bills deemed objectionable or unimportant, and to substitute for reports upon them a few bills of the Committee's own drafting; so that thousands of bills expire with the expiration of each congress, not having been rejected, but having been simply neglected. There was not time to report upon them.

Of course it goes without saying that the practical effect of this Committee organization of the House is to consign to each of the Standing Committees the entire direction of legislation upon those subjects which properly come to its consideration. As to those subjects it is entitled to the initiative, and all legislative action with regard to them is under its overruling guidance. It gives shape and course to the determinations of the House. In one respect, however, its initiative is limited. Even a Standing Committee cannot report a bill whose subject-matter has not been referred to it by the House, "by the rules or otherwise"; it cannot volunteer advice on questions upon which its advice has not been asked. But this is not a serious, not even an operative, limitation upon its functions of suggestion and leadership; for it is a very simple matter to get referred to it any subject it wishes to introduce to the attention of the House. Its chairman, or one of its leading members, frames a bill covering the point upon which the Committee wishes to suggest legislation; brings it in, in his capacity as a private member, on Monday, when the call of States is made; has it referred to his Committee; and thus secures an opportunity for the making of the desired report.

It is by this imperious authority of the standing Committees that the new member is stayed and thwarted whenever he seeks to take an active part in the business of the House. Turn which way he may, some privilege of the Committees stands in his path. The rules are so framed as to put all business under their management; and one of the discoveries which the new member is sure to make albeit after many trying experiences and sobering adventures and as his first session draws towards its close, is, that under their sway freedom of debate finds no place of allowance, and that his long-delayed speech must remain unspoken. For even a long congressional session is too short to afford time for a full consideration of all the reports of the forty-seven Committees, and debate upon them must be rigidly cut short, if not altogether excluded, if any considerable part of the necessary business is to be gotten through with before adjournment. There are some subjects to which the House must always give prompt attention; therefore reports from the Committees on Printing and on Elections are always in order; and there are some subjects to which careful consideration must always be accorded; therefore the Committee of Ways and Means and the Committee on Appropriations are clothed with extraordinary privileges; and revenue and supply bills may be reported, and will ordinarily be considered, at any time. But these four are the only specially licensed Committees. The rest must take their turns in fixed order as they are called on by the Speaker, contenting themselves with such crumbs of time as fall from the tables of the four Committees of highest prerogative.

Can We Be Good Without God?
Chuck Colson

December 1993 *Imprimis*

Charles Colson was special counsel to President Richard Nixon. He was involved in the coverup of the Watergate scandal and served time in prison for what he had done. In 1973, while in prison, he was converted to Christ. Since then he has written many books and articles about Christianity and about politics and culture. He is co-founder of Prison Fellowship, which ministers to prisoners, ex-prisoners, victims, and their families. He has a daily five-minute radio commentary called Breakpoint. He received the 1993 Templeton Prize for Progress in Religion.

Last December, newspapers ran a striking photograph of a group of people held at bay by armed guards. They were not rioters or protesters; they were Christmas carolers. The town of Vienna, Virginia, had outlawed the singing of religious songs on public property. So these men, women, and children were forced to sing "Silent Night" behind barricades, just as if this were Eastern Europe under communist rule instead of Christmas in America in 1992.

We have spent the past 30 years determined to secularize our society. Some months before the incident in Virginia, the U.S. Supreme Court ruled in *Lee v. Weisman* that a rabbi who delivered a very politically correct "To Whom It May Concern" prayer at a Rhode Island junior high school commencement had violated the constitutional rights of a fifteen-year-old student in the audience. The Court said, in effect, that the girl must be legally protected against listening to views she disagreed with. There was a time when it was a mark of civility to listen respectfully to different views; now you have a constitutional right to demand that those views are not expressed in your presence.

In another case that went all the way to the Supreme Court, visual religious symbols have been banned. Zion, Illinois, in the "heartland of America," was forced to eliminate the cross featured in its city seal, because the Justices ruled it a breach of the First Amendment.

In education, the same kind of court-enforced secularism has been so successful that teachers . . . are forbidden to display a copy of the Ten Commandments on a bulletin board. Students, meanwhile, may indulge in almost any kind of activity in school, but they are forbidden to pray.

The Supreme Court is not the only institution out to protect us from the "threat" faith poses. The media assault upon religious believers has been fierce. Cardinal O'Connor has been excoriated by the *New York Times* for even suggesting that he might deny the sacraments to a pro-choice legislator. (This was the same *New York Times* that praised a Louisiana archbishop who refused to administer communion to a segregationist legislator in 1962.)

In February of 1993, the *Washington Post* featured a front-page article that characterized evangelical Christians as "largely poor, uneducated, and easy to command." If a journalist said that about any other group in America, he would be fired on the spot, but the *Post* didn't fire anyone. It merely expressed surprise that many readers found the description offensive. A few days later, one of the bemused editors explained that they felt they were simply printing something that is "universally accepted."

It is no wonder that Peter Berger, professor of sociology at Boston University, says that if you look around the world you will find that the most religious county is India, and the

most irreligious country is Sweden—and America is an interesting combination of Indians who are governed by Swedes.

A Post-Christian Society

These Swedes have done their job well. In 1962, polls indicated that at least 65 percent of all Americans believed the Bible to be true. In 1992, polls indicate that only 32 percent do, while 50 percent say they actually fear fundamentalists. If the polls are right, our Judeo-Christian heritage is no longer the foundation of our values. We have become a post-Christian society.

The process of "shedding" our religion began with the cultural revolution of the 1960s, which exalted existentialism and a kind of "live-for-the-moment-God-is-dead-or-irrelevant" philosophy. Today, that Sixties philosophy has become mainstream; it is in the White House, it is in the poetry of Maya Angelou, it is in every walk of life. This is not to say that people aren't going to church. Forty-four percent of the American people still attend religious services regularly. But we live in a Donahue-ized culture in which we sit and watch, hour by hour, the banality that passes for knowledge on television, and we rarely think about issues in terms of Judeo-Christian truth. We hear carolers singing "Silent Night" or an invocation at a public ceremony and we are filled with trepidation; we are worried that we are infringing upon the rights of nonbelievers. We see the symbol of the cross and we feel compelled to paint it out because it might violate the principle of separation between church and state. We exalt tolerance not truth as the ultimate virtue.

The City of Man

Can we really sustain the city of man without the influence of the City of God? St. Augustine argued that it was impossible.

Any society, especially a free society, depends on a moral consensus and on shared assumptions: What is ultimate reality? What is meaningful in life? By what standards should we be governed? These common values are the glue that holds society together.

In America, the glue is wearing pretty thin. We are in the middle of an identity crisis in which we are attempting to redefine our basic values all over again. We can no longer assume that right and wrong have clear meanings or that there is universal truth. After all, pollsters tell us that sixty-seven percent of the American people say there is no such thing.

What we fail to realize, however, is that rejecting transcendental truth is tantamount to committing national suicide. A secular state cannot cultivate virtue—an old-fashioned word you don't hear much in public discourse these days. In his classic novel, *The Brothers Karamazov*, the nineteenth century Russian novelist Dostoyevsky asked, essentially, "Can man be good without God?" In every age, the answer has been no. Without a restraining influence on their nature, men will destroy themselves. That restraining influence might take many abstract forms, as it did for the Greeks and Romans, or it might be the God of the Old and New Testaments. But it has always served the same purpose.

Even before Dostoyevsky posed his timeless question, an eighteenth century German professor of logic and metaphysics, Immanuel Kant, had already dismissed it as irrelevant. God exists, said Kant, but he is separate from the rest of life. Over here are the things that we can empirically know; over there are things we can accept only on faith. What does that do to ethics? Kant's answer was to separate them from faith; we can, on our own, with only our rational capacities to depend upon, develop what he called the "categorical imperative." He explained: "Act as if the maxim from which you act were to become through your will a universal law."

This rational, subjective view is the basis of ethics being taught in nearly every school in American today, from Public Grammar School No. 1 to Harvard Business School. Students are never exposed to traditional moral teaching in school, only to rationalism. Pragmaticism and utilitarianism are substituted for Judeo-Christian ethics, and students are taught that they have the inner capacity to do good rationally, apart from God.

The Danger of Self-Righteousness

Nothing could be more dangerous. Let me give you a case study: Chuck Colson. I grew up in the Depression years. My dad, who was the son of a Swedish immigrant, used to tell me two things on Sunday afternoon. Although no one in my family had ever gone to college, he said, "If you work hard, you can get to the top. That's the American dream." And the second thing he used to say was, "Always tell the truth. No matter what you do in life, always tell the truth." (One could not go through Watergate and claim much distinction for anything, but the fact was that I testified under oath 44 times and I was the only defendant who was not charged with perjury. My dad's lesson stuck: tell the truth.)

I kept both of these pieces of advice in mind as I grew up, earned a scholarship to college and then went on to law school. I also remembered them when I joined a very successful law firm and years later in 1969 when President Nixon asked me to come to work at the White House. I took everything I had earned and put it into a blind trust. (If you want to make a small fortune, let me tell you how: You take a large fortune and put it in a blind trust.) I did everything to avoid even the appearance of a conflict of interest. I passed unsolicited gifts on to my employees. I refused to see people whom I had practiced law with or made business deals with—I mean, I *really* had studied Kant's categorical imperative, and I *knew* that I would always do right.

What happened? I went to prison.

Why? Because we are never more dangerous than when we are feeling self-righteous. We have an infinite capacity for this feeling and for the self-justification that accompanies it. It was only when Jesus Christ came into my life that I was able to see myself for who I am. Indeed, it is only when we all turn to God that we begin to see ourselves as we really are—as fallen sinners desperately in need of His restraint and His grace.

Kant's philosophy, like much Enlightenment thought, was based on a flawed view of human nature that held that men are basically good and, if left to their own devices, will almost always do good things. It was also dead wrong in assuming that the categorical imperative could take the place of moral law. Just because men can think the right thing, it does not mean that they will heed it. Remember Pierre, one of the central characters in Tolstoy's *War and Peace*? Torn by spiritual agonies, he cried out to God, "Why is it that I know what is right and I do what is wrong?" We can know what is right, but we don't always have the will to do what is right.

How Shall We Live?

In books like *Mere Christianity* and *The Abolition of Man*, the twentieth-century British Christian apologist C.S. Lewis attempted to refute Kant and make a powerful intellectual case for the City of God that did not wall it off from the city of man. In an essay entitled, "Men Without Chests," he drew an analogy between the spiritual life and the body that sums up his objections to the supreme rationalism of the Enlightenment. The head, Lewis said, is reason, and the stomach is passion or appetite. The head alone cannot control the stomach. It needs the chest, which is spirit, to restrain our baser passions and appetites.

Yet after World War II schools began to teach ethics based on subjective standards without transcendent moral truths. Lewis challenged this, writing, "We make men without chests and we expect of them virtue and enterprise. We laugh at honor and we are shocked to find traitors in our midst. . . ." That is what we are doing in America today. We are taking away the spiritual element and abandoning morality based on religious truths, counting instead on our heads and our subjective feelings to make us do what is right.

In our zeal to accommodate our so-called enlightened and tolerant age, we have lost the ideal of public virtue. I am reminded of Samuel Johnson, who, upon learning that one of his dinner guests believed morality was merely a sham, said to his butler, "Well, if he really believes that there is no distinction between virtue and vice, let us count the spoons before he leaves." Today, there aren't any spoons left to count. Look at Washington, Wall Street, academia, sports, the ministry—all the spoons are gone because we can no longer distinguish between virtue and vice.

Recovering that ability depends on asking the right questions. Our brightest and best leaders are concerned with the question, "How shall we be governed?" But in the Book of Ezekiel the Jews asked: "How shall we live?" It doesn't matter who governs if society has no spiritual element to guide it. Unless we learn how to live—as men with chests—we are doomed.

The City of God

I have seen this truth most powerfully in the area in which I've been called to spend my life. With the help of my friend Jack Eckerd and others, I work with men and women in prison in 54 countries around the world. The crisis is grave. In Washington, D.C., for example, 46 percent of the inner city black population between the ages of 18 and 31 is either in prison, on parole, or on probation. America as a whole has the highest per capita rate of incarceration in the world, and, for the last 25 years, the crime rate has gone up every year. We can't build prisons fast enough. . . . According to some sources, twenty percent of all schoolchildren carry a weapon.

Criminologist James Q. Wilson, among others, has tried to identify the root cause of this epidemic of violence. When he began his inquiry, he was certain that he would discover that in the great period of industrial revolution in the latter half of the nineteenth century there was a tremendous increase in crime. But, to his astonishment, he discovered a decrease. And then he looked at the years of the Great Depression. Again, there was a significant decrease in crime. Frustrated by these findings which upset all our preconceived notions, Wilson decided to search for a single factor to correlate. The factor he found was religious faith.

When crime should have been rising in the late 1800s because of rapid urbanization, industrialization, and economic dislocation, Victorian morality was sweeping across America. It was a time of intense spirituality. It was not until the conscious rejection of Victorian morality during the Roaring Twenties that crime went up. This was the era when Sigmund Freud's views were coming into vogue among "thinking" Americans: people weren't evil, just misguided or mistreated, or they required better environments. Sin was regarded as a lot of religious claptrap.

The crime rate did not decline again until the Great Depression, a time of people banding together in the face of crisis. Wilson concluded, therefore, that crime was in large part caused by a breakdown of morality. Since 1965 the crime rate has steadily risen. In the same period, religious faith has waned. We have told people there are no absolutes and that they are not responsible for their own behavior. They are simply victims of a system that isn't working anymore and they don't have to worry about it because the government is going to fix it for them. We thought that in this brave new world we could create the perfect secular utopia. But the secular utopia is in reality the nightmare we see as we walk through the dark, rotten holes we call prisons all across America.

In this context, it always amazes me when I listen to politicians say, "We are going to win the war on drugs by building prisons, appointing more judges, and putting more police on the beat." I remember when President [George H. W.] Bush announced the "War on Drugs." Having spent seven months in prison, there wasn't one night that I did not smell marijuana burning. If you can get marijuana into a prison, with watchtowers, inspections, and prison guards, you can get it into a country. You can send the U.S. Marines to Colombia to burn all the fields, seal all the borders, and build all the prisons you want, but you won't stop drug use in this country because it isn't a problem of supply; it is a problem of demand. When there is no greater value in the lives of so many people than simply fulfilling individual desires and gratifications, then crime and drug abuse become inevitable. The soaring crime rate is powerful testimony to the failure of the city of man, deprived of the moral influence of the City of God.

If we cannot be good without God, how do we sustain public virtue in society? We cannot do it through the instrument of politics. Alasdair MacIntyre, moral philosopher at Notre Dame, says that "Politics has become civil war carried on by other means." Without moral authority to call upon, our elected leaders are reduced to saying, "We can't say that this is right and that's wrong. We simply prefer that you wouldn't murder." And crime and drug abuse are not the only results of this loss of moral authority. Forty-four percent of the baby boomers say that there is no cause that would lead them to fight and die for their country.

In the city of man, there is no moral consensus, and without a moral consensus there can be no law. Chairman Mao expressed the alternative well: in his view, morality begins at the muzzle of a gun.

There has never been a case in history in which a society has been able to survive for long without a strong moral code. And there has never been a time when a moral code has not been informed by religious truth. Recovering our moral code—our religious truth—is the only way our society can survive. The heaping ash remains at Auschwitz, the killing fields of Southeast Asia, and the frozen wastes of the gulag remind us that the city of man is not enough; we must also seek the city of God.

Reprinted by permission from Imprimis, *the national speech digest of Hillsdale College, www.hillsdale.edu.*

The Religious Roots of Freedom
M. Stanton Evans

April 1995 *Imprimis*

M. Stanton Evans has had a distinguished career in journalism. He was managing editor of Human Events, *associate editor of* National Review, *and editor of the* Indianapolis Star. *He is also a political columnist and author of several books.*

As the renewed debate over prayer in the public schools suggests, the cultural conflict of the modern era finds vivid and enduring focus in the legal dispute about the place of religion in the civic order. Here the battle is overt, relentless, and pervasive—with traditional belief and custom retreating before a secularist onslaught in our courts and other public institutions.

During the past three decades, the U.S. Supreme Court has handed down a series of rulings that decree a "wall of separation" between affairs of state and the precepts of religion. In the most controverted of these cases, in 1962, the Court said an officially sponsored prayer recited in the New York public schools was an abridgement of our freedoms. This prayer read, in its entirety: "Almighty God, we acknowledge our dependence on Thee, and we beg Thy blessings upon us, our parents, our teachers, and our country." In the Court's opinion, this supplication triggered the First Amendment ban against an "establishment of religion," logic that was later extended to reading the Bible and reciting the Lord's Prayer in the classroom.

In adopting the First Amendment, according to the Court, the Founders meant to sever all connection between religious faith and government, requiring that religion be a purely private matter.

First Prayer in Congress, 1774

As Justice Hugo Black put it in an oft-quoted statement: "The 'establishment of religion' clause of the First Amendment means at least this: Neither a state nor the federal government can set up a church. Neither can pass laws which aid one religion, aid all religions, or prefer one religion over another. . . . No tax in any amount, large or small, can be levied to support any religious activities or institutions, whatever they may be called, or whatever form they may adopt to teach or practice religion."

This doctrine has been affirmed and amplified in many rulings since. In support of it, Black and his successors (most recently Justice David Souter) have offered a reading of our history that supposedly shows the intentions of the people who devised the First Amendment. In a nutshell, this tells us that the Founders chiefly responsible for the Constitution's religion clauses were Madison and Jefferson; that they held views intensely hostile toward any governmental backing for religion; and that the amendment was a triumph for their separationist position.

Of Whole Cloth

The First Amendment depicted by Justice Black and other liberal jurists is, unfortunately, a fabrication. The Supreme Court's alleged history is a prime example of picking and choosing elements from the past to suit the ideological fashions of the present. If we consult the history of the nation's founding, we find that the Court and its supporters have misstated the material facts about the issue in every possible fashion. To begin with, state papers, legal arrangements, and political comment of the founding generation show that American culture in that period was suffused with religious doctrine. The point is made by the very concept of an "establishment of religion." This term had a definite meaning in England and the colonies that is critical to understanding the debate about the First Amendment. It signified an official church that occupied a privileged position with the state, was vested with certain powers denied to others, and was supported from the public treasury. Such was the Church of England in Great Britain, and such also were numerous churches in the colonies at the beginning of our revolution.

The States' Churches

In 1775, no fewer than nine colonies had such arrangements. Massachusetts, Connecticut, and New Hampshire had systems of local church establishment in favor of the Congregationalists. In the South, from Maryland on down, the establishments were Episcopal. In New York, there was a system of locally supported Protestant clergy. Because of growing religious diversity within the states, pressure mounted to disestablish these official churches. In particular, increasingly numerous Baptists and Presbyterians made headway against the Anglican position, which was further weakened by the identification of many Episcopal ministers with the English.

Even so, at the time of the Constitutional Convention, the three New England states still had their Congregational establishments. In other states, there remained a network of official sanctions for religious belief, principally the requirement that one profess a certain kind of Christian doctrine to hold public office or enjoy other legal privilege. With local variations, these generally tended in the same direction, and they make instructive reading alongside the statements of Justices Black and Souter about the supposed history of our institutions.

In South Carolina, for example, the Constitution of 1778 said that "the Christian Protestant religion shall be deemed . . . the established religion of the state." It further said that no religious society could be considered a church unless it agreed "that there is one eternal God and a future state of rewards and punishment; that the Christian religion is the true religion; that that Holy Scriptures of the Old and New Testaments are of divine inspiration." South Carolina also asserted that "no person who denies the existence of a Supreme Being shall hold any office under this Constitution."

Similar statements can be gleaned from other state enactments of the period. The Maryland Constitution of 1776 decreed, for instance, "a general and equal tax for the support of the Christian religion." New Jersey that year expressed its idea of toleration by saying that "no Protestant inhabitant of this colony shall be denied the enjoyment of any civil right." Massachusetts, in 1780, authorized a special levy to support "public Protestant teachers of piety, religion, and morality"—a formula adopted verbatim by New Hampshire.

Official support for religious faith and state religious requirements for public office persisted well after adoption of the First Amendment. The established church of Massachusetts was not abolished until 1833. In New Hampshire, the requirement that one had to be Protestant to serve in the legislature was continued until 1877. In New Jersey, Roman Catholics were not permitted to hold office until 1844. In Maryland, the stipulation that one had to be a Christian lasted until 1826. As late as 1835, one had to be a Protestant to take office in North Carolina; until 1868, the requirement was that one had to be a Christian; thereafter that one had to profess a belief in God.

The official sanction for religious belief provided by the states was equally apparent at the federal level, during and after the Revolution. Appeals for divine assistance, days of prayer and fasting, and other religious observance were common in the Continental Congress. Among its first items of business, in 1774, the Congress decided to appoint a chaplain and open its proceedings with a prayer. When it was objected that this might be a problem because of diversity in religious doctrine, Sam Adams answered: "I am not a bigot. I can hear a prayer from a man of piety and virtue, who is at the same time a friend of his country."

On June 12, 1775, the Congress called for "a day of public humiliation, fasting, and prayer," wherein "[we] offer up our joint supplications to the all-wise, omnipotent, and merciful disposer of all events." In observance of this fast day, Congress attended an Anglican service in the morning and a Presbyterian service in the afternoon.

During the Revolutionary War, Congress made provision for military chaplains, recommended that officers and men attend religious service, and threatened court martial for anyone who misbehaved on such occasions. It also adopted the Northwest Ordinance, stressing the need for "religion and morality," appropriated money for the Christian education of Indians and encouraged the printing of a Bible. The Northwest Ordinance and the measures regarding chaplains, official prayer, and education of the Indians were re-adopted by the first Congress under the new Constitution and maintained for many years thereafter.

Crumbling Wall

Such was the body of doctrine and official practice that surrounded the First Amendment—immediately predating it, adopted while it was being discussed and voted on, and enduring long after it was on the books. The resulting picture is very different from any notion of America as a country run by secularists and Deists. Nor does it look very much like a country in which the governing powers were intent on creating a "wall of separation" between church and state, denying official support to the precepts of religion.

This was the background to Madison's motion on June 8, 1789, introducing a set of amendments to the Constitution, culled from the proposals of [the state ratifying] conventions. Among the measures that he offered was this pertaining to an establishment of religion: "The civil rights of none shall be abridged on account of religious belief, nor shall any national religion be established . . . ." In view of the weight that has been given to Madison's personal opinions on the subject, his comments on this occasion are of special interest. For example, challenged by Roger Sherman as to why such guarantees were needed, given the doctrine of "enumerated powers," Madison said:

> *he apprehended the meaning of the words to be* that Congress shall not establish a religion and enforce the legal observation of it by law, nor compel men to worship God in any manner contrary to their conscience. *Whether the words are necessary or not, he did not mean to say, but they have been required by some of the state conventions, who seemed to entertain an opinion that* [under the "necessary and proper" clause] . . . Congress . . . might infringe the rights of conscience and establish a national religion; to prevent these effects *he presumed the amendment was intended,* and he thought it as well expressed as the nature of language would admit. [Italics added.]

In this and other exchanges, the House debate made two things clear about the Bill of Rights and its religion clauses: (1) Madison was introducing the amendments not because *he* thought they were needed but because others did, and because he had promised to act according to their wishes; (2) the aim was to prevent Congress from establishing a "national" religion that would threaten the religious diversity of the states. Given the varied practices we have noted, ranging from establishments and doctrinal requirements for public office to relative toleration, any "national" religion would have been a source of angry discord.

Against that backdrop, the meaning of the establishment clause as it came out of conference should be crystal clear: "Congress shall make no law respecting an establishment of religion." The agency prohibited from acting is the national legislature; what it is prevented from doing is passing any law "respecting" an establishment of religion. In other words, Congress was forbidden to legislate at all concerning church establishment—either for or against. It was prevented from setting up a national established church; equally to the point, *it was prevented from interfering with the established churches in the states.*

Shield Becomes Sword

Though this history is blurred or ignored, it is no secret, and its general features are sometimes acknowledged by liberal spokesmen. It may be conceded, for example, that the First Amendment was intended to be a prohibition against the *federal* government. But that guarantee was supposedly broadened by the Fourteenth Amendment, which "applied" the Bill of Rights against the states. Thus what was once prohibited only to the federal government is now also prohibited to the states.

Here we meet the Orwellian concept of "applying" a protection *of* the states *as a weapon against them*—using the First Amendment to achieve the very thing it was intended to prevent. The legitimacy of this reversal has been convincingly challenged by such constitutional scholars as Raoul Berger, Lino Graglia, and James McClellan. But for present purposes, let us simply *assume* the First Amendment restrictions on Congress were "applied" against the states. What then? What did this prohibit?

One thing we know for sure is that it *did not prohibit officially sponsored prayer*. As we have seen, Congress itself engaged in officially sponsored, tax-supported prayer, complete with paid official chaplains, from the very outset—and continues to do so to this day. Indeed, in one of the greatest ironies of this historical record, we see the practice closely linked with passage of the First Amendment—supplying a refutation of the Court's position that is as definitive as could be wished.

The language that had been debated off and on throughout the summer and then hammered out in conference finally passed the House of Representatives on September 24, 1789. *On the very next day*, the self-same House of Representatives passed a resolution calling for *a day of national prayer and thanksgiving*. Here is the language the House adopted: "We acknowledge with grateful hearts the many single favors of Almighty God, especially by affording them an opportunity peacefully to establish a constitutional government for their safety and happiness."

The House accordingly called on President Washington to issue a proclamation designating a national day of prayer and thanksgiving (the origin of our current legal holiday). This was Washington's response:

> It is the duty of all nations to acknowledge the providence of Almighty God, to obey His will, to be grateful for His benefits, and humbly to implore His protection and favor. . . . That great and glorious Being who is the beneficent author of all the good that was, that is, or that ever will be, that we may then unite in rendering unto Him our sincere and humble thanks for His kind care and protection of the people.

Such were the official sentiments of Congress and the President immediately after the adoption of the First Amendment. These statements are far more doctrinal and emphatic than the modest prayer schoolchildren are forbidden to recite because it allegedly violates the First

Amendment. If we accept the reasoning of the modern Court, as Robert Cord observes, *both Congress and George Washington violated the intended meaning of the First Amendment from its inception.*

The more logical conclusion, of course, is that Congress knew much better what it meant by the language adopted the preceding day than does our self-consciously evolving Court two centuries later. And in the view of Congress, there was nothing either in law or in logic to bar it from engaging in officially sponsored, tax-supported prayer, then or ever. It follows that the amendment can't possibly bar the states from doing likewise.

Madison and Jefferson

To all this the liberal answer is, essentially: James Madison. Whatever the legislative history, we are informed, Madison in his subsequent writings took doctrinaire positions on church-state separation, and these should be read into the First Amendment. This, however, gets the matter topsy-turvy. Clearly, if the Congress that passed the First Amendment and the states that ratified it didn't agree with Madison's more stringent private notions, as they surely didn't, then these were *not* enacted. It is the common understanding of the relevant parties, not the ideas of a single individual, especially those expressed in other settings, that defines the purpose of a law or constitutional proviso.

Furthermore, the Court's obsession with the individual views of Madison is highly suspect. It contrasts strangely with judicial treatment of his disclaimers in the House debate, and of his opinions on other constitutional matters. Madison held strict-constructionist views on the extent of federal power, arguing that the Constitution reserved undelegated authority to the states. These views of Madison are dismissed entirely by the Court. Thus we get a curious inversion: Madison becomes the Court's authority on the First Amendment, even though the notions he later voiced about this subject were not endorsed by others involved in its adoption. On the other hand, he isn't cited on the residual powers of the states, even thought his statements on this topic were fully endorsed by other supporters of the Constitution and relied on by the people who voted its approval. It is hard to find a thread of consistency in this—beyond the obvious one of serving liberal ideology.

As peculiar as the Court's selective use of Madison is its resort to Jefferson. The anomaly here is that Jefferson was not a member of the Constitutional Convention, or of the Congress that considered the Bill of Rights, or of the Virginia ratifying convention. But he had strongly separationist views (up to a point) and had worked with Madison for disestablishment and religious freedom in Virginia. For the Court, this proves the First Amendment embodied Jefferson's statement in 1802 in a letter to the Baptists of Connecticut, about a "wall of separation."

Again we pass over the Lewis Carroll logic—in this case deducing the intent of an amendment adopted in 1789 from a letter written 13 years later by a person who had no official role in its adoption. Rather than dwelling on this oddity, we shall simply go to the record and see what Jefferson actually said about the First Amendment and its religion clauses. In his second inaugural address, for example, he said:

> In matter of religion, I have considered that its free exercise is placed by the Constitution independent of the powers of the general government. I have therefore undertaken on no occasion to prescribe the religious exercises suited to it. But I have left them as the Constitution found them, under the direction or discipline of state or church authorities acknowledged by the several religious societies.

Jefferson made the same point a few years later to a Presbyterian clergyman, who inquired about his attitude toward Thanksgiving proclamations:

> I consider the government of the United States as interdicted from inter-meddling with religious institutions, their doctrines, discipline, or exercises. This results from the provision that no law shall be made respecting the establishment of religion or the free exercise thereof, but also from that which reserves to the states the powers not delegated to the United States. Certainly no power over religious discipline has been delegated to the general government. It must thus rest with the states as far as it can be in any human authority.

The irresistible conclusion is that there was no wall of separation between religious affirmation and civil government in the several states, nor could the First Amendment, with or without the Fourteenth Amendment, have been intended to create one. The wall of separation, instead, was between the *federal government and the states* and was meant to make sure the central authority didn't meddle with the customs of local jurisdictions.

As a matter of constitutional law, the Court's position in these religion cases is an intellectual shambles—results-oriented jurisprudence at its most flagrant. An even greater scandal is the extent to which the Justices have rewritten the official record to support a preconceived conclusion: a performance worthy of regimes in which history is tailored to the interests of the ruling powers. In point of fact, America's constitutional settlement—up to and including the First Amendment—was the work of people who believed in God, and who expressed their faith as a matter of course in public prayer and other governmental practice.

Reprinted by permission from Imprimis, *the national speech digest of Hillsdale College, www.hillsdale.edu.*

It's Time to End the Filibuster Rule
Ray Notgrass

We can all imagine it happening. A group of boys in the neighborhood have gotten together in the empty lot to play football. The smallest kid doesn't like being chosen last; so he grabs the football and runs away, preventing all the other boys from even playing the game. The big kids stand around muttering about how the culprit was so childish and wondering what they are going to do now.

It's a frustrating situation, but it only affects the boys in the neighborhood—except that the playing field is the United States Senate, and the little boy running away with the ball are the members of the greatest deliberative body in the world who are threatening a filibuster. You don't have to be a child to act childishly.

We wouldn't stand for it if one member of a three-member board of city aldermen talked for hours trying to prevent an action he didn't like from being taken. We'd roll our eyes if the grown men and women in our state legislature pulled stunts like this. Yet if the wise members of the U.S. Senate act this way, we are supposed to be impressed by their mature and insightful concern for the rights of the minority. Poppycock.

Real maturity is shown by being a good loser. If one party loses the election and are in the minority, they just need to decide to work harder, fine tune their message, perhaps change their stances, and do a better job of getting out their supporters next time, not paralyze the workings of government by running off the field with the ball.

Notice who filibustered civil rights legislation for many years: Southern Democrats. Notice who now threatens to filibuster the President's judicial nominees: Democrats. This does not mean that Republicans showed mature statesmanship by running off with the ball when they didn't want to vote on Clinton's nominees. Republican-controlled committees just didn't report the nominations out of committee to the entire Senate, and guess what—the Democrats cried foul. It just shows that neither party knows how to be good losers or good winners.

Defenders of the filibuster say that it protects the country against unwise legislation or an unwise judicial nomination who would be a threat to personal freedom (in other words, a nominee who might vote to overturn *Roe v. Wade*). It is true that America offers many rights and protections to minorities, but a minority should not be able to run the show—or, in this case, to stop the show. Otherwise, what is the purpose of a majority? What is the purpose of voting? Why not let the losers in an election take office? Now there's a plan for protecting minority rights!

Today, a real filibuster never even has to take place. Senators only have to give notice that they will filibuster. The little boy only has to threaten to run away with the ball, and the game stops. This is not an example of good leadership by the majority. The majority needs to let the filibusterers make good on their threat. Let them bring the work of Congress to a screeching halt (would that be such a terrible thing, at least for a while?). Let it be played out on C-SPAN and reported on the news channels and the networks. I believe the American people will see it for what it is, and the filibusterers will lose even more. As it is, they are winning by hiding behind the mantra of "maintaining the traditional rules of the Senate." Unfortunately, since the Senate makes its own rules, and since there is a polite collegiality maintained among the members, letting the bratty little boys trip and go splat as they run away with the ball is not likely to happen.

The House many years ago permitted unlimited debates, but the increasing number of members there led to the rule change that limits the time each member has to speak on the floor. That was a good reason for a rule change, and another good reason exists now for eliminating the rule in the Senate. The reason is that the well-being of our country demands it. The members of Congress should put aside pettiness and their desire to protect their special little club and do what is best for the country.

Congress has the responsibility to consider legislation. The President has the responsibility to nominate judges and Cabinet members and submit treaties to the Senate. The Senate has the responsibility to advise and consent—or reject—but not to advise and block. Let bills, treaties, and nominations come to the floor. Let the august, wise, and eloquent members of the Senate debate, discuss, cajole, persuade, appeal, threaten—and then, after a reasonable time, vote.

Let's get on with the game.

Our Unconstitutional Congress
Stephen Moore

July 1997 *Imprimis*

Stephen Moore has worked with the Cato Institute in Washington, D.C. He has served as a Congressional staffer and has authored numerous articles and books.

In 1800, when the nation's capital was moved from Philadelphia to Washington, D.C., all of the paperwork and records of the United States government were packed into twelve boxes and then transported the one hundred and fifty miles to Washington in a horse and buggy. That was truly an era of lean and efficient government.

In the early years of the Republic, government bore no resemblance to the colossal empire it has evolved into today. In 1800, the federal government employed three thousand people and had a budget of less than $1 million ($100 million in today's dollars). That's a far cry from today's federal budget of $1.6 trillion and total government workforce of eighteen million.

Since its frugal beginnings, the U.S. federal government has come to subsidize everything from Belgian endive research to maple syrup production to the advertising of commercial brand names in Europe and Japan. In a recent moment of high drama before the

Interior of the United States Capitol Dome

Supreme Court, during oral arguments involving the application of the interstate commerce clause of the Constitution, a bewildered Justice Antonin Scalia pressed the solicitor general to name a single activity or program that our modern-day Congress might undertake that would fall outside the bounds of the Constitution. The stunned Clinton appointee could not think of one.

During the debate in Congress over the controversial 1994 Crime Bill, not a single Republican or Democrat challenged the $10 billion in social spending on the grounds that it was meant to pay for programs that were not the proper responsibility of the federal government. No one asked, for example, where is the authority under the Constitution for Congress to spend money on midnight basketball, modern dance classes, self-esteem training, and the construction of swimming pools? Certainly, there was plenty of concern about "wasteful spending," but none about unconstitutional spending.

Most federal spending today falls in this latter category because it lies outside Congress's spending powers under the Constitution and it represents a radical departure from the past. For the first one hundred years of our nation's history, proponents of limited government in Congress and the White House routinely argued—with great success—a philosophical and legal case against the creation and expansion of federal social welfare programs.

A Rulebook for Government

The U. S. Constitution is fundamentally a rulebook for government. Its guiding principle is the idea that the state is a source of corruptive power and ultimate tyranny. Washington's responsibilities were confined to a few enumerated powers, involving mainly national security and public safety. In the realm of domestic affairs, the Founders sought to guarantee that federal interference in the daily lives of citizens would be strictly limited. They also wanted to make sure that the minimal government role in the domestic economy would be financed and delivered at the state and local levels.

The enumerated powers of the federal government to spend money are defined in the Constitution under Article I, Section 8. These powers include the right to "establish Post Offices and post roads; raise and support Armies; provide and maintain a Navy; declare War . . . " and to conduct a few other activities related mostly to national defense. No matter how long one searches, it is impossible to find in the Constitution any language that authorizes at least 90 percent of the civilian programs that Congress crams into the federal budget today.

The federal government has no authority to pay money to farmers, run the health care industry, impose wage and price controls, give welfare to the poor and unemployed, provide job training, subsidize electricity and telephone service, lend money to businesses and foreign governments, or build parking garages, tennis courts, and swimming pools. The Founders did not create a Department of Commerce, a Department of Education, or a Department of Housing and Urban Development. This was no oversight: They did not believe that government was authorized to establish such agencies.

Recognizing the propensity of governments to expand, and, as Thomas Jefferson put it, for "liberty to yield," the Founders added the Bill of Rights to the Constitution as an extra layer of protection. The government was never supposed to grow so large that it could trample on the liberties of American citizens. The Tenth Amendment to the Constitution states clearly and unambiguously: "The powers not delegated to the United States by the Constitution . . . are reserved to the States respectively, or to the people." In other words, if the Constitution doesn't specifically permit the federal government to do something, then it doesn't have the right to do it.

The original budget of the U.S. government abided by this rule. The very first appropriations bill passed by Congress consisted of one hundred and eleven words—not pages, mind you, *words*. The main expenditures were for the military, including $137,000 for "defraying the expenses" of the Department of War, $190,000 for retiring the debt from the Revolutionary War, and $95,000 for "paying the pensions to invalids." As for domestic activities, $216,000 was appropriated. This is roughly what federal agencies spend in fifteen seconds today.

As constitutional scholar Roger Pilon has documented, even expenditures for the most charitable of purposes were routinely spurned as illegitimate. In 1794, James Madison wrote disapprovingly of a $15,000 appropriation for French refugees: "I cannot undertake to lay my finger on that article of the Constitution which granted a right to Congress of expending, on objects of benevolence, the money of their constituents." This view that Congress should follow the original intent of the Constitution was restated even more forcefully on the floor of the House of Representatives two years later by William Giles of Virginia. Giles condemned a relief measure for fire victims and insisted that it was not the purpose nor the right of Congress to "attend to what generosity and humanity require, but to what the Constitution and their duty require."

In 1827, [while Davy Crockett of Tennessee was serving in the U.S. House of Representatives], a $10,000 relief bill for the widow of a naval officer was proposed. Colonel Crockett rose in stern opposition and gave the following eloquent and successful rebuttal:

> We must not permit our respect for the dead or our sympathy for the living to lead us into an act of injustice to the balance of the living. I will not attempt to prove that Congress has no power to appropriate this money as an act of charity. Every member upon this floor knows it. We have the right as individuals to give away as much of our own money as we please in charity; but as members of Congress we have no right to appropriate a dollar of the public money.

In a famous incident in 1854, President Franklin Pierce courageously vetoed an extremely popular bill intended to help the mentally ill, saying: "I cannot find any authority in the Constitution for public charity." To approve such spending, he argued, "would be contrary to the letter and the spirit of the Constitution and subversive to the whole theory upon which the Union of these States is founded." Grover Cleveland, the king of the veto, rejected hundreds of congressional spending bills during his two terms as president in the late 1800s, because, as he often wrote: "I can find no warrant for such an appropriation in the Constitution."

Were Jefferson, Madison, Crockett, Pierce, and Cleveland merely hardhearted and uncaring penny pinchers, as their critics have often charged? Were they unsympathetic toward fire victims, the mentally ill, widows, or impoverished refugees? Of course not. They were honor bound to uphold the Constitution. They perceived—we now know correctly— that once the government genie was out of the bottle, it would be impossible to get it back in.

With a few notable exceptions during the nineteenth century, Congress, the president, and the courts remained faithful to the letter and spirit of the Constitution with regard to government spending. As economic historian Robert Higgs noted in *Crisis and Leviathan,* until the twentieth century, "government did little of much consequence or expense" other than running the military. The total expenditures for the federal budget confirm this assessment. Even as late as 1925, the federal government was still spending just 4 percent of national output.

Abandoning Constitutional Protections

Several major turning points in American history mark the reversal of this ethic. The first was the passage in 1913 of the Sixteenth Amendment, which permitted a federal income tax. This was the first major tax that was not levied on a proportional or uniform basis. Hence, it allowed Congress a political free ride: It could provide government benefits to many by imposing a disproportionately heavy tax burden on the wealthy. Prior to enactment of the income tax, Congress's power to spend was held in check by its limited power to tax. Most federal revenues came from tariffs and land sales. Neither source yielded huge sums. The income tax, however, soon became a cash cow for a Congress needing only the feeblest of excuses to spend money.

The second major event that weakened constitutional protections against big government was the ascendancy of Franklin Roosevelt and his New Deal agenda to the White House during the Great Depression. One after another, constitutional safeguards against excessive government were ignored or misinterpreted. Most notable and tragic was the perversion of the "general welfare" clause. Article 1, Section 8 of the Constitution says: "The Congress shall have power to lay and collect taxes, duties, imposts, and excises to pay the debts, provide for the common defense, and promote *the general welfare* of the United States." Since the 1930s, the courts have interpreted this phrase to mean that Congress may spend money for any purpose, whether there is an enumerated power of government or not, as long as legislators deem it to be in the general welfare of certain identifiable groups of citizens like minorities, the needy, or the disabled. This *carte blanche* is exactly the opposite of what the Founders intended. The general welfare clause was supposed to limit government's taxing and spending powers to purposes that are in the national interest.

Jefferson had every reason to be concerned that the general welfare clause might be perverted. To clarify its meaning, he wrote in 1798: "Congress has not unlimited powers to provide for the general welfare but only those specifically enumerated." In fact, when some early lawmakers suggested that the general welfare clause gave Congress a generalized spending authority, they were always forcefully rebuked. In 1828, for example, South Carolina Senator William Drayton reminded his peers, "If Congress can determine what constitutes the general welfare and can appropriate money for its advancement, where is the limitation to carrying into execution whatever can be effected by money?"

Exactly.

Nonetheless, by the late nineteenth century, Congress had adopted the occasional practice of enacting spending bills for public charity in the name of "promoting the general welfare." These laws often made a mockery of this clause. In 1884, Senator John Morgan of Alabama stormed to the Senate floor to describe the impact of a relief bill approved by Congress to provide $400,000 of funds for victims of a flood on the Tombigbee River. Morgan lamented:

> The overflow had passed away before the bill passed Congress, and new crops were already growing upon the land. The funds were distributed in the next October and November elections upon the highest points of the sand mountains throughout a large region where the people wanted what was called "overflow bacon." I cannot get the picture out of my mind. There was the General Welfare of the people invoked and with success, to justify this political fraud; the money was voted and the bacon was bought, and the politicians went around with their greasy hands distributing it to men who cast greasy ballots. And in that way the General Welfare was promoted!

But the real avalanche of such special interest spending did not start until some fifty years later in the midst of the Depression. In their urgency to spend public relief funds to combat hard times, politicians showed their contempt for constitutional restraints designed to prevent raids on the public purse. "I have no patience whatever with any individual who tries to hide behind the Constitution, when it comes to providing foodstuffs for our citizens," argued New York Representative Hamilton Fish in support of a 1931 hunger relief bill. James O'Conner, a congressman from Louisiana, opined, "I am going to give the Constitution the flexibility . . . as will enable me to vote for any measure I deem of value to the flesh and blood of my day."

Pork-barrel spending began in earnest. In the same year, for instance, Congress introduced an act to provide flood relief to farmers in six affected states. By the time the bill made its way through Congress, farmers in fifteen states became its beneficiaries. One Oklahoma congressman succinctly summarized the new beggar-thy-neighbor spending ethic that had overtaken Capitol Hill: "I do not believe in this pie business, but if we are making a great big pie here . . . then I want to cut it into enough pieces so that Oklahoma will have its piece."

In 1932, Charles Warren, a former assistant attorney general, wrote a popular book titled *Congress as Santa Claus*. "If a law to donate aid to any farmer or cattleman who has had poor crops or lost his cattle comes within the meaning of the phrase 'to provide for the General Welfare of the United States,'" he argued, "why should not similar gifts be made to grocers, shopkeepers, miners, and other businessmen who have made losses through financial depression, or to wage earners out of employment? Why is not their prosperity equally within the purview of the General Welfare?"

Of course, we now know Congress's answer: All of these things are in the "general welfare." This is why we now have unemployment compensation, the Small Business Administration, the Department of Commerce, food stamps, and so on. Of course, all this special interest spending could have been—no, should have been—summarily struck down as unconstitutional. However, the courts have served as a willing co-conspirator in congressional spending schemes.

In a landmark 1936 decision, the Supreme Court inflicted a mortal blow to the Constitution by ruling that the Agricultural Adjustment Act was constitutional. The Court's interpretation of the spending authority of Congress was frightful and fateful. Its ruling read: "The power of Congress to authorize appropriations of public money for public purposes is not limited by the grants of legislative power found in the Constitution."

James M. Beck, a great American legal scholar and former solicitor general, likened this astounding assault on the Constitution to the *Titanic*'s tragic collision with the iceberg. "After the collision," wrote Beck, "which was hardly felt by the steamer at the time, the great liner seemed to be intact and unhurt, and continued to move. But a death wound had been inflicted under the surface of the water, which poured into the hold of the steamer so swiftly that in a few hours the great ship was sunk."

The New Deal Court essentially told Congress: It doesn't matter what the Constitution says or what limits on government it establishes, you are empowered to spend money on whatever you please. And so Congress does, even though its profligacy has placed the nation in great economic peril.

Other than the Great Depression, by far the most important events that have fostered the growth of government in this century have been the two world wars. Periods of national crisis tend to be times in which normal constitutional restraints are suspended and the nation willingly bands together under government for a national purpose of fighting a common enemy. Yet the recurring lesson of history is that once government has seized new powers, it seldom gives them back after the crisis ends. Surely enough, this phenomenon is one of Parkinson's famous laws of the public sector:

> Taxes (and spending) become heavier in times of war and should diminish, by rights, when the war is over. This is not, however, what happens. Taxes never regain their pre-war level. That is because the level of expenditure rises to meet the wartime level of taxation.

In the five years prior to World War I, total federal outlays averaged 2 percent of GDP. In the five years after the war, they averaged 5 percent of GDP. In the years prior to that war the top income tax rate was 7 percent. During the war the tax rate shot up to 70 percent, which was reduced afterward, but only to 24 percent—or more than three times higher than it had originally been.

Government regulations of the private economy also proliferate during times of war and often remain in force afterward. Robert Higgs notes that during World War I, the federal government nationalized the railroads and the telephone lines, requisitioned all ships over 2,500 tons, and regulated food and commodity prices. The Lever Act of 1917 gave the government the power to regulate the price and production of food, fuels, beverages and distilled spirits. It is entirely plausible that, without the war, America would never have suffered through the failed experiment of Prohibition.

World War II was also the genesis of many modern-day government intrusions—which were and still are of dubious constitutionality. These include wage and price controls, conscription (which lasted until the 1970s), rent control in large cities, and, worst of all, federal income tax withholding. In the post-World War II era, Congress has often relied on a war theme to extend its authority into domestic life. Lyndon Johnson launched the modern welfare state in the 1960s when he declared a "war on poverty." In the early 1970s, Richard Nixon imposed across-the-board wage and price controls—the ultimate in government command and control—as a means of winning the "inflation war." In the late 1970s, Jimmy Carter sought to enact a national energy policy with gas rationing and other draconian measures by pleading that the oil crisis had become the "moral equivalent of war."

While government has been the principal beneficiary of national emergency, the principal casualty has been liberty. As Madison warned, "Crisis is the rallying cry of the tyrant." This should give us pause as Congress now sets out to solve the health care crisis, the education crisis, and the crime crisis. To Congress, a crisis is an excuse to expand its domain.

Shortly before his death, Benjamin Franklin was asked how well the Constitution would survive the test of time. He responded optimistically that "everything appears to promise it will last." Then he added his famous warning, "But in this world nothing is certain but death and taxes." Ironically, the mortal wounds of the Constitution have been inflicted by precisely those who insist that they want to make it "a living document." Yet to argue that we return to the spirit and the true meaning of this living document is to invite scorn, malice, or outright disbelief from modern-day intellectuals.

Those few brave souls (mainly outside the Beltway) who urge that government should be guided by the original intent of the Constitution are always accused of trying to "turn back the clock." But turning back the clock in order to right a grievous wrong is precisely what we ought to do. There is nothing reactionary or backward-looking about dedicating ourselves to the ideas and principles that guided our Founders and formed the bedrock of our free society.

By all means, let's turn back the clock. Who knows? In the process we might even encourage a few Jeffersons and Madisons to run for Congress.

Reprinted by permission from Imprimis, *the national speech digest of Hillsdale College, www.hillsdale.edu.*

The Real Cost of Regulation
John Stossel

May 2001 *Imprimis*

John Stossel is an investigative reporter with ABC News.

When I started 30 years ago as a consumer reporter, I took the approach that most young reporters take today. My attitude was that capitalism is essentially cruel and unfair, and that the job of government, with the help of lawyers and the press, is to protect people from it. For years I did stories along those lines—stories about Coffee Association ads claiming that coffee "picks you up while it calms you down," or Libby-Owens-Ford Glass Company ads touting the clarity of its product by showing cars with their windows rolled down. I and other consumer activists said, "We've got to have regulation. We've got to police these ads. We've got to have a Federal Trade Commission." And I'm embarrassed at how long it took me to realize that these regulations make things worse, not better, for ordinary people.

The damage done by regulation is so vast, it's often hard to see. The money wasted consists not only of the taxes taken directly from us to pay for bureaucrats, but also of the indirect cost of all the lost energy that goes into filling out the forms. Then there's the distraction of creative power. Listen to Jack Faris, president of the National Federation of Independent Business: "If you're a small businessman, you have to get involved in government or government will wreck your business." And that's what happens. You have all this energy going into lobbying the politicians, forming the trade associations and PACs, and trying to manipulate the leviathan that's grown up in Washington, D.C. and the state capitals. You have many of the smartest people in the country today going into law, rather than into engineering or science. This doesn't create a richer, freer society. Nor do regulations only depress the economy. They depress the spirit. Visitors to Moscow before the fall of communism noticed a dead-eyed look in the people. What was that about? I don't think it was about fear of the KGB. Most Muscovites didn't have intervention by the secret police in their daily lives. I think it was the look that people get when they live in an all-bureaucratic state. If you go to Washington, to the Environmental Protection Agency, I think you'll see the same thing.

One thing I noticed that started me toward seeing the folly of regulation was that it didn't even punish the obvious crooks. The people selling [bogus products] got away with it. The Attorney General would come at them after five years, they would hire lawyers to gain another five, and then they would change the name of their product or move to a different state. But regulation did punish legitimate businesses.

When I started reporting, all the aspirin companies were saying they were the best, when in fact aspirin is simply aspirin. So the FTC sued and demanded corrective advertising. Corrective ads would have been something like, "Contrary to our prior ads, Excedrin does not relieve twice as much pain." Of course these ads never ran. Instead, nine years of costly litigation finally led to a consent order. The aspirin companies said, "We don't admit doing anything wrong, but we won't do it again." So who won? Unquestionably the lawyers did. But did the public? Aspirin ads are more honest now. They say things like, "Nothing works better than Bayer"—which, if you think about it, simply means, "We're all the same." But I came to see that the same thing would have happened without nearly a decade of litigation, because markets police themselves. I can't say for certain how it would have happened. I think it's a fatal conceit to predict how markets will work. Maybe Better Business Bureaus would have gotten involved. Maybe the aspirin companies would have sued each other. Maybe the press would have embarrassed them. But the truth would have gotten out. The more I watched the market, the more impressed I was by how flexible and reasonable it is compared to government-imposed solutions.

Market forces protect us even where we tend most to think we need government. Consider the greedy, profit-driven companies that have employed me. CBS, NBC, and ABC make their money from advertisers, and they've paid me for 20 years to bite the hand that feeds them. Bristol-Myers sued CBS and me for $23 million when I did the story on aspirin. You'd think CBS would have said, "Stossel ain't worth that." But they didn't. Sometimes advertisers would pull their accounts, but still I wasn't fired. Ralph Nader once said that this would never happen except on public television. In fact the opposite is true: Unlike PBS, almost every local TV station has a consumer reporter. The reason is capitalism: More people watch stations that give honest information about their sponsors' products. So although a station might lose some advertisers, it can charge the others more. Markets protect us in unexpected ways.

Alternatives to the Nanny State

People often say to me, "That's okay for advertising. But when it comes to health and safety, we've got to have OSHA, the FDA, the CPSC" and the whole alphabet soup of regulatory agencies that have been created over the past several decades. At first glance this might seem to make sense. But by interfering with free markets, regulations almost invariably have nasty side effects. Take the FDA, which saved us from thalidomide—the drug to prevent morning sickness in pregnant women that was discovered to cause birth defects. To be accurate, it wasn't so much that the FDA saved us, as that it was so slow in studying thalidomide that by the end of the approval process, the drug's awful effects were being seen in Europe. I'm glad for this. But since the thalidomide scare, the FDA has grown ten-fold in size, and I believe it now does more harm than good. If you want to get a new drug approved today, it costs about $500 million and takes about ten years. This means that there are drugs currently in existence that would improve or even save lives, but that are being withheld from us because of a tiny chance they contain carcinogens. Some years ago, the FDA held a press conference to announce its long-awaited approval of a new beta-blocker, and predicted it would save 14,000 American lives per year. Why didn't anybody stand up at the time and say, "Excuse me, doesn't that mean you killed 14,000 people last year by not approving it?" The answer is, reporters don't think that way.

Why, in a free society, do we allow government to perform this kind of nanny-state function? A reasonable alternative would be for government to serve as an information agency. Drug companies wanting to submit their products to a ten-year process could do so. Those of us who choose to be cautious could take only FDA-approved drugs. But others, including people with terminal illnesses, could try non-approved drugs without sneaking off to Mexico or breaking the law. As an added benefit, all of us would learn something valuable by their doing so. I'd argue further that we don't need the FDA to perform this research. As a rule, government agencies are inefficient. If we abolished the FDA, private groups like the publisher of *Consumer Reports* would step in and do the job better, cheaper, and faster. In any case, wouldn't that be more compatible with what America is about? Patrick Henry never said, "Give me absolute safety or give me death!"

Lawyers and Liability

If we embrace the idea of free markets, we have to accept the fact that trial lawyers have a place. Private lawsuits could be seen as a supplement to Adam Smith's invisible hand: the invisible fist. In theory they should deter bad behavior. But because of how our laws have evolved, this process has gone horribly wrong. It takes years for victims to get their money, and most of the money goes to lawyers. Additionally, the wrong people get sued. A Harvard study of medical malpractice suits found that most of those getting money don't deserve it, and that most people injured by negligence don't sue. The system is a mess. Even the cases the trial lawyers are most proud of don't really make us safer. They brag about their lawsuit over football helmets, which were thin enough that some kids were getting head injuries. But now the helmets are so thick that kids are butting each other and getting other kinds of injuries. Worst of all, they cost over $100 each. School districts on the margin can't afford them, and as a result some are dropping their football programs. Are the kids from these schools safer playing on the streets? No.

An even clearer example concerns vaccines. Trial lawyers sued over the Diphtheria-Pertussis-Tetanus Vaccine, claiming that it wasn't as safe as it might have been. Although I suspect this case rested on junk science, I don't know what the truth is. But assuming these lawyers were right, and that they've made the DPT vaccine a little safer, are we safer? When they sued, there were twenty companies in America researching and making vaccines. Now there are four. Many got out of the business because they said, "We don't make that much on vaccines. Who needs this huge liability?" Is America better off with four vaccine makers instead of twenty? No way.

These lawsuits also disrupt the flow of information that helps free people protect themselves. For example, we ought to read labels. We should read the label on tetracycline, which says that it won't work if taken with milk. But who reads labels anymore? I sure don't. There are 21 warning labels on stepladders—"Don't dance on stepladders wearing wet shoes," etc.—because of the threat of liability. Drug labels are even crazier. . . . My point is that government and lawyers don't make us safer. Freedom makes us safer. It allows us to protect ourselves. Some say, "That's fine for us. We're educated. But the poor and the ignorant need government regulations to protect them." Not so. I sure don't know what makes one car run better or safer than another. Few of us are automotive engineers. But it's hard to get totally ripped off buying a car in America. The worst car you can find here is safer than the best cars produced in planned economies. In a free society, not everyone has to be an expert in order for markets to protect us. In the case of cars, we just need a few car buffs who read car magazines. Information gets around through word-of-mouth. Good companies thrive and bad ones atrophy. Freedom protects the ignorant, too.

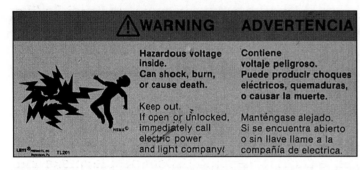

Admittedly there are exceptions to this argument. I think we need some environmental regulation, because now and then we lack a market incentive to behave well in that area. Where is the incentive for me to keep my waste-treatment plant from contaminating your drinking water? So we need some rules, and some have done a lot of good. Our air and water are cleaner thanks to catalytic converters. But how much regulation is enough? President Clinton set a record as he left office, adding 500,000 new pages to the Federal Register—a whole new spiderweb of little rules for us to obey. How big should government be? For most of America's history, when we grew the fastest, government accounted for five percent or less of GDP. The figure is now 40 percent. This is still less than Europe. But shouldn't we at least have an intelligent debate about how much government should do? The problem is that to have such a debate, we need an informed public. And here I'm embarrassed, because people in my business are not helping that cause.

Fear-Mongering: A Risky Business

A turning point came in my career when a producer came into my office excited because he had been given a story by a trial lawyer—the lazy reporter's best friend—about Bic lighters spontaneously catching fire in people's pockets. These lighters, he told me, had killed four Americans in four years. By this time I'd done some homework, so I said, "Fine. I'll do the exploding lighter story after I do stories on plastic bags, which kill 40 Americans every four years, and five-gallon buckets, which kill 200 Americans (mostly children) every four years." This is a big country, with 280 million people. Bad things happen to some of them. But if we frighten all the rest about ant-sized dangers, they won't be prepared when an elephant comes along. The producer stalked off angrily and got Bob Brown to do the story. But several years later, when ABC gave me three hour-long specials a year in order to keep me, I insisted the first one be called, "Are We Scaring Ourselves to Death?" In it, I ranked some of these risks and made fun of the press for its silliness in reporting them.

Risk specialists compare risks not according to how many people they kill, but according to how many days they reduce the average life. The press goes nuts over airplane crashes, but airplane crashes have caused fewer than 200 deaths per year over the past 20 years. That's less than one day off the average life. There is no proof that toxic-waste sites like Love Canal or Times Beach have hurt anybody at all, despite widely reported claims that they cause 1,000 cases of cancer a year. (Even assuming they do, and assuming further that all these cancer victims die, that would still be less than four days off the average life.) House fires account for about 4,500 American deaths per year—18 days off the average life. And murder, which leads the news in most towns, takes about 100 days off the average life. But to bring these risks into proper perspective, we need to compare them to far greater risks like driving, which knocks 182 days off the average life. I am often asked to do scare stories about flying—"The Ten Most Dangerous Airports" or "The Three Most Dangerous Airlines"—and I refuse because it's morally irresponsible. When we scare people about flying, more people drive to Grandma's house, and more are killed as a result. This is statistical murder, perpetuated by regulators and the media.

Even more dramatic is the fact that Americans below the poverty line live seven to ten fewer years than the rest of us. Some of this difference is self-induced: poor people smoke and drink more. But most of it results from the fact that they can't afford some of the good things that keep the rest of us alive. They drive older cars with older tires; they can't afford the same medical care; and so on. This means that when bureaucrats get obsessed about flying or toxic-waste sites, and create new regulations and drive up the cost of living in order to reduce these risks, they shorten people's lives by making them poorer. Bangladesh has floods that kill 100,000 people. America has comparable floods and no one dies. The difference is wealth. Here we have TVs and radios to hear about floods, and cars to drive off in. Wealthier is healthier, and regulations make the country poorer. Maybe the motto of OSHA should be: "To save four, kill ten."

Largely due to the prevalence of misleading scare stories in the press, we see in society an increasing fear of innovation. Natural gas in the home kills 200 Americans a year, but we accept it because it's old. It happened before we got crazy. We accept coal, which is awful stuff, but we're terrified of nuclear power, which is probably cleaner and safer. Swimming pools kill over 1,000 Americans every year, and I think it's safe to say that the government wouldn't allow them today if they didn't already exist. What about vehicles that weigh a ton and are driven within inches of pedestrians by 16-year-olds, all while spewing noxious exhaust? Cars, I fear, would never make it off the drawing board in 2001.

What's happened to America? Why do we allow government to make decisions for us as if we were children? In a free society we should be allowed to take risks, and to learn from them. The press carps and whines about our exposure to dangerous new things—invisible chemicals, food additives, radiation, etc. But what's the result? We're living longer than ever. A century ago, most people my age were already dead. If we were better informed, we'd realize that what's behind this longevity is the spirit of enterprise, and that what gives us this spirit—what makes America thrive—isn't regulation. It's freedom.

Reprinted by permission from Imprimis, *the national speech digest of Hillsdale College, www.hillsdale.edu.*

The Threat from Lawyers is No Joke
Walter Olson

March 2004 *Imprimis*

Walter Olson is a senior fellow at the Manhattan Institute. He is a political commentator and writer.

Many of us have wondered over the years what the difference is between satire and reality in the American legal system. I now have the answer: one year, 11 months, and ten days. Let me explain.

It was on August 3, 2000, that *The Onion*—America's favorite satirical newspaper—published an article entitled, "Hershey's Ordered to Pay Obese Americans $135 Billion." This piece of comic fiction reported that the chocolate company had been sued by state attorneys general in a class action over the lack of warnings on its product, over its marketing of products to children, and over its having—most insidiously of all—artificially spiked its products with nuts and crisped rice to keep people addicted. The jury, by this satirical account, had responded by granting an enormous award. "This is a vindication for myself and all chocolate victims," said one of the plaintiffs. In addition, the company was ordered to place a warning on all of its products reading: "The Surgeon General has determined that eating chocolate may lead to being really fat."

Well, on July 24, 2002—less than two years later—the wire services reported that Mr. Caesar Barber of the Bronx, New York, was filing a lawsuit against McDonald's. (He was soon joined by various other plaintiffs suing Wendy's, Burger King, and other fast food chains.) Mr. Barber had for years been wandering into McDonald's restaurants, apparently under the impression that they served health food, and had been receiving hamburgers and French fries instead of celery stalks. He had no idea that you could get fat from such products, and sure enough he developed heart problems and other medical conditions associated with obesity.

Although many of us greeted this lawsuit with incredulity, it was taken quite seriously by some veterans of the tobacco litigation that had succeeded so gloriously a few years earlier. Here is a law professor from George Washington University, quoted in *Time*: "A fast food company like McDonald's may not be responsible for the entire obesity epidemic. But let's say they're five percent responsible. Five percent of 117 billion dollars is still an enormous amount of money." Northeastern University organized a conference on how to sue food makers that was attended by scores of lawyers, one of whom—a recent Rutgers law graduate—told *Time*: "It's a very important and pressing issue and its outcome will be with us for years to come. I'm hoping to be able to build a career out of this issue." Lawsuits against fast food restaurants were also taken seriously by the *New York Times*, which defended them as socially beneficial. Its general argument seemed to be, "We're not saying these lawsuits should win, but what can they hurt?"

We used to know the answer to that question. We knew that they could hurt a lot.

The Older View

. . . [T]he proprietor of [a parking lot] in Framingham, Massachusetts, was sued after a thief broke into the lot, stole a car, drove off at high speed and crashed. Indeed, the family of the thief sued the lot owner for negligently making it too easy to steal a car from the lot. We used to know what was wrong with that, too.

A California man who passed out drunk on the railroad tracks sued the Union Pacific railroad because its engineer and conductor did not sound the train's horn after seeing him—they were too busy trying to engage its emergency brakes. . . .

Throughout most of American history, we understood quite clearly that litigation is for most people one of the most expensive, unpleasant things that ever happens to them in their lives. It is incredibly expensive, not only monetarily, but in the time and energy it absorbs. It is an assault on the reputation of at least one party, and often both parties, as charges are leveled back and forth. It is an assault on privacy, forcing those involved to answer questions under oath, involuntarily, about what they have done. It is a breach of the social peace. It is something that tends to corrupt the participants into doing things that they would not do otherwise. So while of course it was recognized that litigation is necessary sometimes as a last resort, it was seen as just that—a last resort. And if you accept the idea that litigation ought to be a last resort—and ought to be embarked on only in strong cases—you will want to arrange the rules of your legal system in a way to discourage weaker cases from going forward. We do not do this today. In fact, we have intentionally dismantled such rules.

Courtroom, Denver, Colorado

In almost every country but the U.S., legal systems incorporate a "loser pays" principle. If you sue someone and lose, you can't just walk away. You have to contribute something to making the victim of the lawsuit whole for what he has paid. We had that same principle in our legal system throughout much of American history, but it gradually died out. We also had procedural rules discouraging ill-conceived litigation. And we had rules of legal ethics prohibiting lawyers from stirring up litigation for their own benefit. But something changed around the 1960s and 1970s. It started in the world of ideas—in the universities and the law schools. Litigation came to be seen not as a necessary evil, but as a positive good. This view can be identified with the career of Ralph Nader, and with many of the professors who began to dominate elite law schools during that period.

The Newer View

According to this new view, litigation deters wrongful conduct: The more lawsuits that are filed, the more people will behave carefully. Litigation also came to be seen as a way to redistribute wealth from those who have it to those who need it. From this perspective, the more litigation there is, the more redistributive justice the courts can impose on society. And who can be against justice?

From being a last resort, then, litigation came to be seen as socially beneficial. And lawyers who advertise with billboards saying, "Sue someone and let's see how much money I can get for you," are seen not as sleazy but as public-spirited.

Given this new view of litigation, rules discouraging lawsuits ceased to make sense. This is why, starting in the 1960s and 1970s, we began changing the rules to make it easier to sue. We liberalized the rules of discovery—the rules governing how a person can demand information from his opponent. We opened the door to the "fishing expedition": "I don't know for sure whether you have done me any legal wrong, but please hand over the contents of your filing cabinets so that I can find out." We made it much easier to organize class actions, by which most Americans are periodically dragged into lawsuits as plaintiffs without even knowing it. We dropped many of the rules against lawyers stirring up litigation. And we weakened traditional legal principles like "assumption of risk." Here's what that means: If you go to a baseball game and get conked on the head by a foul ball, the old courts would have said that you have no grounds to sue because everyone knows that foul balls happen at baseball games. This no longer makes sense, however, if the point of lawsuits is to encourage ball clubs to be careful about where they let their players send their foul balls—and to redistribute wealth. So out it went, at least in many courts.

All these developments were bound to give us more litigation, and sure enough they did. The share of America's GNP that is devoted to litigation has tripled over 50 years. We spend two to three times more on it, in terms of percentage of GNP, as the other industrial democracies. The figure for how much is spent annually on liability insurance in the U.S.—a relatively easy thing to measure—is now $721 per citizen, which comes to over $2,800 per year for a family of four. So are we getting our money's worth?

Everyone has heard about the medical malpractice crisis that is driving doctors out of high-risk fields like obstetrics and neurosurgery. The Harvard University study of New York hospitals that is cited by both sides in this controversy is very revealing. On the one hand—and this is the part that has been best advertised—it found that in the majority of cases where people are injured by negligent care in a hospital, they never sue. True enough. But the same study also found that in the majority of cases where people do sue, experienced reviewers could not identify any negligence. So you have a lot of negligence with no lawsuits and a lot of lawsuits with no negligence. Is the latter somehow supposed to balance out the former?

The Harvard study also found that a great many of the lawsuits filed where no negligence was identified were nonetheless successful in obtaining money. Even though we could go on at great length about the monetary costs of lawsuits, those costs are not, in the final analysis, of prime importance. Indeed, we are a very rich country and can afford to spend a small percent of our GNP on litigation, if only for the entertainment value. The non-monetary costs, however, should give us real pause. For instance, at the real heart of the medical malpractice crisis is the demoralization that spreads in a profession like medicine at the knowledge that being the best possible doctor will not save you from being sued. Most doctors, I think, would be willing to pay high insurance premiums if they could have confidence that the legal system works rationally in identifying the doctors who ought not to be practicing. Few of them, I believe, have that confidence today.

Think of the knots that people tie themselves into, attempting to keep from being sued. We've all seen crazy warning labels, and each of us has his favorite. There's the one on an artificial fireplace log saying, "Caution: Risk of Fire"; the one on a bag of peanuts saying, "Warning: Contains Nuts"; and the one on a baby stroller saying, "Warning: Remove Child Before Folding." My favorite is the warning on the cardboard windshield sunscreen that keeps the car from getting too hot in the summer: "Do not drive with sunshield in place." This unhealthy level of caution infects many areas of our national life. Consider the unwillingness of most businesses today to give honest job references. That was one factor behind the recent case of the alleged killer nurse in Pennsylvania and New Jersey, who bounced from hospital to hospital, usually leaving under suspicion. The hospitals hadn't even bothered calling each other, because they knew they wouldn't get honest answers due to fears about lawsuits.

Effects on American Politics

This revolution in the legal system has begun to transform American politics. The part of this that gets the most press today is the litigation lobby—"big law," if you will—which has become one of the most financially robust and effective lobbies in American politics. It is among the three or four most important financial bases of the Democratic Party, and also contributes to some Republicans. But this financial involvement in politics was just a prologue to a more disturbing trend: In recent years, litigation has evolved into a kind of substitute for politics.

Until quite recently, a group of Americans who saw the need for some sweeping new law would march in the streets, organize a letter-writing campaign to Congress or the state legislature, or try to replace congressmen or state legislators with candidates sympathetic to their cause. That was how politics was done. But today, politics is not necessary. If you want gun control or tighter control over tobacco or more environmental regulations, you can simply call 1-800-LAWSUIT. Operators will be standing by around the clock, and once you agree to give the lawyers a share of the monetary reward, you can lean back and watch them go to work.

Take tobacco. Despite years of agitation, Congress had not acted rapidly enough for anti-tobacco activists who wanted an increase in taxes on cigarettes and more regulation of advertising. The states were doing some of this, but not fast enough for activists. So what happened? We saw private lawyers flying around the country in their Lear jets, signing up state attorneys general and brokering a

Courtroom, Baltimore, Maryland

settlement that obtained $246 billion for state governments and $10 or 20 billion in fees for the lawyers. The settlement also resulted in the adoption of regulations that the elected branches of government had been unwilling to enact. We also got what amounted to a new tax on cigarettes—a tax increase unlike any other tax hike in that it did not originate in a legislature.

Soon we saw this same process of bypassing the political system being tried in other areas as well. *American Lawyer* magazine published an article on the origins of gun litigation, in which it interviewed the private lawyer (a multi-millionaire, needless to say) who had dreamed it up and flown around the country selling it to mayors. The article explained that it fit his thinking—that the plaintiff's bar should act as a "de facto fourth branch of government—one that achieved regulation through litigation when legislation failed." Richard "Dickie" Scruggs, the private lawyer who organized the tobacco litigation (and whose firm got an estimated one billion dollars for it), was profiled in *Time*, which reported as follows: "Ask Scruggs if trial lawyers are trying to run America, and he doesn't bother to deny it: 'Somebody's got to do it.'"

What are the differences between this newly contrived fourth branch of government and the three branches that the founders established in the Constitution? The differences begin with the manner of selection. Those in the fourth branch don't have to worry about those pesky things called elections—or even about getting confirmed by the Senate, as federal judges do. Nor do they have to worry about the safeguards of transparency that are built into our political system. Much of their activity takes place behind the scenes. Indeed, these cases nearly always are meant to be settled instead of tried, and the public is not admitted into the negotiation room. And if the public doesn't like the results, there is, frankly, not much the public can do about it. This is highly ironic: The proclaimed goal of trial lawyers is to hold every profession and industry accountable for their actions, yet they have created a litigation-based policy-making process in which they themselves are almost entirely unaccountable.

Today there are increasing reports about how environmentalists are beginning to place their trust in global warming lawsuits against the auto industry, electric utilities and the like. Racial reparations litigation is beginning to absorb much of the energy that used to go into political agitation for civil rights. You see this occurring now in so many areas that William Greider, a leading left-wing journalist, has proposed in *Rolling Stone*—in the context of discussing Senator John Edwards of North Carolina—that trial lawyers have emerged as the natural leadership of the left in America today. He may be right.

After years of refusing to govern our trial lawyers, it seems they have decided to take it upon themselves to govern us. It is not too late to do something about it. But neither is this a problem that can be solved overnight by a quick fix such as tort reform legislation. As I said before, the ideas that underlie the new legal system and way of governing were born in the academy. This is where our judges and lawyers learned them. And now these ideas are being spread among the general public by the system itself. For instance, these lawsuits teach us again and again the principle that some distant institution with a lot of money is responsible for each individual's problems. It is this distorted view of responsibility that makes thinkable today claims that were unthinkable a few short years ago. So the first step in turning things around, I would say, is to come to a real understanding of exactly what we did wrong in changing the rules of our legal system and handing the trial lawyers so much power.

Until we reverse this process, it will remain the rule that if you want to hurt someone in America, you may not be able to do it with impunity using a scalpel or a car. But you can do it with a lawsuit and no one will lay a glove on you.

Reprinted by permission from Imprimis, *the national speech digest of Hillsdale College, www.hillsdale.edu.*

The Liberal Assault on Freedom of Speech
Thomas G. West

January 2004 *Imprimis*

Thomas G. West is a professor of politics at the University of Dallas. He served as an Army Lieutenant in the Vietnam War. West has authored several books.

America has less freedom of speech today than it has ever had in its history. Yet it is widely believed that it has more. Liberal law professor Archibald Cox has written: "The body of law presently defining First Amendment liberties" grew out of a "continual expansion of individual freedom of expression." Conservative constitutional scholar Walter Berns agrees: "Legally we enjoy a greater liberty [of speech] than ever before in our history." Both are wrong.

Liberals and libertarians applaud what Cox, Berns, and others perceive as an expansion of free speech. Conservatives sometimes deplore it, rightly assuming that the expansion in question leads to greater scope for nude dancers, pornographers and flag burners. But from the point of view of the original meaning of free speech, our speech today is much less free than it was in the early republic.

Campaign Finance Regulation

In 1974, for the first time in American history, amendments to the Federal Elections Campaign Act (FECA) made it illegal in some circumstances for Americans to publish their opinions about candidates for election. Citizens and organizations who "coordinate" with a candidate for public office were prohibited from spending more than a set amount of money to publish arguments for or against a candidate. Those who "coordinate" with a candidate are his friends and supporters. In other words, publication was forbidden to those with the greatest interest in campaigns and those most likely to want to spend money publishing on behalf of candidates.

The Bipartisan Campaign Reform Act of 2002 goes well beyond the 1974 law, imposing substantial limits on the right of political parties and nonprofit organizations to publicize their views on candidates during election campaigns. Imagine the shock of the Founders if they were here to see that government was heavily into the business of banning private citizens from pooling their fortunes to publicize their opinions about candidates for elections.

These laws do contain a notable exception. Newspaper owners may spend as much money as they wish publishing arguments in support of candidates with whom they "coordinate." This solitary exemption from restrictions on free speech is, of course, no mistake: The dominant newspapers in America are liberal, and the 1974 law was passed by a

Democratic Congress on the day before Richard Nixon resigned in disgrace from the presidency.

Campaign finance regulation stands in direct opposition to the Founders' understanding of the First Amendment. For a large class of people, it effectively prohibits and punishes the most important thing that the right to free speech is supposed to guarantee: open discussion of candidates and issues at election time.

Those who favor campaign finance regulation sometimes claim that their primary concern is with "corruption and the appearance of corruption"—that is, what used to be called bribery or the appearance of bribery. But that is not the real agenda of the reformers. There is a good reason why the 2002 Act, like the 1974 law, was voted for by almost every House and Senate Democrat, and opposed by a large majority of Republicans: These laws are primarily about limiting the speech of conservatives.

Here are some quotations from the 2002 congressional debate:

Sen. Maria Cantwell (Dem., Wash.): "This bill is about slowing the ad war. . . . It is about slowing political advertising and making sure the flow of negative ads by outside interest groups does not continue to permeate the airwaves."

Sen. Barbara Boxer (Dem., Calif.): "These so-called issues ads are not regulated at all and mention candidates by name. They directly attack candidates without any accountability. It is brutal. . . . We have an opportunity in the McCain-Feingold bill to stop that."

Sen. Paul Wellstone (Dem., Minn.): "I think these issue advocacy ads are a nightmare. I think all of us should hate them . . . . [By passing the legislation], [w]e could get some of this poison politics off television."

In other words, the law makes it harder for citizens to criticize liberal politicians when they disagree with their policy views.

Some congressmen were willing to be even more open about the fact that the new law would cut down on conservative criticism of candidates. Rep. Jan Schakowsky (Dem.-Ill.) said: "If my colleagues care about gun control, then campaign finance is their issue so that the NRA does not call the shots." Democratic Reps. Marty Meehan (Mass.) and Rosa DeLauro (Conn.), and Democratic Sens. Harry Reid (Nev.) and Dick Durbin (Ill.) also cited the National Rifle Association's political communications as a problem that the Act would solve. Several liberal Republicans chimed in.

What this means is that government is now in the business of silencing citizens who believe in the Second Amendment right to keep and bear arms.

Sen. Jim Jeffords (Ind.-Vt.) said that issue ads "are obviously pointed at positions that are taken by you, saying how horrible they are." "Negative advertising is the crack cocaine of politics," added Sen. Tom Daschle (Dem.-S.D.). What these quotations show—and there are many more like them—is that the purpose of campaign finance regulation is to make it harder for conservatives to present their views to the public about candidates and issues in elections.

In its shocking December 2003 decision in *McConnell v. Federal Election Commission*, the five most liberal members of the Supreme Court upheld this law and saw no conflict with the First Amendment guarantee of freedom of speech and of the press. Yet it is impossible to imagine a more obvious violation of the First Amendment, unless the government were explicitly to authorize the Federal Election Commission to close down conservative newspapers and magazines. In his powerful dissent in the *McConnell* case, Justice Clarence Thomas wrote:

> The chilling endpoint of the Court's reasoning is not difficult to foresee: outright regulation of the press. None . . . of the reasoning employed by the Court exempts the press. . . . What is to stop a future Congress from determining that the press is 'too influential,' and that the 'appearance of corruption' is significant when media organizations endorse candidates or run 'slanted' or 'biased' news stories in favor of candidates or parties? Or, even easier, what is to stop a future Congress from concluding that the availability of unregulated media corporations creates a loophole that allows for easy 'circumvention' of the limitations of the current campaign finance laws?

With the National Rifle Association announcement that it intends to acquire a media outlet in order to get around Congress's unconstitutional restrictions on issue ads during elections, Justice Thomas's nightmare might come true even sooner than he anticipated. We are already hearing statements suggesting that any media owned by the NRA will not count as "real" media. At some point, perhaps in the very near future, the Federal Election Commission may find itself deciding which newspapers and broadcast stations are "real" news media (and can therefore be permitted their First Amendment rights) and which ones are "slanted" or "biased" (thus whose First Amendment rights must be denied).

Censorship Through Broadcast Licensing

Reading today's scholarship on freedom of speech, one would hardly guess that government control over the content of speech through licensing requirements—supposedly outlawed long ago—is alive and well. The amazing ignorance with which this matter is usually discussed today may be seen in the following quote from legal scholar Benno Schmidt, the former president of Yale:

> The First Amendment tolerates virtually no prior restraints [on speech or the press]. This doctrine is one of the central principles of our law of freedom of the press. . . . [T]he doctrine is presumably an absolute bar to any wholesale system of administrative licensing or censorship of the press, which is the most repellent form of government suppression of expression. . . ."

Schmidt fails to notice that every radio, television, and cable broadcaster in America is subject to a "wholesale system of administrative licensing," i.e., the "most repellent form of government suppression of expression."

Broadcasters have to obtain a license from the Federal Communications Commission. Stations receive licenses only when the FCC judges it to be "in the public interest, convenience, or necessity." Licenses are granted for a limited period, and the FCC may choose not to renew. The FCC has never defined what the "public interest" means. In the past, it preferred a case-by-case approach, which has been called "regulation by raised eyebrow."

During most of its history, the FCC consistently favored broadcasters who shared the views of government officials, and disfavored broadcasters who did not.

The first instance of serious and pervasive political censorship was initiated by Franklin Roosevelt's FCC in the 1930s. The Yankee Radio network in New England frequently editorialized against Roosevelt. The FCC asked Yankee to provide details about its programming. Sensing the drift, Yankee immediately stopped broadcasting editorials in 1938. In order to drive its point home, the FCC found Yankee deficient at license renewal time. They announced,

> Radio can serve as an instrument of democracy only when devoted to the communication of information and exchange of ideas fairly and objectively presented. . . . It cannot be devoted to the support of principles he [the broadcaster] happens to regard most favorably. . . .

In other words, if you want your broadcasting license renewed, stop criticizing Roosevelt.

The FCC soon afterwards made exclusion of "partisan" content a requirement for all broadcasters. It was understood, of course, that radio stations would continue to carry such supposedly "nonpartisan" fare as presidential speeches and "fireside chats" attacking Republicans and calling for expansions of the New Deal. In the name of "democracy," "fairness" and "objectivity," the FCC would no longer permit stations to engage in sustained criticism of Roosevelt's speeches and programs.

In 1949, the FCC announced its Fairness Doctrine. Broadcasters were required "to provide coverage of vitally important controversial issues . . . and . . . a reasonable opportunity for the presentation of contrasting viewpoints on such issues." In practice, the Fairness Doctrine only worked in one direction: against conservatives.

During the Republican Eisenhower years, the FCC paid little attention to broadcasting content, and a number of conservative radio stations emerged. After John Kennedy was elected in 1960, his administration went on the offensive against them. Kennedy's Assistant Secretary of Commerce, Bill Ruder, later admitted, "Our massive strategy was to use the Fairness Doctrine to challenge and harass right-wing broadcasters and hope that the challenges would be so costly to them that they would be inhibited and decide it was too expensive to continue."

Moniters at a Federal Communications Commission Listening Post, 1944

This strategy was highly successful. Hundreds of radio stations cancelled conservative shows that they had been broadcasting. The FCC revoked the license of one radio station, WXUR of Media, Pennsylvania, a tiny conservative Christian broadcaster. When WXUR appealed to the courts, one dissenting judge noted "that the public has lost access to information and ideas . . . as a result of this doctrinal sledge-hammer [i.e., the Fairness Doctrine]." The Supreme Court refused to hear the appeal. It saw no free speech violation in the government shutdown of a radio station for broadcasting conservative ideas.

The government also revoked the license of a television station in Jackson, Mississippi. WLTB was unapologetically and openly opposed to federal civil rights policies at the time, and would introduce NBC's news reports with this warning: "What you are about to see is an example of biased, managed, Northern news. Be sure to stay tuned at 7:25 to hear your local newscast." The D.C. Circuit Court ordered the FCC to revoke WLTB's license. In an outrageous opinion authored by Warren Burger, who was shortly afterward appointed by President Nixon as Chief Justice of the Supreme Court, the Circuit Court demanded in indignant tones that WLTB's owner be silenced: "After nearly five decades of operation, the broadcast industry does not seem to have grasped the simple fact that a broadcast license is a public trust subject to termination for breach of duty." Again, the Supreme Court refused to hear the station's appeal.

Conservatives tried to use the Fairness Doctrine as well, but failed in every case. Liberal author Fred Friendly writes, "After virtually every controversial program [on the major TV networks]—'Harvest of Shame,' . . . 'Hunger in America' [1960s programs advocating liberal anti-poverty policies]—fairness complaints were filed, and the FCC rejected them all. As FCC general counsel Henry Geller explained, 'We just weren't going to get trapped into determining journalistic judgments. . . .'" In other words, when liberals were on the air, the FCC called it journalism. When conservatives were on the air, the FCC called it partisan and political, and insisted that the liberal point of view be given equal time.

In the 1980s, President Reagan appointed a majority to the Federal Communications Commission, and it abolished the Fairness Doctrine in 1987. The effect was dramatic. Immediately, conservative talk radio blossomed. Rush Limbaugh was the biggest winner. He came along at just the moment when, for the first time since the 1950s, stations could be confident that conservative broadcasting would no longer lead to license renewal problems or Fairness Doctrine complaints and litigation.

The end of the Fairness Doctrine was a tremendous victory for the First Amendment. But it does not mean that broadcast media are now free. The authority of the FCC over broadcasters remains in place. It can be brought back with the full partisan force of the Roosevelt and Kennedy administrations as soon as one party gets control over all three branches of the federal government and chooses to do so.

Harassment Law

For about 25 years, government has required businesses and educational institutions to punish speech that can be characterized as "hostile environment" harassment. This standard is so vague that the question of what constitutes a "hostile working environment" is endlessly litigated. One court ordered employees to "refrain from any racial, religious, ethnic, or other remarks or slurs contrary to their fellow employees' religious beliefs." Another court banned "all offensive conduct and speech implicating considerations of race." Of course, there are some who find any criticism of affirmative action offensive, even racist. Others are offended when someone alludes to his own religious convictions. So this policy, in effect, makes it potentially illegal for employees to say anything about their own religious beliefs or to defend the "wrong" kind of political opinions. UCLA law professor Eugene Volokh has cited a headline in a major business magazine that sums up this denial of free speech in the workplace: "Watch What You Say, or Be Ready to Pay."

The Founders' Approach

Let us turn to the original meaning of free speech in the Constitution to see how far we have abandoned the original meaning of that document.

The Declaration of Independence calls liberty an inalienable right with which we are "endowed by our Creator." As human beings are born free in all respects, they are also born free to speak, write and publish.

Nevertheless, although all human beings possess the same natural right to liberty, the Founders believed there is a law of nature that teaches us that no one has the right to injure another. The most obvious kind of injurious speech is personal libel. Here is a quotation from an early libel case:

> [T]he heart of the libeller . . . is more dark and base than . . . his who commits a midnight arson. . . . [T]he injuries which are done to character and reputation seldom can be cured, and the most innocent man may, in a moment, be deprived of his good name, upon which, perhaps, he depends for all the prosperity, and all the happiness of his life.

But the Founders knew very well that allowing government to punish abuses of speech is potentially dangerous to legitimate free speech. So they relied on three pillars to secure this right of free speech while setting limits on injurious speech.

First, no speech could be prohibited by government except that which is clearly injurious. Today, as we have seen, noninjurious political and religious speech is routinely prohibited and punished through campaign finance and other laws.

Second, there could be no prior restraint of speech. Government was not permitted to withhold permission to publish if it disapproved of a publisher or his views. Today, the media from which most Americans get their news is subject to a government licensing scheme that is strikingly similar to the system by which England's kings kept the press in line in the sixteenth and seventeenth centuries.

Third, injurious speech had to be defined in law, and punishment of it could only be accomplished by due process of law. Guilt or liability could be established only by juries—that is, by people who are not government officials. Today, clear legal standards, formal prosecutions and juries are mostly avoided in the convoluted censorship schemes employed by government in broadcasting law, campaign finance law, harassment law and the like. . . .

Today's Liberal View

Why have liberals rejected the Founders' idea of free speech?

The Founders looked toward a society in which each person's right to life, liberty, property, free exercise of religion, and pursuit of happiness would be protected by government. . . . [G]overnment would be mostly indifferent to the manner in which citizens lived their private lives. Laws would protect everyone's rights equally, but it was understood that equal rights lead to unequal results, because of differences in talent, character and luck. About a century ago, liberals began to argue that the Founders' view, which is embodied in the Constitution, is unjust in two ways.

First, they argued that by protecting everyone's property equally, government in effect sides with the rich against the poor. It protects the rich and leaves the poor open to oppression. It is not enough, in the liberal view, for government to be neutral between business and labor, between men and women, between whites and racial minorities, and so on. In each case, liberals say, justice requires that government must put burdens on the rich and powerful and give special advantages to the weak and vulnerable.

Applied to free speech, the liberal view leads to the conclusion that government must limit spending by those who can afford to publish or broadcast their views. As University of Chicago law professor Cass Sunstein writes, the traditional autonomy of newspapers "may itself be an abridgment of the free speech right." Government interference with broadcasting content through FCC licensing is from this standpoint a positive good for free speech. Without it, rich white males will dominate, and the poor, women and minorities will be marginalized and silenced. Therefore, in the liberal view, speech rights must be redistributed from the rich and privileged to the poor and excluded.

University of Maryland professor Mark Graber endorses this view: "Affluent Americans," he writes, "have no First Amendment right that permits them to achieve political success through constant repetition of relatively unwanted ideas." In other words, if you publish or broadcast "too much," government has the right, and the duty, to silence you. Yale law professor Stephen Carter agrees: "Left unregulated, the modern media could present serious threats to democracy." Sunstein calls for a "New Deal for Speech," in which government will treat speech in exactly the same way as it already treats property, namely, as something that is really owned by government, and which citizens are only permitted to use or engage in when they meet conditions established by government to promote fairness and justice.

Arguments like these are the deepest reason that liberals no longer follow the Constitution, and why Americans today no longer know what the free speech clause really means.

One might raise the objection that these are only law professors. But their view turns out to be squarely in the mainstream. Several candidates for the presidency in 2000 from both political parties (but not George W. Bush) called for much more stringent limitations on free speech in the name of campaign finance reform. One of those candidates, Bill Bradley, proposed a constitutional amendment in 1996 that would have repealed the free speech clause of the First Amendment. Dick Gephardt, the former minority leader of the House of Representatives, has made the same proposal. In the end, even President Bush signed the Bipartisan Campaign Reform Act of 2002.

I am reminded by this of Abraham Lincoln's remark in the 1850s about those who would read blacks out of the Constitution and the Declaration of Independence: If that view is to prevail, why not move to Russia, he asked, where we can take our despotism unalloyed? Liberals today are on the verge of throwing off all pretense and admitting openly that what they mean by equality is the abolition of liberty.

There is a second reason that today's liberals see the Founders' view of free speech as oppressive. . . . A famous passage from a Supreme Court pro-abortion decision sums up this liberal view. It reads, "At the heart of liberty is the right to define one's own concept of existence, of meaning, of the universe, and of the mystery of human life."

The Founders would have replied that we are precisely not free to define our own concept of existence and meaning. God and nature have established the "laws of nature and of nature's God," which have already defined it for us. Human beings, Jefferson wrote, are "inherently independent of all but moral law." If men defy that law, they are not free. They are slaves, at first to their own passions, eventually to political tyranny. For men who cannot govern their own passions cannot sustain a democratic government.

Our task today is to recover the cause of constitutionalism. In doing so, the recovery of a proper understanding and respect for free speech must be a high priority.

Reprinted by permission from Imprimis, *the national speech digest of Hillsdale College, www.hillsdale.edu.*

Constitutional Myths and Realities
Stephen Markman

August 2005 *Imprimis*

Stephen Markman is an associate justice on the Michigan Supreme Court.

The United States has enjoyed unprecedented liberty, prosperity and stability, in large part because of its Constitution. I would like to discuss a number of myths or misconceptions concerning that inspired document.

Myth or Misconception 1: Public policies of which we approve are constitutional and public policies of which we disapprove are unconstitutional.

It might be nice if those policies that we favor were compelled by the Constitution and those policies that we disfavor were barred by the Constitution. But this is not, by and large, what the Constitution does. Rather, the Constitution creates an architecture of government that is designed to limit the abuse of governmental power. The delegates to the Constitutional Convention of 1787 sought to create a government that would be effective in carrying out its essential tasks, such as foreign policy and national defense, while not coming to resemble those European governments with which they were so familiar, where the exercise of governmental power was arbitrary and without limits. Therefore, while the Constitution constrains government, it does not generally seek to replace the representative processes of government.

Governments may, and often do, carry out unwise public policies without running afoul of the Constitution. As a Justice of the Michigan Supreme Court, I often uphold policies that have been enacted in the state legislature, or by cities and counties and townships, that I believe are unwise. But lack of wisdom is not the test for what is or is not constitutional, and lack of wisdom is not what allows me—a judge, not the adult supervisor of society—to exercise the enormous power of judicial review and strike down laws that have been enacted by "we the people" through their elected representatives. Redress for unwise public policies must generally come as the product of democratic debate and at the ballot box, not through judicial correction.

Constitutional Convention

Myth or Misconception 2: The Constitution principally upholds individual rights and liberties through the guarantees of the Bill of Rights.

It is not to denigrate the importance of the Bill of Rights to suggest that the Founders intended that individual rights and liberties would principally be protected by the architecture of the Constitution—the structure of government set forth in its original seven articles. The great animating principles of our Constitution are in evidence everywhere within this architecture. First, there is federalism, in which the powers of government are divided between the national government and the states. To the former belong such powers as those relating to foreign policy and national defense; to the latter such powers as those relating to the criminal justice system and the protection of the family. Second, there is the separation of powers, in which each branch of the national government—the legislative, the executive, and the judicial branch—has distinct responsibilities, yet is subject to the checks and balances of the other branches. Third, there is the principle of limited government of a particular sort in which the national government is constrained to exercise only those powers set forth by the Constitution, for example, issuing currency, administering immigration laws, running the post office and waging war. Together, these principles make it more difficult for government to exercise power and to abuse minority rights, and they limit the impact of governmental abuses of power.

Many of the Founders, including James Madison, believed that a Bill of Rights was unnecessary because the Constitution's architecture itself was sufficient to ensure that national power would not be abused. As Alexander Hamilton remarked in *Federalist* 84, "the Constitution is itself, in every rational sense, and to every useful purpose, a Bill of Rights." And practically speaking, until 1925, the Bill of Rights was not even thought to apply to the states, only to Congress; yet the individual rights of our citizens remained generally well protected.

Myth or Misconception 3: The national government and the state governments are regulated similarly by the Constitution.

As the 10th Amendment makes clear, the starting point for any constitutional analysis is that the national, i.e., the federal, government can do nothing under the Constitution unless it is affirmatively authorized by some provision of the Constitution. The states, on the other hand, can do anything under the Constitution unless they are prohibited by some provision of the Constitution. Why then, one might ask, throughout the 19th century and well into the 20th century—before the Bill of Rights was thought to apply to the states—did Michigan and other states not generally infringe upon such indispensable freedoms as the freedoms of speech or religion? How were individual rights protected? Well, in two ways principally: First and most obviously, there was simply not majority sentiment on the part of the people of Michigan or other states to encroach upon such freedoms. Second, Michigan and all other states had their own Constitutions that protected such freedoms.

Today the Bill of Rights has been construed by the U.S. Supreme Court to apply to the states, creating more uniform and more centralized constitutional policy. It remains true, however, that the impact of the Constitution upon the national and state governments varies substantially.

Myth or Misconception 4: Federalism is the same thing as states' rights.

"States' rights" in the constitutional sense refers to all of the rights of sovereignty retained by the states under the Constitution. But in this sense, states' rights refers to only half of what federalism is, the other half consisting of those powers either reserved for the national government or affirmatively prohibited to the states.

In popular use, "states' rights" has had a checkered history. Before the Civil War, it was the rallying cry of southern opponents of proposals to abolish or restrict slavery. By the 20th century, it had become the watchword of many of those who supported segregation in the public schools, as well as those who criticized generally the growing power of the central government.

While I share the view that federal power has come to supplant "states' rights" in far too many areas of governmental responsibility, "states' rights" are truly rights only where an examination of the Constitution reveals both that the national government lacks the authority to act and that there is nothing that prohibits the state governments from acting. There is no "state right," for example, for one state to impose barriers on trade coming from another, or to establish a separate foreign policy. These responsibilities are reserved to the national government by the Constitution.

Myth or Misconception 5: The Constitution is a document for lawyers and judges.

The Constitution was written for those in whose name it was cast, "we the people." It is a relatively short document, and it is generally straightforward and clear-cut. With only a few exceptions, there is an absence of legalese or technical terms. While the contemporary constitutional debate has focused overwhelmingly on a few broad phrases of the Constitution such as "due process" and "equal protection," the overwhelming part of this document specifies, for example, that a member of the House of Representatives must be 25 years of age, seven years a citizen, and an inhabitant of the state from which he is chosen; that a bill becomes a law when approved by both Houses and signed by the president, etc. One willing to invest just a bit more time in understanding the Constitution need only peruse *The Federalist Papers* to see what Madison, Hamilton or Jay had to say about its provisions to a popular audience in the late-18th century.

One reason I believe that the Constitution, as well as our laws generally, should be interpreted according to the straightforward meaning of their language, is to maintain the law as an institution that belongs to all of the people, and not merely to judges and lawyers. Let me give you an illustration: One creative constitutional scholar has said that the requirement that the president shall be at least 35 years of age really means that a president must have the maturity of a person who was 35 back in 1789 when the Constitution was written. That age today, opines this scholar, might be 30 or 32 or 40 or 42. The problem is that whenever a word or phrase of the Constitution is interpreted in such a "creative" fashion, the Constitution—and the law in general—becomes less accessible and less comprehensible to ordinary citizens, and more the exclusive province of attorneys who are trained in knowing such things as that "35" does not always mean "35."

One thing, by the way, that is unusual in the constitutional law course that I teach at Hillsdale College is that we actually read the language of the Constitution and discuss its provisions as we do so. What passes for constitutional law study at many colleges and universities is exclusively the study of Supreme Court decisions. While such decisions are obviously important, it is also important to compare what the Supreme Court has said to what the Constitution says. What is also unusual at Hillsdale is that, by the time students take my course, they have been required to study such informing documents as the Declaration of Independence, *The Federalist Papers*, Washington's First Inaugural Address—and, indeed, the Constitution itself.

Myth or Misconception 6: The role of the judge in interpreting the Constitution is to do justice.

The role of a judge is to do justice under law, a very different concept. Each of us has his or her own innate sense of right and wrong. This is true of every judge I have ever met. But judges are not elected or appointed to impose their personal views of right and wrong upon the legal system. Rather, as Justice Felix Frankfurter once remarked, "The highest example of judicial duty is to subordinate one's personal will and one's private views to the law." The responsible judge must subordinate his personal sense of justice to the public justice of our Constitution and its representative and legal institutions.

I recall one judicial confirmation hearing a number of years ago when I was working for the Senate Judiciary Committee. The nominee was asked, "If a decision in a particular case was required by law or statute and yet that offended your conscience, what would you do?" The nominee answered, "Senator, I have to be honest with you. If I was faced with a situation like that and it ran against my conscience, I would follow my conscience." He went on to explain: "I was born and raised in this country, and I believe that I am steeped in its traditions, its mores, its beliefs and its philosophies, and if I felt strongly in a situation like that, I feel that it would be the product of my very being and upbringing. I would follow my conscience." To my mind, for a judge to render decisions according to his or her personal conscience rather than the law is itself unconscionable.

Myth or Misconception 7: The great debate over the proper judicial role is between judges who are activist and judges who are restrained.

In the same way that excessively "activist" judges may exceed the boundaries of the judicial power by concocting law out of whole cloth, excessively "restrained" judges may unwarrantedly contract protections and rights conferred by the laws and the Constitution. It is inappropriate for a judge to exercise "restraint" when to do so is to neglect his obligation of judicial review—his obligation to compare the law with the requirements set forth by the Constitution. Nor am I enamored with the term "strict construction" to describe the proper duties of the judge, for it is the role of the judge to interpret the words of the law reasonably—not "strictly" or "loosely," not "broadly" or "narrowly," just reasonably.

I would prefer to characterize the contemporary judicial debate in terms of interpretivism verses non-interpretivism. In doing this, I would borrow the description of the judicial power used by Chief Justice John Marshall, who 200 years ago in *Marbury v. Madison* stated that it is the duty of the judge to say what the law is, not what it ought to be (which is the province of the legislature). For the interpretivist, the starting point, and usually the ending point, in giving meaning to the law are the plain words of the law. This is true whether we are construing the law of the Constitution, the law of a statute, or indeed the law of contracts and policies and deeds. In each instance, it is the duty of the judge to give faithful meaning to the words of the lawmaker and let the chips fall where they may.

One prominent illustration of the differing approaches of interpretivism and non-interpretivism arises in the context of the constitutionality of capital punishment. Despite the fact that there are at least six references in the Constitution to the possibility of capital punishment—for example, both the 5th and 14th Amendments assert that no person shall be "deprived of life, liberty or property without due process of law," from which it can clearly be inferred that a person can be deprived of these where there is due process—former Justice William Brennan held, in dissent, that capital punishment was unconstitutional on the grounds apparently that, since 1789, there had arisen an "evolving standard of decency marking the progress of a maturing society" on whose behalf he spoke. Purporting to speak for "generations yet unborn," Justice Brennan substituted his own opinions on capital punishment for the judgments reached in the Constitution by the Founders. His decision in this regard is the embodiment, but certainly not the only recent example, of non-interpretivism.

Myth or Misconception 8: The Constitution is a living document.

The debate between interpretivists and non-interpretivists over how to give meaning to the Constitution is often framed in the following terms: Is the Constitution a "living" document, in which judges "update" its provisions according to the "needs" of the times? Or is the Constitution an enduring document, in which its original meanings and principles are permanently maintained, subject only to changes adopted in accordance with its amending clause? I believe that it is better described in the latter sense. It is beyond dispute, of course, that the principles of the Constitution must be applied to new circumstances over time—the Fourth Amendment on searches and seizures to electronic wiretaps, the First Amendment on freedom of speech to radio and television and the Internet, the interstate commerce clause to automobiles and planes, etc. However, that is distinct from allowing the words and principles themselves to be altered based upon the preferences of individual judges.

Our Constitution would be an historical artifact—a genuinely dead letter—if its original sense became irrelevant, to be replaced by the views of successive waves of judges and justices intent on "updating" it, or replacing what some judges view as the "dead hand of the past" with contemporary moral theory. This is precisely what the Founders sought to avoid when they instituted a "government of laws, not of men."

There is no charter of government in the history of mankind that has more wisely set forth the proper relationship between the governed and their government than the American Constitution. For those of us who are committed to constitutional principles and fostering respect for that document, there is no better homage that we can pay it than to understand clearly its design and to take care in the manner in which we describe it.

Reprinted by permission from Imprimis, *the national speech digest of Hillsdale College, www.hillsdale.edu.*

The Late, Great Doctrine of States' Rights
Ray Notgrass

At the founding of our republic, the general understanding in government and politics was that the states that made up the Union had certain, definite rights regarding their sovereignty and power. The states had been founded as independent colonies, and they clung to this independence through the Revolution. The Confederation government, under which the country fought the War for Independence, was something less than the sum of its parts because of this independence of the states, since states could ignore requests by Congress for troops and funds.

In some areas of government, both before and after the adoption of the Constitution, states were understood to have paramount rights. The national government was to have nothing to do with those areas. Slavery, for instance, was seen as a state issue which the national government had no right to address. Voting and the conducting of elections were also seen as entirely under the purview of the states and were not to be addressed by the Federal government. The states formulated policies for public education; the national government did not.

The growth of the Federal government's power over the course of the Twentieth Century, especially during the New Deal of the 1930s and the Great Society of the 1960s, came largely at the expense of the powers of state government. To be sure, some endeavors which the Federal government undertook were not pursued previously by any governmental authority. However, where power has flowed from one level of government to another, the flow has been almost completely in the direction of going from the states to the national level. Little power has flowed in the opposite direction. Now, to cite two examples, the Federal government is heavily involved in elections and in education.

Advocates of states' rights bemoan this concentration of power in Washington and the loss of power by the states. In theory, and in some areas of practice, the exercise of power by the states was good. However, the states have sometimes been their own worst enemies. Some states did not sufficiently regulate the banks that they chartered, and this failure led to frequent financial panics. States did not always protect the right of every legally qualified citizen to vote. States did not always treat people of color with fairness and equality. In many cases, states hid behind the doctrine of states' rights to deny people the individual rights to which they were entitled by the Constitution.

The high water mark of states' rights was the secession of slave states to form the Confederacy. Political leaders in these states were indignant at what they saw as the danger of encroachment by the Federal government on the states' proper sphere of power, especially with regard to slavery. The issue was portrayed by the South as one of states' rights. However, the states were not protesting Federal encroachment in education or in the conduct of elections. The states feared what a Republican government might do with regard to slavery, even though the Lincoln Administration had in fact done absolutely nothing about slavery when the Southern states seceded.

Read what Alexander Stephens, Vice-President of the Confederacy, said on March 21, 1861 in Savannah, Georgia, in what came to be called the "Cornerstone Speech." No official transcript of this extemporaneous speech exists. The text we have comes from a reporter's notes, but Stephens never denied this portion of the speech.

> The new [Confederate] constitution has put at rest, forever, all the agitating questions relating to our peculiar institution—African slavery as it exists amongst us—the proper status of the negro in our form of civilization. This was the immediate cause of the late rupture and present revolution. Jefferson, in his forecast, had anticipated this, as the "rock upon which the old Union would split." He was right. What was conjecture with him, is now a realized fact. But whether he fully comprehended the great truth upon which that rock stood and stands, may be doubted. The prevailing ideas entertained by him and most of the leading statesmen at the time of the formation of the old constitution, were that the enslavement of the African was in violation of the laws of nature; that it was wrong in principle, socially, morally, and politically. It was an evil they knew not well how to deal with, but the general opinion of the men of that day was that, somehow or other in the order of Providence, the institution would be evanescent and pass away. This idea, though not incorporated in the constitution, was the prevailing idea at that time. The constitution, it is true, secured every essential guarantee to the institution while it should last, and hence no argument can be justly urged against the constitutional guarantees thus secured, because of the common sentiment of the day. Those ideas, however, were fundamentally wrong. They rested upon the assumption of the equality of races. This was an error. It was a sandy foundation, and the government built upon it fell when the "storm came and the wind blew."
>
> Our new government is founded upon exactly the opposite idea; its foundations are laid, its cornerstone rests, upon the great truth that the negro is not equal to the white man; that slavery—subordination to the superior race—is his natural and normal condition. This, our new government, is the first, in the history of the world, based upon this great physical, philosophical, and moral truth.

There it is, from the Vice-President of the Confederacy. The Southern government was not based on states' rights but on the foundational, cornerstone belief that blacks were inferior to whites. Thus, in the minds of white Southern leaders, slavery was justified. Probably the majority of Americans North and South in the 1860s believed that blacks were inferior to whites—intellectually, socially, and morally. Many of those who opposed slavery also opposed complete integration of blacks into American society. But let us have no more blather about the idea that the issue underlying the Civil War was states' rights. The issue was slavery, even though it was sometimes cloaked in arguments that appealed to states' rights.

It is not as though state governments are holy and just and good and the Federal government is corrupt and unjust and evil. The Federal government does its share of wrong and ridiculous things and often encroaches on our freedoms, but we cannot trust state governments to protect our rights either. They do not have a good record of doing so.

There is something even more basic to the nature of American government and society than states' rights, and that is individual rights, our rights as Americans. State governments did not make sure that those rights were protected. When the cry of states' rights arose the loudest again, it was in the 1960s, and the real issue was race. States did not want the Federal government deciding how blacks were to be treated. Surely we can understand why, when blacks saw their rights denied by the states, they sought relief wherever they thought they could find it. As a result, they looked to the Federal government, even though the Federal government did not have a great record of protecting the rights of blacks either.

I lament the loss of power and sovereignty by the states at the hands of the Federal government. The Federal government is too big, and big government leads to inefficiency, impersonal treatment, and a lack of accountability. States have rights, but not the right to discriminate against citizens on the basis of race. Their doing so is why states lost some of their rights. States had their chance to do a better job of governing and protecting American citizens than the national government did, and they blew it. The states only have themselves to blame for a great measure of what they have lost.

The Moral Case for the Flat Tax
Steve Forbes

October 1996 *Imprimis*

Steve Forbes is President and Chief Executive Officer of Forbes, Inc., and Editor-in-Chief of Forbes *magazine. He ran for the Republican presidential nomination in 1996 and 2000.*

Capitalism works better than any of us can conceive. It is also the only truly *moral* system of exchange. It encourages individuals to devote their energies and impulses freely to peaceful pursuits, to the satisfaction of others' wants and needs, and to constructive action for the welfare of all. The basis of capitalism is not greed. You don't see misers creating Wal-Marts and Microsofts.

Think about it for a moment. Capitalism is truly miraculous. What other system enables us to cooperate with millions of other ordinary people—whom we will never meet but to whom we will gladly provide goods and services—in an incredible, complex web of commercial transactions? And what other system perpetuates itself, working every day, year in, year out, with no single hand guiding it?

Capitalism is a moral system if only because it is based on *trust*. When we turn on a light, we assume there will be electricity. When we drive into a service station, we assume there will be fuel. When we walk into a restaurant, we assume there will be food. If we were to make a list of all the basic things that capitalism provides—things that we take for granted—it would fill an encyclopedia.

Three years have passed since I wrote those words in a September 1993 issue of Hillsdale College's speech digest, *Imprimis*, called "Three Cheers for Capitalism." I still firmly believe in them, but the vast majority of liberals—and, sadly, many conservatives—persist in viewing capitalism as merely an economic system, forgetting, as Warren Brookes wrote in *The Economy in Mind* (1982), that economics is a metaphysical rather than a mathematical science, "in which intangible spiritual values and attitudes are at least as important as physical assets and morals more fundamental than the money supply." He concluded that "a national economy, like an individual business or a specific product, is the sum of the spiritual and mental qualities of its people, and its output of value will be only as strong as the values of society."

Flat tax advocates like myself are often criticized for focusing too much on "dollars and cents" issues instead of on moral issues. But as the philosopher and essayist Ralph Waldo Emerson said 150 years ago: "A dollar is not value, but representative of value, and, at last, of moral value." More recently, scholars like former education secretary Bill Bennett and Nobel Prize winning economist Milton Friedman have pointed out that every time you take a dollar out of one person's pocket and put it into another's, you are making a moral decision.

The High Price of Taxes

Taxes are not simply a means of raising revenue; they are also a price. The taxes on our income, capital gains, and corporate profits are the price we pay for the privilege of working, the price we pay for being productive, and the price we pay for being innovative and successful. If the price we pay becomes too high, we get less of these things. If the price we pay is lowered, we get more of them. So taxes are a barrier to progress, and they punish rather than reward success.

The Kemp-Roth bill of 1981 and the tax reform bill of 1986 reduced individual income tax rates to levels we hadn't seen in more than half a century, and they helped create an unrivaled period of prosperity. Yet today, many of our policymakers ignore or deny the positive benefits of those tax cuts. They also fail to realize that it is people, not policies, who make an economy run.

Remember, says investor and philanthropist Theodore J. Forstmann, "No government has ever borne the cost of anything. Taxes cost *people*. Tax cuts do not cost *government*." Families with children are hardest hit by high taxes. According to the Family Research Council, a family of four at the median income in 1948 paid 2 percent of its income in taxes; in 1994 the figure was 25 percent. That is why families feel they are on a treadmill and the treadmill is winning.

If we want to do something to help families in this country, I can't think of a better option than the flat tax. True, the across-the-board tax cuts proposed by Republican and even

some Democratic leaders are an important step in the right direction and will do enormous good, but we should not stop there. We should scrap the existing tax code. Just think about what a monstrosity this code is. The Gettysburg Address runs about 200 words. The Declaration of Independence runs about 1,300 words. The Holy Bible runs about 773,000 words. But our federal income tax code runs about seven million words and is growing longer every year.

How Taxes Corrupt

Political Corruption. Today's tax code is incomprehensible, even to tax collectors, and it is the principal source of corruption in our nation's capital. Politicians have been trading favors and loopholes for political contributions and support for so long that they have come to think that this is acceptable, even virtuous, behavior. And there are now almost 13,000 registered lobbyists and special interest groups who together represent the largest private sector industry in Washington, D.C. Over half of them are there for the precise purpose of manipulating the tax code to their own advantage. As House Majority Leader Dick Armey warns, this not only costs our economy billions of dollars but turns the political process into a free-for-all for special interests.

Washington attorney Leonard Garment says, "Whatever corruption may exist here is what happens wherever government is given large amounts of money to dispense, great power over people's lives, and great discretion in using that power, whether it is in a poverty program, or the Small Business Administration, or the Department of Defense. . . . It is a corruption that occurs almost universally when government has too much discretionary power and individuals too little."

Civic Corruption. Taxes also have a corrosive impact on our civic life. Our individual sense of responsibility and trust is destroyed—eaten by the acid of big government spending sprees and confiscatory taxes. Today, many of us view taxes as a form of legalized plunder, and we have little faith that the earnings we are forced to surrender to Uncle Sam will be used wisely or properly. So we do not scruple to look for ways to avoid compliance with the tax code whenever possible. We don't think of ourselves as "tax cheats" but as "tax rebels." But no matter what we call ourselves, we have the uneasy sense that high taxes, like welfare, can steal our sense of self-reliance and integrity.

Cultural Corruption. When we look around our nation, we see more illegitimacy, more illiteracy, more crime, more drug abuse, more broken families, and more members of a permanent underclass than ever before. In the name of "compassion," we have spent trillions of tax dollars on all these crises, and all we have done is to make them worse.

If we truly wish to be compassionate, we should adopt a flat tax that exempts the poorest citizens and offers all Americans real and practical ways to climb the ladder of successful living. Moreover, the flat tax allows us, not the federal government, to decide how best to solve our own problems. It puts responsibility back into the equation and sends a powerful moral message.

What Is the Flat Tax?

The flat tax is a simple, fair, and uniform system. It is a sound system, with widespread support from Nobel Prize winning economists as well as former cabinet members and other political leaders. And it is a moral system because it means more take-home pay for wage earners, more savings and investment, more businesses, more jobs, more efficiency, more products and services, more price cuts, and more personal decisions as opposed to state planning. When people can keep more of what they earn, they tend to spend it on their children's education, on preparing for careers, on solving social problems, on going to church, and on volunteering instead of working overtime. The flat tax can actually provide a moral imperative to rebuild our lives and our communities.

Under my flat tax proposal, every individual would have a tax exemption of $13,000; every child $5,000. For a family of four, the first $36,000 of income would be free. (There would be generous exemptions for smaller and larger families and for single individuals, too.) Currently, a family of four typically owes over $3,000 in taxes for the first $36,000 in income. With the flat tax, they would owe nothing, and their income over $36,000 would be taxed at a flat 17 percent rate. There would be no tax on personal savings, pensions, Social Security benefits, capital gains, or inheritances. For businesses, the 17 percent rate on net profits would also apply, and investments would be written off in the first year. Constantly changing and complicated depreciation schedules would be eliminated. The IRS would no longer be able to define arbitrarily the life of an asset.

The flat tax would get America's economy moving again. But it has been attacked through a nationwide campaign of misinformation based mainly on six myths:

Myth 1: *The flat tax would raise taxes on the middle class.* How many families of four do you know that have $36,000 of exemptions under the current tax code? The flat tax will actually lower taxes on the middle class. Yet one New Hampshire state official ran ads during the last presidential primary saying the flat tax would hike taxes on families of four in his state by $2,000-$3,000. How did he come up with these numbers? He ignored the $36,000 tax exemption and applied the 17 percent to their entire income.

Myth 2: *The flat tax would hurt the housing industry and property owners.* But even President Clinton's Treasury Department acknowledges that the flat tax would lower interest rates by one-fourth to one-third. Lower interest rates mean lower down payments and monthly mortgage payments. More people can become homeowners for the first time, and current homeowners can save more of their earnings for other expenses. The need for mortgage deductions (which would be phased out gradually rather than all at once) would end because the flat tax would bring far greater savings and superior benefits.

Myth 3: *The flat tax would destroy municipal bonds.* The lower interest rates introduced by the flat tax would not hurt existing municipal bonds or future ones. New purchasers would be more concerned with where their money was going than how their taxes were affected. This would lead to greater accountability in public finance, and bond prices would even be likely to rise a little as general interest rates came down.

Myth 4: *The flat tax would hurt charitable giving.* The American people don't need to be bribed by the tax code to give when they live under a fair and equitable system. We were a generous and giving nation long before the federal income tax was instituted. And the tax cuts in the 1980s actually resulted in a huge, historic increase in charitable giving. In short, when the American people have more, they give more.

Myth 5: *The flat tax is a giveaway because investment income, or what liberal economists love to call "unearned income," would not be taxed.* Wrong: Under the flat tax, all income would be taxed. But investment income would be taxed only once instead of two or three times as the current code mandates. When a company makes a profit, it would pay a 17 percent rate tax.

Myth 6: *The flat tax would increase the budget deficit.* The only way we are going to cure the budget deficit is by cutting government spending and cutting taxes. This will lead to an economic boom. In the 1960s and 1980s, tax cuts increased rather than decreased government revenues. Why? Because, as I mentioned earlier, taxes are a price. When the American people can keep more of the resources they create, they create more resources. And whenever tax rates are reduced, compliance goes up because people find it easier to work productively than to figure out how to get around the shoals of the tax code.

The flat tax would mean more than just a financial savings—it would save time, too. Right now, individuals and businesses spend more than five billion hours a year filling out tax forms. The flat tax form would be the size of a postcard and would take almost no time to fill out. Imagine what we could achieve with all the time we would save. Imagine the benefits for our families, our schools, our churches, our charities, our communities, and our businesses.

Let Individuals Choose

There is a moral case for the flat tax because the flat tax is fundamentally about freedom. I am not talking about the freedom that the great free market economist Ludwig von Mises condemned as the freedom to "let soulless forces operate." That is not freedom at all; that is just tyranny in another guise. Rather, I am talking about the freedom to "let individuals choose."

Time and time again, the evidence has shown that the federal government cannot preserve our families, reawaken our faith, restore our values, solve our social problems, or create prosperity. Only free individuals can.

Reprinted by permission from Imprimis, *the national speech digest of Hillsdale College, www.hillsdale.edu.*

Morality and Foreign Policy:
Reagan and Thatcher
Edwin Meese III

August 2002 *Imprimis*

Edwin Meese III served as Attorney General under President Ronald Reagan from 1985 to 1988. Prior to that, he served in several positions in the Reagan White House.

Ronald Reagan revitalized the American economy and began an unprecedented period of economic growth. He rebuilt our armed forces. He restored the spirit of the American people. But most important to our discussion today, he developed a new set of strategic principles to deal with the Soviet Union and the threat of communist imperialism. According to those principles, the United States would oppose rather than accommodate the Soviet Union, insofar as it sought to expand its power and impose totalitarianism around the globe.

Prime Minister Margaret Thatcher and President Ronald Reagan

The first way in which Reagan took on the Soviet Union—and the basis of everything else—was to defend strongly the moral superiority of freedom. He rejected absolutely the idea of moral equivalence—the idea, prevalent at the time, and still prevalent today, that there is no moral difference between free government and tyranny. Second, Reagan stood up to Soviet aggression. In 1979 and 1980, before he took office, the Soviets had marched into Afghanistan with virtual impunity. Reagan made it clear, through his discussions with the Soviet ambassador and through other means, that the United States would not allow the Soviet Union to occupy one square foot of additional ground anywhere in the world. And third, Reagan adopted the policy of rolling back communism wherever possible, by supporting freedom fighters in Poland, Angola, Nicaragua and elsewhere around the world.

The public unveiling of Reagan's anti-communist strategy took place 20 years ago today, [on June 8, 1982], when he spoke to the British Parliament at Westminster Palace. It was in that speech that he announced his battle plan for dealing with communism in the future. Writing about that speech later, he said,

> When I came into office, I believed there had been mistakes in our policy toward the Soviets in particular. I wanted to do some things differently, like speaking the truth about them for a change, rather than hiding reality between the niceties of diplomacy.

So he spoke openly about the conflict between the principles of constitutional government and those of communism. In retrospect, I'm amazed that previous national leaders had not attacked the ideas behind Marxism-Leninism in this direct way. We had come to be too worried that we would offend the Soviet leaders if we did so. Reagan portrayed Marxism-Leninism as an "empty cupboard." Everyone knew this by the 1980s, he believed, but no one was saying it. Being honest about it, he thought, would help the Soviets to face up to their own weaknesses, and to their uncertain future.

Scaring the "Striped-Pants Diplomats"

It was in that speech that Reagan said,

> What I am describing now is a plan and a hope for the long-term. The march of freedom and democracy will leave Marxism-Leninism on the ash heap of history, as it has left other tyrannies which stifled the freedom and muzzled the self-expression of the people.

As you might imagine, those words scared . . . the people whom Reagan used to call "striped-pants diplomats." It was not at all what the State Department would have preferred him to say in such a widely broadcast speech. But honesty was Reagan's way, and it turned out to be effective.

The following year, in March of 1983, Reagan gave a speech to the National Association of Evangelicals, in which he said that those who promote the total sovereignty of the state over the individual are the focus of evil in the modern world. This is the speech in which he called the Soviet Union an "evil empire"—again, much to the dismay of the State Department. And in that same month, and in the same spirit, Reagan declared the importance of the Strategic Defense Initiative—what we know today as ballistic missile defense—and announced his intention to begin to develop it.

There are several other milestones in Reagan's campaign against communism. In October of 1983, at the request of the Organization of Eastern Caribbean States, the United States used military force for the first time since Vietnam, rescuing nearly a thousand American citizens and putting down an oppressive totalitarian regime on the island of Grenada.

After that there was the series of meetings with Mikhail Gorbachev, beginning in 1985, in which Reagan set forth the understanding that the United States posed no threat to the Soviet Union, but that we would not accept peace at the expense of other peoples' freedom.

The most important of these meetings—which came to be called "summits"—was at Reykjavik in 1986. It was at this meeting that Gorbachev put on the table what would have been the greatest reduction of offensive weapons in the history of the world. But he had one requirement: the United States would have to give up the Strategic Defense Initiative. Reagan already knew that ballistic missile defense was important, and had explained why to the American people. But it wasn't until that moment that he realized how important it was *to the Soviets*. The Soviet Union had been cheating on the Anti-Ballistic Missile Treaty—the 1972 treaty which forbade the Soviet Union and the United States from going beyond a certain level of ballistic missile defense—for 10 or 15 years. But already in 1986, Gorbachev recognized that the United States was eclipsing the Soviet Union in its technological development of missile defense.

Reagan turned down Gorbachev's offer. At the time, the news media, along with many others in our country and around the world, argued that Reagan had made a mistake by not giving in to Gorbachev's demand. But in hindsight, we can say that this was one of the critical moments in the entire Cold War. The Soviets realized the importance of SDI. They also knew, because of Reagan's refusal to give it up—as many Soviet leaders have written since that time—that they would never be able to prevail over the United States.

Following Reykjavik was Reagan's visit to Berlin on June 12, 1987. In his speech that day at the Brandenburg Gate, Reagan reviewed the history of the Cold War. He compared the progress that was taking place in the West with the technological backwardness and privation in the communist world. He suggested that the Soviets themselves may be coming to understand the importance of freedom, noting that under Gorbachev there had been some changes. Political prisoners had been released. Economic enterprises had been permitted to operate with greater freedom from state control. "Are these the beginnings of profound changes in the Soviet state," Reagan asked, "or are they token gestures intended to raise false hopes in the West, or to strengthen the Soviet system without changing it?"

"We welcome change and openness," he continued. "We believe that freedom and security go together, that the advance of human liberty can only strengthen the cause of world peace." And then Reagan went on to make the challenge that we've heard repeated so many times since, and that turned out to be so momentous in the history of Berlin and of the Cold War:

> There is one sign the Soviets can make that would be unmistakable, that would advance dramatically the cause of freedom and peace. General Secretary Gorbachev, if you seek peace, if you seek prosperity for the Soviet Union and Eastern Europe, if you seek liberalization, come here to this gate. Mr. Gorbachev, open this gate. Mr. Gorbachev, tear down this wall!

That was in many ways the beginning of the end of the Cold War. From that point on, there was a marked difference in the goings-on within the communist world. Reagan had accurately perceived the weaknesses of the Soviet Union. He had formulated American policy in a way that those weaknesses couldn't be hidden. He had been honest about the immoral reason for those weaknesses. And so, as he predicted at the end of his speech at the Brandenburg Gate, the Berlin Wall—and all it represented—fell. "For it cannot withstand faith," Reagan said. "It cannot withstand truth. The Wall cannot withstand freedom."

Reagan and Thatcher

Ronald Reagan said that his principles were formed out of his upbringing in middle America. His boyhood was in a poor, but very upright, family. He learned religious faith from his mother. He learned friendship and respect toward others, including a strong opposition toward racial discrimination, from his father. He learned the importance of public service, and of neighbors helping each other, from the community in which he lived.

Margaret Thatcher came from a similar, although slightly more affluent, background. She learned a great deal from her father's work as a grocer—particularly the lesson that letting people make their own decisions was vastly superior to government-controlled economic systems. It was this background, she said, that gave her the mental outlook and tools of analysis for reconstructing an economy in England that had been ravaged by socialism.

Reagan and Thatcher were of like mind in world affairs, particularly in regard to dealing with the Soviet Union. Their joint leadership during the Cold War resembled in many ways the collaboration between Roosevelt and Churchill during World War II. But there was one big difference: Churchill knew the importance of United States participation and support of Britain in World War II, and he was tremendously grateful to Roosevelt for his leadership in that war and for his friendship toward Britain. Together, they agreed on most major decisions about international affairs. But concerning a philosophy of government and domestic policy, Churchill did not share Roosevelt's penchant for centralizing power and regulating the economy. By contrast, Reagan and Thatcher saw eye-to-eye on both international affairs and government generally—particularly on the need for limited government as a protection for individual liberty.

Thatcher wrote about Reagan,

> Above all, I knew that I was talking to someone who instinctively felt and
> thought as I did. Not just about policies, but about a philosophy of government,
> a view of human nature.

The key element of Reagan's strategy in dealing with the Soviet Union was NATO. He had exerted his leadership to move NATO policies into line with a more assertive response to the Soviet Union, inaugurating the principle that an attack on one would be an attack on all. He also worked with the other NATO leaders to gain support for freedom fighters in places such as Poland, and to give hope to captive nations. In all of this, Thatcher had a very important role. She was, as she described herself, Reagan's principal cheerleader in NATO—not only in NATO councils, but also privately as she met with other NATO leaders, and also, perhaps even more importantly, as she met with leaders of the Warsaw Pact. In talking to leaders in Hungary, Czechoslovakia and other places, she explained that the United States and NATO were not threats to the Warsaw Pact, but that they would resist any actions by the Soviets to engage in aggression. In a sense, she was trying in these meetings to create a wedge between the leaders of the Warsaw Pact countries and the Soviet Union itself.

Nowhere was Thatcher's help to Reagan more pronounced than in his dealings with Gorbachev. Reagan had delayed meeting with Soviet leaders until 1985, largely because he wanted the United States to be able to negotiate from a position of strength, and it had taken a few years to build up our military forces to the point where he was in a position to do so. Thatcher agreed with and supported this strategy, whereas other leaders, particularly in Europe, were pressing for Reagan to meet immediately with the Soviet leadership.

When Gorbachev came to power in 1985, Mrs. Thatcher met with him first. She had studied his statements and his background. She knew of his education, and knew that he understood the West better than his predecessors. After she had talked with him and before he had met with Reagan, she shared with Reagan her view that he was "a man we can do business with." Her insights helped Reagan greatly in preparing for his first meeting with Gorbachev. She was of critical help also in demonstrating to Gorbachev that she and Reagan were in total agreement. By presenting a united front, she was instrumental in creating the right background for Reagan's meetings with Gorbachev in Geneva, Reykjavik, Washington, D.C. and Moscow.

The close personal and political friendship between Reagan and Thatcher had obvious long-term significance for world history. It also illustrates an important lesson to keep in mind as we navigate the future. It embodied the principles that have characterized the histories of the United States and England. The origins of those principles date back many centuries to a common beginning, and to the fundamental ideas which guide both our countries today—the ideas of freedom and the rule of law.

Thatcher put it well recently when she said—at a Hillsdale event, interestingly enough–"Being democratic is not enough, for a majority cannot turn what is wrong into right. In order to be considered truly free, countries must also have a deep love of liberty and an abiding respect for the rule of law."

That is a moral creed to which both Reagan and Thatcher subscribed, and which both preserved. And our world is the better for it.

Reprinted by permission from Imprimis, *the national speech digest of Hillsdale College, www.hillsdale.edu.*

American Unilateralism
Charles Krauthammer

January 2003 *Imprimis*

Charles Krauthammer is a national political columnist and past recipient of the Pulitzer Prize. Before beginning his career in journalism, he earned a medical degree and practiced psychiatry. Unilateralism means the decision by a country to act by itself, as opposed to two countries involved in an action (bilateralism) or the action of several countries (multilateralism).

American unilateralism has to do with the motives and the methods of American behavior in the world, but any discussion of it has to begin with a discussion of the structure of the international system. The reason that we talk about unilateralism today is that we live in a totally new world. We live in a unipolar world of a sort that has not existed in at least 1500 years.

At the end of the Cold War, the conventional wisdom was that with the demise of the Soviet Empire, the bipolarity of the second half of the 20th century would yield to a multi-polar world. You might recall the school of thought led by historian Paul Kennedy, who said that America was already in decline, suffering from imperial overstretch. There was also the Asian enthusiasm, popularized by James Fallows and others, whose thinking was best captured by the late-1980s witticism: "The United States and Russia decided to hold a Cold War. Who won? Japan."

Well, they were wrong, and ironically no one has put it better than Paul Kennedy himself, in a classic recantation emphasizing America's power: "Nothing has ever existed like this disparity of power, nothing. Charlemagne's empire was merely Western European in its reach. The Roman Empire stretched farther afield, but there was another great empire in Persia and a larger one in China. There is, therefore, no comparison."

We tend not to see or understand the historical uniqueness of this situation. Even at its height, Britain could always be seriously challenged by the next greatest powers. It had a smaller army than the land powers of Europe, and its navy was equaled by the next two navies combined. Today, the American military exceeds in spending the next twenty countries combined. Its Navy, Air Force and space power are unrivaled. Its dominance extends as well to every other aspect of international life—not only military, but economic, technological, diplomatic, cultural, even linguistic, with a myriad of countries trying to fend off the inexorable march of MTV English.

Ironically, September 11 accentuated and accelerated this unipolarity. It did so in three ways. The first and most obvious was the demonstration it brought forth of American power.

In Kosovo, we had seen the first war ever fought and won exclusively from the air, which gave the world a hint of the recent quantum leap in American military power. But it took September 11 for the U.S. to unleash, with concentrated fury, a fuller display of its power in Afghanistan. Being a relatively pacific commercial republic, the U.S. does not go around looking for demonstration wars. This one being thrust upon it, it demonstrated that at a range of 7,000 miles, with but a handful of losses and a sum total of 426 men on the ground, it could destroy, within weeks, a hardened fanatical regime favored by geography and climate in a land-locked country that was already well known as the graveyard of empires. Without September 11, the giant would surely have slept longer. The world would have been aware of America's size and potential, but not its ferocity and full capacities.

New York City Firemen in the Rubble of the World Trade Center

Secondly, September 11 demonstrated a new kind of American strength. The center of our economy was struck, aviation was shut down, the government was sent underground and the country was rendered paralyzed and fearful. Yet within days, the markets reopened, the economy began its recovery, the President mobilized the nation and a unified Congress immediately underwrote a huge worldwide war on terror. The Pentagon, with its demolished western façade still smoldering, began planning the war. The illusion of America's invulnerability was shattered, but with the demonstration of its recuperative powers, that sense of invulnerability assumed a new character. It was transmuted from impermeability to resilience—the product of unrivaled human, technological and political reserves.

The third effect of September 11 was the realignment it caused among the great powers. In 1990, our principal ally was NATO. A decade later, the alliance had expanded to include some of the former Warsaw Pact countries. But several major powers remained uncommitted: Russia and China flirted with the idea of an anti-hegemonic alliance, as they called it. Some Russian leaders made ostentatious visits to little outposts of the ex-Soviet Empire like North Korea and Cuba. India and Pakistan sat on the sidelines.

Then came September 11, and the bystanders lined up. Pakistan immediately made a strategic decision to join the American camp. India enlisted with equal alacrity. Russia's Putin, seeing a coincidence of interests with the U.S. in the war on terror and an opportunity to develop a close relation with the one remaining superpower, fell into line. Even China, while remaining more distant, saw a coincidence of interest with the U.S. in fighting Islamic radicalism, and so has cooperated in the war on terror and has not pressed competition with the U.S. in the Pacific.

This realignment accentuated a remarkable historical anomaly. All of our historical experience with hegemony suggests that it creates a countervailing coalition of weaker powers. Think of Napoleonic France, or of Germany in the 20th century. Nature abhors a vacuum and history abhors hegemony. But in the first decade of post-Cold War unipolarity, not a single great power, let alone a coalition of great powers, arose to challenge America. On the contrary, they all aligned with the U.S. after September 11.

So we bestride the world like a colossus. The question is, how do we act in this new world? What do we do with our position?

Secretary of Defense Rumsfeld gave the classic formulation of unilateralism when he said, regarding Afghanistan—but it applies equally to the war on terror and to other conflicts—that "the mission determines the coalition." This means that we take our friends where we find them, but only in order to help us accomplish our mission. The mission comes first and we define the mission.

This is in contrast with what I believe is a classic case study in multilateralism: the American decision eleven years ago to conclude the Gulf War. As the Iraqi Army was fleeing, the first Bush administration had to decide whether its goal in the war was the liberation of Kuwait or the liberation of Iraq. National Security Advisor Brent Scowcroft, who was instrumental in making the decision to stop with Kuwait, has explained that going further would have fractured the coalition, gone against our promises to our allies, and violated the U.N. resolutions under which we had gone to war. "Had we added occupation of Iraq and removal of Saddam Hussein to those objectives," he wrote, "our Arab allies, refusing to countenance an invasion of an Arab colleague, would have deserted us." Therefore we did not act. The coalition defined the mission.

Liberal Internationalism

There are two schools of committed multilateralists, and it is important to distinguish between them. There are the liberal internationalists who act from principle, and there are the realists who act from pragmatism. The first was seen in the run-up to the congressional debate on the war on Iraq. The main argument from opposition Democrats was that we should wait and hear what the U.N. was saying. Senator Kennedy, in a speech before the vote in Congress, said, "I'm waiting for the final recommendation of the Security Council before I'm going to say how I'm going to vote." Senator Levin, who at the time was the Chairman of the Senate Armed Services Committee, actually suggested giving authority to the President to act in Iraq only upon the approval of the U.N. Security Council.

The liberal internationalist position is a principled position, but it makes no internal sense. It is based on a moral vision of the world, but it is impossible to understand the moral logic by which the approval of the Security Council confers moral legitimacy on this or any other enterprise. How does the blessing of the butchers of Tiananmen Square, who hold the Chinese seat on the Council, lend moral authority to anything, let alone the invasion of another country? On what basis is moral legitimacy lent by the support of the Kremlin, whose central interest in Iraq, as all of us know, is oil and the $8 billion that Iraq owes Russia in debt? Or of the French, who did everything that they could to weaken the resolution, then came on board at the last minute because they saw that an Anglo-American train was possibly leaving for Baghdad, and they didn't want to be left at the station?

My point is not to blame the French or the Russians or the Chinese for acting in their own national interest. That's what nations do. My point is to express wonder at Americans who find it unseemly to act in the name of our own national interest, and who cannot see the logical absurdity of granting moral legitimacy to American action only if it earns the prior approval of others which is granted or withheld on the most cynical grounds of self-interest.

Practical Multilateralism

So much for the moral argument that underlies multilateralism. What are the practical arguments? There is a school of realists who agree that liberal internationalism is nonsense, but who argue plausibly that we need international or allied support, regardless. One of their arguments is that if a power consistently shares rulemaking with others, it is more likely to get aid and assistance from them.

I have my doubts. The U.S. made an extraordinary effort during the Gulf War to get U.N. support, share decision-making and assemble a coalition. As I have pointed out, it even denied itself the fruits of victory in order to honor coalition goals. Did this diminish anti-Americanism in the region? Did it garner support for subsequent Iraq policy—policy dictated by the original acquiescence to that coalition? The attacks of September 11 were planned during the Clinton administration, an administration that made a fetish of consultation and did its utmost to subordinate American hegemony. Yet resentments were hardly assuaged, because extremist rage against the U.S. is engendered by the very structure of the international system, not by our management of it.

Pragmatic realists value multilateralism in the interest of sharing burdens, on the theory that if you share decision-making, you enlist others in your own hegemonic enterprise. As proponents of this school argued recently in Foreign Affairs, "Straining relationships now will lead only to a more challenging policy environment later on." This is a pure cost-benefit analysis of multilateralism versus unilateralism.

If the concern about unilateralism is that American assertiveness be judiciously rationed and that one needs to think long-term, hardly anybody will disagree. One does not go it alone or dictate terms on every issue. There's no need to. On some issues, such as membership in the World Trade Organization, where the long-term benefit both to the U.S. and to the global interest is demonstrable, one willingly constricts sovereignty. Trade agreements are easy calls, however, free trade being perhaps the only mathematically provable political good. Other agreements require great skepticism. The Kyoto Protocol on climate change, for example, would have had a disastrous effect on the American economy, while doing nothing for the global environment. Increased emissions from China, India and other third-world countries which are exempt from its provisions clearly would have overwhelmed and made up for whatever American cuts would have occurred. Kyoto was therefore rightly rejected by the Bush administration. It failed on its merits, but it was pushed very hard nonetheless, because the rest of the world supported it.

The same case was made during the Clinton administration for chemical and biological weapons treaties, which they negotiated assiduously under the logic of, "Sure, they're useless or worse, but why not give in, in order to build good will for future needs?" The problem is that appeasing multilateralism does not assuage it; appeasement only legitimizes it. Repeated acquiescence on provisions that America deems injurious reinforces the notion that legitimacy derives from international consensus. This is not only a moral absurdity. It is injurious to the U.S., because it undermines any future ability of the U.S. to act unilaterally, if necessary.

The key point I want to make about the new unilateralism is that we have to be guided by our own independent judgment, both about our own interests and about global interests. This is true especially on questions of national security, war making, and freedom of action in the deployment of power. America should neither defer nor contract out such decision-making, particularly when the concessions involve permanent structural constrictions, such as those imposed by the International Criminal Court. Should we exercise prudence? Yes. There is no need to act the superpower in East Timor or Bosnia, as there is in Afghanistan or in Iraq. There is no need to act the superpower on steel tariffs, as there is on missile defense.

The prudent exercise of power calls for occasional concessions on non-vital issues, if only to maintain some psychological goodwill. There's no need for gratuitous high-handedness or arrogance. We shouldn't, however, delude ourselves as to what psychological goodwill can buy. Countries will cooperate with us first out of their own self-interest, and second out of the need and desire to cultivate good relations with the world's unipolar power. Warm feelings are a distant third.

After the attack on the USS *Cole*, Yemen did everything it could to stymie the American investigation. It lifted not a finger to suppress terrorism at home, and this was under an American administration that was obsessively multilateralist and accommodating. Yet today, under the most unilateralist American administration in memory, Yemen has decided to assist in the war on terrorism. This was not the result of a sudden attack of Yemeni goodwill, or of a quick re-reading of the *Federalist Papers*. It was a result of the war in Afghanistan, which concentrated the mind of recalcitrant states on the price of non-cooperation.

Coalitions are not made by superpowers going begging hat in hand; they are made by asserting a position and inviting others to join. What even pragmatic realists fail to understand is that unilateralism is the high road to multilateralism. It was when the first President Bush said that the Iraqi invasion of Kuwait would not stand, and made it clear that he was prepared to act alone if necessary, that he created the Gulf War coalition.

America's Special Role

Of course, unilateralism does not mean seeking to act alone. One acts in concert with others when possible. It simply means that one will not allow oneself to be held hostage to others. No one would reject Security Council support for war on Iraq or for any other action. The question is what to do if, at the end of the day, the Security Council or the international community refuses to back us? Do we allow ourselves to be dictated to on issues of vital national interest? The answer has to be "no," not just because we are being willful, but because we have a special role, a special place in the world today, and therefore a special responsibility.

Let me give you an interesting example of specialness that attaches to another nation. During the 1997 negotiations in Oslo over the land mine treaty, when just about the entire Western world was campaigning for a land mine ban, one of the holdouts was Finland. The Finnish prime minister found himself scolded by his Scandinavian neighbors for stubbornly refusing to sign on to the ban. Finally, having had enough, he noted tartly that being foursquare in favor of banning land mines was a "very convenient" pose for those neighbors who "want Finland to be their land mine."

Simulated Land Mine Used in Military Training

In many parts of the world, a thin line of American GIs is the land mine. The main reason that the U.S. opposed the land mine treaty is that we need them in places like the DMZ in Korea. Sweden and Canada and France do not have to worry about an invasion from North Korea killing thousands of their soldiers. We do. Therefore, as the unipolar power and as the guarantor of peace in places where Swedes do not tread, we need weapons that others do not. Being uniquely situated in the world, we cannot afford the empty platitudes of allies not quite candid enough to admit that they live under the protection of American power. In the end, we have no alternative but to be unilateralist. Multilateralism becomes either an exercise in futility or a cover for inaction.

The futility of it is important to understand. The entire beginning of the unipolar age was a time when this country, led by the Clinton administration, eschewed unilateralism and pursued multilateralism with a vengeance. Indeed, the principal diplomatic activity of the U.S. for eight years was the pursuit of a dizzying array of universal treaties: the comprehensive test ban treaty, the chemical weapons convention, the biological weapons convention, Kyoto and, of course, land mines.

In 1997, the Senate passed a chemical weapons convention that even its proponents admitted was useless and unenforceable. The argument for it was that everyone else had signed it and that failure to ratify would leave us isolated. To which we ought to say: So what? Isolation in the name of a principle, in the name of our own security, in the name of rationality is an honorable position.

Multilateralism is at root a cover for inaction. Ask yourself why those who are so strenuously opposed to taking action against Iraq are also so strenuously in favor of requiring U.N. support. The reason is that they see the U.N. as a way to stop America in its tracks. They know that for ten years the Security Council did nothing about Iraq; indeed, it worked assiduously to weaken sanctions and inspections. It was only when President Bush threatened unilateral action that the U.N. took any action and stirred itself to pass a resolution. The virtue of unilateralism is not just that it allows action. It forces action.

I return to the point I made earlier: The way to build a coalition is to be prepared to act alone. The reason that President Bush has been able and will continue to be able to assemble a coalition on Iraq is that the Turks, the Kuwaitis and others in the region will understand that we are prepared to act alone if necessary. In the end, the real division between unilateralists and multilateralists is not really about partnerships or about means or about methods. It is about ends.

We have never faced a greater threat than we do today, living in a world of weapons of mass destruction of unimaginable power. The divide before us, between unilateralism and multilateralism, is at the end of the day a divide between action and inaction. Now is the time for action, unilaterally if necessary.

Reprinted by permission from Imprimis, *the national speech digest of Hillsdale College, www.hillsdale.edu.*

America and the United Nations
Mark Steyn

February 2006 *Imprimis*

Mark Steyn is a columnist for the Chicago Sun-Times. *Steyn has some harsh words for the United Nations in this speech; but his criticisms are based on facts, some of which he cites. Whether or not you believe that the United States should get out of the United Nations, Steyn makes a strong case that our security and well-being as a nation in today's world cannot and should not depend on the opinion held about us in the United Nations.*

At one level, the United Nations is merely the latest variant on the Congress of Vienna held almost two centuries ago—a venue where the great powers sit down to resolve the problems of the world to their mutual satisfaction. Unfortunately, unlike Lord Castlereagh, Prince Metternich and Talleyrand, none of whom would be asked to audition for a "We Are The World" charity fundraising single, the UN has become the repository of all the West's sappiest illusions of one-worldism.

United Nations Building in New York City

Let me give an example. Nearly three years ago, the space shuttle Columbia crashed, and Katie Couric on NBC's *Today* show saluted the fallen heroes as follows: "They were an airborne United Nations—men, women, an African-American, an Indian woman, an Israeli. . . ." By contrast, there's a famous terror-supporting Islamist imam in Britain, Abu Hamza, who, when the shuttle crashed, claimed it was God's punishment "because it carried Americans, an Israeli and a Hindu, a trinity of evil against Islam." Say what you like about the old Islamofascist nutcake, but he was at least paying attention to the particulars of the situation, not just peddling, as Katie Couric did, vapid "multi-culti" bromides.

Why couldn't Katie have said the Columbia was an airborne America? After all, the "Indian woman," Kalpana Chawla, was the American Dream writ large upon the stars: she emigrated to the U.S. in the 1980s and became an astronaut within a decade. What an incredible country. But somehow it wasn't enough to see in the crew's multiple ethnicities a stirring testament to the possibilities of her own land; instead, Katie upgraded them into an emblem of what seemed to her a far nobler ideal—the UN.

In the days before Miss Couric's observation—this was in 2003, just before the Iraq war—there had been two notable news items about the United Nations: (1) The newly elected chair of the UN Human Rights Commission was Colonel Gaddafi's Libya; and (2) it was announced that in May, the presidency of the UN Conference on Disarmament would pass to Saddam Hussein's Iraq. But as Katie demonstrated, no matter what the UN actually is, the very initials evoke in her and many others some vague blurry memory of a long-ago UNESCO benefit with Danny Kaye or Audrey Hepburn surrounded by smiling children of many lands. There were many woozy Western leftists who felt—and still feel—that the theoretical idealism of Communism excused all its terrible failures in practice. The UN gets a similar pass, but from a far larger number of people. How else to explain all the polls in Europe, Australia, Canada and even America that show large numbers of people will only support war if it's approved by the UN?

The Real UN

In fact, however, the UN is a shamefully squalid organization whose corruption is almost impossible to exaggerate. If you think—as the media and the left do in this country—that Iraq [rebuilding after the fall of Saddam] is a . . . mess (which it's not), then try being the Balkans or Sudan or even Cyprus or anywhere where the problem's been left to the United Nations. . . .

Developed peoples value resilience: when disaster strikes, you bounce back. A hurricane flattens Florida, you patch things up and reopen. As the New Colonial Class, the UN doesn't look at it like that: when disaster strikes, it just proves that you and your countrymen are children who need to be taken under the transnational wing. The folks who have been under the UN wing the longest—indeed, the only ones with their own permanent UN agency and semi-centenarian "refugee camps"—are the most comprehensively wrecked people on the face of the earth: the Palestinians. UN territories like Kosovo are the global equivalent of inner-city housing projects with the blue helmets as local enforcers for the absentee slum landlord. By contrast, a couple of years after imperialist warmonger Bush showed up, Afghanistan and Iraq have elections, presidents and prime ministers.

Let's just take one of the scandals that go widely unreported in the American media—the UN Oil-for-Food program. Among the targets of the corruption investigation was Kofi Annan's son Kojo—who had a $30,000-a-year job but managed to find a spare quarter-million dollars sitting around to invest in a Swiss football club. The investigators then broadened their sights to include Kofi's brother Kobina Annan, the Ghanaian Ambassador to Morocco, who has ties to a businessman behind several of the entities involved in the scandal—one Michael Wilson, the son of the former Ghanaian Ambassador to Switzerland and a childhood friend of young Kojo. Mr. Wilson is currently being investigated for bribery involving a $50 million contract to renovate the Geneva offices of the UN World Intellectual Property Organization.

The actual head of the Oil-for-Food racket, Kofi sidekick Benon Sevan, has resigned, having hitherto insisted that a mysterious six-figure sum in his bank account was a gift from his elderly aunt, a lady of modest means who lived in a two-room flat in Cyprus. Paul Volcker's investigators had planned to confirm with auntie her nephew's version of events, but unfortunately she fell down an elevator shaft and died. It now seems likely that the windfall had less to do with Mr. Sevan's late aunt than with his soliciting of oil allocations for a company run by a cousin of Kofi Annan's predecessor, Boutros Boutros-Ghali.

Despite current investigations into his brother, his son, his son's best friend, his predecessor's cousin, his former chief of staff, his procurement officer and the executive director of the UN's biggest ever program, the Secretary-General insists he remains committed to staying on and tackling the important work of "reforming" the UN. Unfortunately, his Executive Coordinator for United Nations Reform has also had to resign.

You'd think that by now, respect for the UN would be plummeting faster than Benon Sevan's auntie down that lift shaft. After all, these aren't peripheral figures or minor departments. They reach right into the heart of UN policy on two of the critical issues of the day—Iraq and North Korea. Most of the Ghanaian diplomatic corps and their progeny seem to have directorships at companies with UN contracts and/or Saddamite oil options.

What's important to understand is that Mr. Annan's ramshackle UN of humanitarian money-launderers . . . and a Human Rights Commission that looks like a lifetime-achievement awards ceremony for the world's torturers is not a momentary aberration. Nor can it be corrected by bureaucratic reforms designed to ensure that the failed Budget Oversight Committee will henceforth be policed by a Budget Oversight Committee Oversight Committee. The Oil-for-Food fiasco is the UN—the predictable spawn of its utopian fantasies and fetid realities. If Saddam grasped this more clearly than, say, Katie Couric or John Kerry, well, that's why he is—was—an A-list dictator and they're not.

Why was there an Oil-for-Food program in the first place? Because back in the 90s, having thrown a big old multilateral Gulf War and gotten to the gates of Baghdad, the grand UN coalition then decided against toppling Saddam. So, having shirked the responsibilities that come with having a real policy, America and its allies were in the market for a pseudo-policy. And where does an advanced Western democracy go when it wants a pseudo-policy? Why, the UN! Saddam correctly calculated that the great powers were over-invested in Oil-for-Food as a figleaf for their lack of will, and reasoned that in such an environment their figleaf would also serve as a discreet veil for all kinds of other activities. He didn't game the system; he simply understood far better than Clinton and Bush Sr., John Major and Tony Blair how it worked.

Failures of Transnationalism

Transnationalism is the mechanism by which the world's most enlightened progressives provide cover for its darkest forces. It's a largely unconscious alliance, but not an illogical one. Western proponents of Kyoto and some of the other loopy NGO [nongovernmental organization]—beloved eco-doom-mongering concepts up for debate in Montreal at the moment have at least this much in common with psychotic Third World thugocracies: they find it hard to win free elections, they regard transnational bodies as useful for conferring a respect unearned at the ballot box, and they are unduly troubled by the lack of accountability in global institutions.

Those of us who believe that big government is by definition remote government—and that therefore the UN's pretensions to world government make it potentially the worst of all—should, in theory, argue for withdrawal from the organization. Outside of a few college towns and coastal enclaves, I don't believe there would be any political downside for candidates campaigning on a platform of pulling out of the UN entirely, and I'd encourage Republicans to do so if only as a way of unnerving those lazy pols like John Kerry who are prone to mindless transnationalist boosterism. But as a matter of practical politics, I can't see the U.S. leaving the UN anytime soon.

Can the U.S. force the UN to reform itself? Look at it this way: With hindsight, the UN was most effective when it was least effective—that's to say, the four decades between Korea and the Gulf War, when the Cold War's mutually-assured vetoes at least accurately represented the global stand-off. Now, however, we're in a unipolar world. As a result, the UN is no longer a permanent talking-shop for the world's powers but an alternative power in and of itself—a sort of ersatz superpower intended to counter the real one. Consider the 85 yes-or-no votes America made in the General Assembly in 2003: Arab League members voted against the U.S. position 88.7% of the time; ASEAN members voted against the U.S. position 84.5% of the time; Islamic Conference members voted against the U.S. position 84.1% of the time; African members voted against the U.S. position 83.8% of the time; Non-Aligned Movement members voted against the U.S. position 82.7% of the time; and European Union members voted against the U.S. position 54.5% of the time.

You can take the view of the European elites that this is proof of America's isolation and that the U.S. now needs to issue a "Declaration of Interdependence" with the world. Or you can be like the proud mom in Irving Berlin's WWI marching song: "They Were All Out Of Step But Jim." But what these figures really demonstrate is that the logic of the post-Cold War UN is to be institutionally anti-American. The U.S. could seize on Kofi Annan's present embarrassment and lean hard on him to reform this and reorganize that and reinvent the other and, if it employs its full diplomatic muscle, it might get those anti-U.S. votes down to . . . a tad over 80%. And along the way it would find that it had "reformed" a corrupt, dysfunctional, sclerotic anti-American club into a lean, mean, functioning, effective anti-American club. Which is, if they're honest, what most reformers mean by "reform."

In the old days, ramshackle dictatorships were proxies for heavyweight patrons, but not any more. These days, psychotic dictators represent only themselves. Yet somehow, in the post-Cold War talking shops, the loony tunes' prestige has been enhanced: the UN, as Canadian writer George Jonas puts it, enables "dysfunctional dictatorships to punch above their weight." Away from Kofi and Co., the world is moving more or less in the right direction: entire regions that were once wall-to-wall tyrannies are now filled with flawed but broadly functioning democracies—e.g., Central and Eastern Europe and Latin America. The UN has been irrelevant to this transformation. Its structures resist reform and the principal beneficiaries are the thug states.

What Actually Works?

What should replace the UN? Some people talk about a "caucus of the democracies." But I'd like to propose a more radical suggestion: nothing. In the war on terror, America's most important relationships have been not transnational but bilateral: Australia's John Howard didn't dispatch troops to Iraq because the Aussies and the Yanks belong to the same international talking shop; Tony Blair's reliability on war and terror isn't because of the European Union but in spite of it. These relationships are meaningful precisely because they're not the product of formal transnational bureaucracies.

When the tsunami hit last year, hundreds of thousands of people died within minutes. The Australians and Americans arrived within hours. The UN was unable to get to Banda Aceh for weeks. Instead, the humanitarian fat cats were back in New York and Geneva holding press conferences warning about post-tsunami health consequences—dysentery, cholera, BSE from water-logged cattle, etc.—that, its spokesmen assured us, would kill as many people as the original disaster. But this never happened, any more than did their predictions of disaster for Iraq: "The head of the World Food Program has warned that Iraq could spiral into a massive humanitarian disaster." Or for Afghanistan: "The UN Children's Fund has estimated that as many as 100,000 Afghan children could die of cold, disease and hunger."

It's one thing to invent humanitarian disasters to disparage Bush's unilateralist warmongering; but in the wake of the tsunami, the UN was reduced to inventing a humanitarian disaster in order to distract attention from the existing humanitarian disaster it wasn't doing anything about.

In fact, the whole idea of multilateral organizations feels a bit last millennium. With hindsight, institutions like the UN seem like a hangover from the Congress of Vienna age when contact between nations was limited to the potentates' emissaries. That's why transnationalism so appeals both to Euro-statists and to dictators—the great men of the world meeting together to decide things for everyone else. But, in the era of the Internet, five-cents-per-minute international phone rates, bank cards issued in Finland that you can use in an ATM in Brazil or Fiji, and blue collar families taking cheap vacations in the Maldives and Bali, the bloated UN bureaucracy seems at best irrelevant and at worst an obstruction to the progress of international relations. I'm all in favor of the Universal Postal Union and the Berne Copyright Convention, but they work precisely because dysfunctional dictators weren't involved. The non-nutcake jurisdictions came together, and others were required to be in compliance before they could join. That's why they work and endure. Transnational institutions should reflect points of agreement: Americans don't mind the Toronto Blue Jays playing in the same baseball league—and even winning it occasionally—because they're all agreed on the rules of baseball. A joint North American Public Health Commission, on the other hand, would be a bureaucratic boondoggle seeking to reconcile two incompatible health systems. Imagine then what happens when you put America, Denmark, Libya and Syria on a human rights committee, and then try and explain why the verdict of such a committee should be given any weight when the U.S. is weighing its vital national interest. . . .

If you make the free nations and the thug states members of the same club, the danger isn't that they'll meet each other half-way but that the free world winds up going three-quarters or seven-eighths of the way. Indeed, the UN has met the thug states so much more than half way that they now largely share the dictators' view of their peoples—as either helpless children who need every decision made for them, or a bunch of dupes whose national wealth can be rerouted to a Swiss bank account.

Perhaps that malign combination of empty European gesture-politics and Third World larceny would be relatively harmless, at least in the geopolitical sense, if these were quieter times. But they're not. This is an age in which America and its real allies—a bigger number than you'd think—need to be free to act without being a latter-day Gulliver ensnared by Lilliputian UN resolutions from head to toe. After all, consider the alternative to American action. As you may have noticed, the good people of Darfur in Sudan have been fortunate enough not to attract the attention of the arrogant cowboy unilateralist Bush and have instead fallen under the care of the UN multilateral compassion set. So, after months of expressing deep, grave concern over whether the graves were deep enough, Kofi Annan managed to persuade the UN to set up a committee to look into what's going on in Darfur. Eventually, they reported back that it's not genocide.

That's great news, isn't it? Because if it had been genocide, that would have been very, very serious. As yet another Kofi Annan-appointed UN committee boldly declared a year ago: "Genocide anywhere is a threat to the security of all and should never be tolerated." So thank goodness what's going on in Sudan isn't genocide. Instead, it's just 100,000 corpses who all happen to be from the same ethnic group—which means the UN can go on tolerating it until everyone's dead, and none of the multilateral compassion types have to worry their pretty heads about it.

That's the transnational establishment's alternative to Bush and his "coalition of the willing": appoint a committee that agrees on the urgent need to do nothing at all. Thus, last year the UN Human Rights Commission announced the working group that will decide which complaints will be heard at its annual meeting in Geneva this spring: the five-nation panel that will select which human-rights violations will be up for discussion comprises the Netherlands, Hungary, Cuba, Saudi Arabia and Zimbabwe. I wouldn't bet on them finding room on their crowded agenda for the question of human rights in Cuba, Saudi Arabia and Zimbabwe.

One of the mystifying aspects of UN worship is the assumption that this embryo world government is a "progressive" concept. It's not. Most of us in our business and family and consumer relationships are plugged into global networks far better for the long-term health of the planet than using American money to set up Eurowimp talking shops manned by African thugs—which is what the UN Human Rights Commission boils down to.

Judging by Results

Go back to that tsunami. While the UN and its agencies were on television badgering and hectoring the West for its stinginess, the actual relief efforts were being made by a couple of diverted U.S. naval groups and the Royal Australian Navy. The Scandinavians can't fly in relief supplies, because they don't have any C-130s. All they can do is wait for the UN to swing by and pick up their check. And it says something for the post-modern decadence of the age that that gives you supposed moral superiority. . . .

[T]he Oxfam international aid organization had paid the better part of a million bucks to Sri Lankan customs officials for the privilege of having 25 four-wheel-drive vehicles allowed into the country to get aid out to remote villages on washed-out roads hit by the tsunami. The Indian-made Mahindras stood idle on the dock in Colombo for a month as Oxfam's representatives were buried under a tsunami of paperwork. Fourteen UNICEF ambulances sent to Indonesia spent two months sitting on the dock of the bay wasting time, as the late Otis Redding so shrewdly anticipated.

The tsunami may have been unprecedented, but what followed was business as usual—the sloth and corruption of government, the feebleness of the brand-name NGOs, the compassion-exhibitionism of the transnational jet set. If we lived in a world where "it's what you do that defines you," we'd be heaping praise on the U.S. and Australian militaries, who in the immediate hours after the tsunami dispatched their forces to save lives, distribute food and restore water, power and communications.

According to my favorite foreign minister these days, Australia's Alexander Downer, "Iraq was a clear example about how outcomes are more important than blind faith in the principles of non-intervention, sovereignty and multilateralism. . . . Increasingly multilateralism is a synonym for an ineffective and unfocused policy involving internationalism of the lowest common denominator. Multilateral institutions need to become more results-oriented."

. . . It's what we do that defines us. And we'll do more without the UN.

Reprinted by permission from Imprimis, *the national speech digest of Hillsdale College, www.hillsdale.edu.*

Immigration,
the War on Terror, and the Rule of Law
Michelle Malkin

April 2003 *Imprimis*

Michelle Malkin is a nationally syndicated columnist. She is the daughter of immigrants who came to the U.S. from the Philippines.

The voice of New Americans who reject political correctness and the cult of multiculturalism has been sorely missing from the debate on immigration policy. September 11 helped shatter that silence. Over the past year, I've heard from countless readers, first- and second-generation Americans like myself and my family, who reject open borders and immigration anarchy. We are sick and tired of watching our government allow illegal line-jumpers, killers, and America-haters to flood our gates and threaten our safety. We are sick and tired of watching ethnic minority leaders cry "racism" whenever Congress attempts to shore up our borders. And we are especially sick and tired of business leaders, lobbyists, and lawmakers from both major parties caving in, forsaking leadership—and selling out our national security.

A year-and-a half after September 11, we have new laws, new agencies, and lots of new government spending to fight off foreign invaders. But our immigration policies leave the door to our nation open wide to the world's law-breakers and evildoers:

> According to the Immigration and Naturalization Service, at least 78,000 illegal aliens from terror-supporting or terror-friendly countries live in the U.S. They are among an estimated seven to eleven million illegal aliens who have crossed our borders illegally, overstayed visas illegally, jumped ship illegally and evaded deportation orders illegally.

> More than 300,000 illegal alien fugitives, including 6,000 from the Middle East, remain on the loose despite deportation orders.

> Last year, at least 105 foreign nationals suspected of terrorist involvement received U.S. visas because of lapses in a new background check system.

> There is still no systematic tracking of criminal alien felons across the country. Sanctuary for illegal aliens remains the policy in almost every major metropolis.

And "catch and release" remains standard operating procedure for untold thousands of illegal aliens who pass through the fingers of federal immigration authorities every day.

My book, *Invasion*, argues in great detail that our current immigration and entrance system is in shambles, partly by neglect, partly by design. From America's negligent consular offices overseas, to our porous air, land, and sea ports of entry, to our ineffective detention and deportation policies, our federal immigration authorities have failed at every level to protect our borders and preserve our sovereignty.

As the daughter of legal immigrants from the Philippines, I have never taken for granted the rights and responsibilities that come with citizenship. The oath my parents took—in English—when they were naturalized resonated even more powerfully with me after September 11:

> I hereby declare, on oath, that I absolutely and entirely renounce and abjure all allegiance and fidelity to any foreign prince, potentate, state, or sovereignty of whom or which I have heretofore been a subject or citizen; that I will support and defend the Constitution and laws of the United States of America against all enemies, foreign and domestic; that I will bear true faith and allegiance to the same; that I will bear arms on behalf of the United States when required by the law; that I will perform noncombatant service in the armed forces of the United States when required by the law; that I will perform work of national importance under civilian direction when required by the law; and that I take this obligation freely without any mental reservation or purpose of evasion; so help me God.

Patriotism surged after the September 11 attacks, but not among some ethnic advocacy groups. Hyphenated leaders who favor lax immigration policies characterized attempts to protect our borders from all enemies, foreign and domestic, as an unnecessary "backlash": Arab-American leaders complained that Arab-Americans were being singled out by the feds, Hispanic leaders complained that Hispanics were being singled out by the feds, etc. Meanwhile, at American airports, grandmothers and Medal of Honor recipients actually were being pulled aside and singled out by the feds.

These ethnic complainers were joined by profit-driven immigration lawyers, university officials and corporate executives, as well as vote-driven political strategists in both major parties, who refused to put the national interest above their own narrow interests. Contrary to their misguided claims, the demand for a more discriminating immigration policy—one that welcomes American Dreamers and bars American Destroyers—does not stem from fear or hatred of foreigners, but from self-preservation and love of country.

An Undeclared War

Last fall, I met a wonderful family from Cadillac, Michigan. Bonnie and Bob Eggle brought their daughter Jennifer, along with several cousins, aunts, uncles, and a family friend, to the nation's capital. But the Eggles were not in Washington, D.C., on a sightseeing tour. Bonnie and Bob traveled to the Beltway because their only son, Kris, was killed over the summer along the U.S.-Mexico border by gun-toting Mexican drug dealers. The Eggles came to town to get someone—anyone—in official Washington to pay attention to the war no one wants to talk about these days: the War On America's Borders.

Kris worked as a U.S. Park Service Ranger at Organ Pipe National Monument in southern Arizona, which is considered one of the most dangerous federal parks in the nation. As many as 1,000 illegal aliens a day trample across Organ Pipe—trashing our fences, ruining the environment, breaking our laws and endangering lives. It's a smugglers' paradise and a national security nightmare.

"We have caught people from China, Pakistan and Yemen coming through," says Bo Stone, an Organ Pipe ranger and close friend of Eggle. "If 1,000 illegal immigrants can walk through the desert here, so can 1,000 terrorists."

Some 200,000 illegal border-crossers and 700,000 pounds of drugs were intercepted at Organ Pipe last year alone. According to Border Patrol agents, foreign invaders are so brazen that they've actually cleared their own private roads through the park. On August 9, 2002, Kris Eggle joined Border Patrol agents in pursuit of armed Mexican bandits. During the chase, he was ambushed. An Eagle Scout, high school valedictorian, champion cross-country runner in college and All-American guy, he was cut down by a sniper hidden in the desert brush with an AK-47. He took a bullet just below his protective vest and died on a dirt path before medics arrived. The Eggles celebrated Kris's 29th birthday at his hometown gravesite.

In his spare time, Kris's father used to volunteer to help fix the fences along our southern border near where his son worked. "It is obscene," Bob Eggle told me, "how little our government cares about protecting the border." Referring to a century-old family farm in northern Michigan, Bob noted, "The worst cow fence on our farm is better than the best fences at the border."

Nor is Kris Eggle's murder an isolated incident. Several shootouts in the Southwest have occurred since last April, some even involving incursions by Mexican military officers suspected of collaborating with criminal drug dealers. Just last week, a Border Patrol agent was stoned in the head along the Tucson sector by a gang of illegal border-crossers. And again—as Kris's friend and fellow park ranger Bo Stone also points out—our southern borders remain open channels not only for illegal aliens and smugglers, but for terrorists.

The story is the same on the northern border, where a few months ago two reporters for the Toronto Star illegally crossed a dozen easy entry points between the boundaries that separate Quebec from Vermont and New York. Mangled fences and battered stop signs spraypainted with "U.S.A." are all that stand in the way. In Washington State, Montana and North Dakota, broken cameras and orange rubber cones are often the only objects that guard against intrusion. Yet calls for increased border patrol resources, park ranger staffing and military help have been ignored in Washington, D.C.

Kris Eggle's murder in August 2002 came just weeks before my book, *Invasion*, hit the shelves. But his death is like so many of the deaths of innocent Americans I document in the book and in subsequent columns—brutal, tragic, unnecessary and undeniably linked to our federal government's systemic refusal to enforce immigration laws:

Six people died and thousands were wounded in the 1993 World Trade Center bombing at the hands of illegal aliens from Palestine, Egypt, Jordan, and Pakistan who freely overstayed their visas and exploited our loophole-ridden asylum system.

Twelve people died from 1997 to 1999 at the hands of illegal alien serial killer Angel Resendiz, who traipsed back and forth freely across the U.S.-Mexican border.

Five law enforcement officers, from Virginia to California, were gunned down in cold blood by illegal border-crossers and visa-violators whom the INS failed to apprehend and deport.

Three thousand people died on September 11, 2001, at the hands of 19 al-Qaeda terrorists who slipped past our snoozing State Department and INS. Five of the terrorist hijackers had freely overstayed student, tourist and business visas.

Last fall, ten people died at the hands of sniper suspects John Muhammad and Lee Malvo. Muhammad had been stopped in Miami for attempted smuggling of illegal aliens, but was never prosecuted. Malvo was himself an illegal alien from Jamaica who had been apprehended by Border Patrol agents in Washington State, but then released pending deportation against Border Patrol recommendation.

In the aftermath of September 11, many advocates of unrestricted immigration on both the left and the right remain stuck in a pre-war mentality. They continue to argue that there is no connection between controlling illegal immigration and protecting national security. This unrepentant "open borders" crowd ranges from liberal Democrats Tom Daschle and Dick Gephardt, to the conservative *Wall Street Journal* editorial page and certain Bush administration officials. They consider it "scapegoating" to link lax immigration enforcement to September 11, and hold to the fatally flawed belief that we can allow millions of "good" illegal immigrants to stream across the borders while retaining the ability to screen out "bad" illegal immigrants who are seeking to destroy us.

Broken Windows, Broken Fences, and Beyond

In my book and columns on U.S. immigration policy, I try to focus on a question that I think is key to framing the border security debate in the post-September 11 world: What do broken fences at the border have to do with the broken buildings at Ground Zero? Or to put it another way: How does preventing another death like Kris Eggle's relate to preventing another September 11?

To answer these questions, we must turn our attention to one of the most influential theories of crime in recent history. It was 21 years ago that criminologists George Kelling and James Q. Wilson introduced this theory in a ground-breaking article in *The Atlantic* called "Broken Windows: The police and neighborhood safety." Their argument was simple: Rampant crime is the inevitable result of disorder. If a window in a building is broken and left unrepaired, people walking by will conclude that no one cares and that no one is in charge. One unrepaired window is an invitation to break more windows, and lawlessness spreads outward from buildings to streets to entire communities.

On the streets, "quality-of-life" crimes—panhandling, vagrants sleeping in doorways, public urination—serve as the equivalent of broken windows. In the subways, low-level crimes like fare-jumping and petty vandalism act similarly as small but unmistakable signals that, left unchecked, invite further chaos and more violent law-breaking. Take graffiti.

The proliferation of graffiti, even when not obscene, confronts the subway rider with the inescapable knowledge that the environment he must endure for an hour or more a day is uncontrolled and uncontrollable, and that anyone can invade it to do whatever damage and mischief the mind suggests. . . .

In such an environment, according to Kelling and Wilson, citizen complaints will often be met with excuses: the police are understaffed, the courts do not punish petty or first-time offenders, etc. Soon, citizens stop calling the police, convinced they can't do anything. Or won't.

In the 1980s, New York City was gripped by an epidemic of violence. Each year, the Big Apple averaged more than 2,000 murders and 600,000 serious felonies, thousands of which occurred in the filthy, fear-choked subway system. Leading law enforcement officials concluded that turning back this epidemic required focusing on the relatively minor transgressions that precipitated the violence. The Transit Police, for example, cracked down on fare-beaters by stationing plain-clothed cops at turnstiles. Thus they demonstrated a clear and consistent commitment to enforcing the law. The same went for graffiti vandals. The battle was fought hour by hour, subway car by subway car.

Many factors contributed to the plummeting crime rates that marked the mid-1990s in New York City. But the turning point came when law enforcement officers shifted their focus to fixing windows, curbing vandalism and stopping low-level cheats. They created a safe environment by restoring order and respect for the law.

What is true of Broken Windows applies to Broken Fences as well. So-called minor immigration crimes—e.g., cutting through rusted barbed wire, overstaying visas, committing marriage fraud and employing illegal day labor—lead to serious national security problems, such as rampant criminal alien gang activity, infiltration by foreign terrorist cells and internal corruption.

One broken fence goes unrepaired; vast miles of borders go undefended; hundreds of illegal border-crossers go unpunished; millions of line-jumpers win amnesty from Congress; thousands of visa overstayers are allowed to violate the rules without consequences; hundreds of thousands of fugitives from deportation are allowed to flout the law. Ultimately it becomes almost impossible for the INS to expel illegal aliens without a political and media backlash. The media even stop referring to these immigrants as illegal, instead using "less judgmental" descriptions such as "undocumented workers." Cities begin declaring themselves "sanctuaries" for illegal immigrants, and governments at all levels begin awarding them free health care, voting rights and discounted college tuition rates. The INS Commissioner begins sending unmistakable signals to immigration law-breakers that he believes it is neither "practical" nor "reasonable" to deport them. Finally, park rangers and Border Patrol agents start taking bullets while Washington looks the other way, even amidst a war on terror.

Meanwhile, those who dare ask whatever happened to our system of laws—those who point to the government's failure to fix its broken fences—are vilified as immigrant-bashers and racists.

The Broken Fences theory explains a lot. When scores of illegal alien day laborers are allowed to congregate openly at 7-11s and near government offices, it sends a signal that no one cares and no one is in charge. This created an environment in which September 11 hijackers Hani Hanjour and Khalid Almihdhar were able to obtain fake photo IDs from illegal alien day laborers hanging out at a 7-11 in Falls Church, Virginia, a stone's throw from the Pentagon. It was in this same environment of disrespect for the rule of law that 1993 World Trade Center bomber Mahmud Abouhalima brazenly filed a bogus application for amnesty—under a federal program for illegal alien farmworkers—and won legal permanent residence; in which the September 11 terrorists got away

Fence in Disrepair on the U.S./Mexico Border, 2007

with filing incomplete visa applications in clear violation of the law; and in which 21 Islamic radicals entered our country illegally during the past decade to carry out terrorist plots, from the 1993 WTC bombing, to the NYC subway bombing conspiracy, to the Los Angeles International Airport Millennium plot, to the September 11 attacks.

Restoring Sovereignty

Open-borders advocates argue that we are a nation of immigrants. But we are first and foremost a nation of laws. Conservatives have traditionally stood for the rule of law. But Republican Party elites in Washington, D.C., continue to turn a blind eye to the immigration crisis. Indeed, as Phyllis Schlafly has noted, the Republican National Committee's mail-order surveys on important national issues omit immigration and border security. And the White House refuses even to meet with the Congressional Immigration Reform Caucus, led by Republican Congressman Tom Tancredo of Colorado.

Opponents of stricter border controls say that all we need to do to fight terrorism is reform our intelligence agencies, nibble at the edge of visa issuance reform and reshuffle INS management. They insist on going only after the big, obvious targets—suspected al-Qaeda operatives applying for visas overseas—and leaving everyone else who is breaking our immigration laws alone. But as long as the stubborn signals of an immigration system in total disrepair persist, the invasion that I describe in my book will go on unabated. Foreign terrorists will read the signs of this disregard for law—driver's licenses for illegal aliens, in-state college discounts for illegal aliens, non-enforcement of employer sanctions, rampant asylum fraud, unpunished document fraud, sanctuary, amnesty—and conclude that they can freely take advantage of it.

So what is to be done? In my book, I offer a number of policy prescriptions—a targeted visa moratorium, reforming the deportation system, increasing detention space and resources for interior enforcement, etc. But I have since come to the conclusion that it will not be the Homeland Security Department—or any top-down legislative fix emanating from Washington—that turns things around. The solution will have to begin with ordinary citizens and local and state officials who understand what Ronald Reagan said nearly two decades ago: "The simple truth is that we've lost control of our own borders . . . and no nation can do that and survive."

We must mend our broken fences, literally and figuratively, one post at a time. And we must—each and every American among us, native-born and naturalized alike—recommit ourselves to the oath of citizenship that binds us to support and defend the laws and Constitution of the United States, against all enemies foreign and domestic, so help us God.

Reprinted by permission from Imprimis, *the national speech digest of Hillsdale College, www.hillsdale.edu.*

Frank Talk About "Mexifornia"
Victor Davis Hanson

November 2003 *Imprimis*

Victor Davis Hanson is a professor of classics at California State University, Fresno. He has written, co-written, or edited over a dozen books; and he has also written articles for a number of publications.

There was a time, not so long ago, when we Americans understood that newcomers did not need to be taught in their own language in our schools. Even less did we believe that their children required special classes in ethnic pride or separate, race-based college graduation ceremonies. The very idea that a national lobbying group would call itself La Raza (The Race)—and have slogans such as: "For La Raza everything; for those outside La Raza, nothing"—would have seemed to us shocking, even chilling. We believed in American civic education for immigrants, which, combined with intermarriage, integration and popular culture, led to rapid parity for those immigrants' children in terms of education, income and influence. Needless to say, in that earlier time, immigrants came to the U.S. from Mexico largely under legal auspices and in measured numbers that did not overwhelm our once formidable powers of assimilation.

What we see going on with Mexican immigration today is a tragedy, and it is not simply a result of the federal government abdicating its responsibility to control our borders (although the federal government has certainly done precisely that). The citizens of my state of California and others are also complicit in this tragedy. For instance, millions of us who used to cut our own lawns and clean our own houses now consider such tasks beneath us, as if America's middle class has embraced as its birthright the culture and leisure once confined to an aristocratic elite. Suddenly our young people, our poor and our unskilled find jobs picking apples or laying tiles somehow demeaning. So-called dead-end jobs are no longer a rite of passage for our youth, but are deemed proper only for unskilled laborers from Mexico, whose toil, we are assured, keeps our produce, restaurants and hotels inexpensive.

The Economics and Morality of Illegal Immigration

Thus do we get in the habit of talking about illegal immigration in economic rather than in moral terms. But consider the situation from a moral perspective. Do we really expect hard-working youths from central Mexico to work 30 years in construction, hotels or the fields without marrying, having children, losing jobs or getting hurt? And how can such workers—without legal status, education or mastery of English—support a family on $10 an hour when most native Americans can't do so on $20? Will we continue to shrug and say, "At least the money is better than in Mexico," or, "None of our own people will do the work," or, "They are going to drive anyway, so let's give them driver's licenses" — all the easy platitudes that justify the current chaos?

Unemployment is high and rising in California, but we are told that even more illegal workers from Mexico are needed. Can it really be the case that the free market can no longer operate to attract American workers through rising wages — even assuming an absence of a pool of unskilled labor? Meanwhile, many who ought to know better champion the employer's right to hire whomever he chooses, and assure us that Mexican immigration poses no more of a problem for the U.S. than nineteenth century Italian immigration — as if they are unaware that multiculturalism did not exist in our schools in the nineteenth century, that we do not share an adjacent open border with Italy, and that Italian immigrants did not flood our country unlawfully as part of the national strategy of the Italian government.

Those who offer up these arguments are either blind to, or shy away from, the hard facts about the tragic cycle that is being perpetuated. The tragedy unfolds like this: Kids in their teens, at great peril, sneak into America from Oaxaca. They work hard for 30 years at roofing, picking, mowing, cleaning or cooking, and then often turn to state agencies when their backs give out or their jobs dry up. Meanwhile, their children too often grow up in the barrios, not with the stern family ethic of Mexico, but instead resentful that their poorly paid and uneducated parents won no security during their decades of hard work. Often these children grow accustomed to think better even of Mexico — which they have never visited — than of the U.S. In reaction, employers express disappointment that this second generation (which has mastered neither Spanish nor English) does not toil as hard and as cheaply as its parents. So at the same time that four out of ten U.S. resident students of Mexican heritage are not graduating from California high schools, and less than one in ten are graduating from college, employers welcome a new cohort of illegal teenagers.

Related to this trafficking in human capital, a serious social and moral dilemma looms a mere decade away, when the Baby Boomers of California finally — and nearly all at once — reach retirement. Influential, affluent, informed — and not shy about self-interested self-promotion — these retirees will demand that Social Security and state retirement programs remain funded at promised levels. But these benefits will remain possible only with a complacent majority population of younger Hispanic immigrants with larger families, working for wages that are less, on average, than what is being paid out to these aging white retirees with no dependents.

Data alone cannot decide for us whether California is saved or ruined by illegal immigration. Liberal economists, for example, offer models that demonstrate that illegal immigrants bring in $25 billion to America in net revenue per annum. Other statisticians employ quite different models showing that these same immigrants cost the United States over $40 billion a year — indeed, that the average California household must contribute at least $1,200 each year to subsidize the deficit between what illegal immigrants cost in services and what they pay in taxes. Who can sort out all the wildcard effects of cash income, fraudulent Social Security numbers and politicized research? Nor do these models customarily account for the insidious costs of the illegal hiring practices of contractors, farmers and factory owners—costs for medical care for uninsured illegals, increased law enforcement, growing entitlements and the need for dual documentation in business and government.

Tragically, political correctness makes it nearly impossible to discuss illegal immigration in any kind of rational way without being labeled racist or nativist. Indeed, even the legal term "illegal alien" is now politically incorrect, and is being replaced by "undocumented worker." But most know that not all illegal immigrants are workers, and that the problem of illegal immigration involves more than a lack of proper documentation.

We are told that blanket amnesty and a grant of legal status will ensure assimilation and prosperity. But statistics suggest that after 20 years, even legal Mexican immigrants have double the welfare rates of American citizens. And in one study, students surveyed at 13 years of age and then again at 17 were 50 percent more likely at 17 to identify themselves as "Mexicans" as opposed to "Mexican-Americans"—this despite, or perhaps even because of, having spent four years in American high schools. In moral terms, it is true that we can hardly hunt out residents of California who have not seen Oaxaca in 40 years and deport them as illegal aliens. On the other hand, every time the issue of amnesty is broached, advocates of open borders offer up no concessions and thereby perhaps reveal their real agenda: a series of rolling amnesties every ten years or so that sends the message far and wide that illegal immigration is now an American institution.

Surreality

We try all sorts of bromides, including an alternate legal universe that is sometimes tougher on citizens than illegal immigrants. Unbelievably, California extends in-state tuition discounts to resident illegal immigrants, even as it charges nearly triple the in-state amount for American citizens from Arizona, Nevada and other states. California's governor, pandering in the recent recall election conundrum, okayed the policy of granting driver's licenses for illegal immigrants—and then discovered that the state's age-old rite of passage whereby citizens produce their birth certificates as proof of age at the Department of Motor Vehicles would be rendered absurd. We now ponder honoring identification documents from Mexico (alone of foreign countries) as legal American identification, even as we read of endemic corruption among police and bureaucrats across the border. In response, aliens from myriad other countries now demand that their own foreign IDs be honored, and the other 49 states of the Union are not so sure they should accept California driver's licenses, given how promiscuously they are granted, at intrastate security check points. Thousands of immigrants from the Punjab, Korea and the Philippines wait patiently for five years or more to become naturalized citizens in the proper and legal fashion, only to watch hundreds of thousands cross illegally from Mexico in the expectation of a periodic and privileged amnesty designed only for them.

Since roughly 1970, the evolving concept of multiculturalism—which holds that Western civilization merits no special consideration, inasmuch as all cultures are of equal merit—has proved to be the force-multiplier of illegal immigration from Mexico. By denying or deprecating the singularity of democracy, capitalism, the rule of law, civic audit and religious freedom, multiculturalism confuses both native Americans and immigrants about why people are leaving Mexico in droves in the first place, and in the second, why they are heading northward rather than southward into Central or South America. Rather than explaining reality, this new ideology emphasizes racial prejudice and economic exploitation in America's past—a topic of increasing interest to comfortable elites, but apparently not seen as an obstacle by the millions of poor and impoverished Mexicans who risk their lives daily to reach the American promised land.

Almost every well-intended and enlightened gesture designed to help immigrants over the last three decades—bilingual education, ever expanding and new state welfare programs, the affirmation of a hyphenated identity and the radical historical revisionism of southwestern American history—has been detrimental to the processes of assimilation and economic improvement. Almost everything stern and uncompromising that for two centuries has helped other immigrants to the United States—entry under legal auspices, language immersion, autonomy from government assistance, rapid assumption of an American identity and eager acceptance of mainstream American culture—has either been dismissed as passé or carried on halfheartedly.

Most Californians of all backgrounds understand the growing social and cultural costs that flow from this situation. Yet the Orwellian alliance of many libertarian-leaning conservatives—who embrace the idea of a perpetual supply of hard-working, unskilled and inexpensive workers—with the race industry of the Left—which envisions an endless influx of unassimilated potential voters who can be appealed to on the basis of group rather than individual identity—tends to demonize any discussion of the issue. Opposition to massive illegal immigration is customarily and cleverly equated with disdain for immigration per se, hence characterized as un-American. Given the demagoguery of our elected state representatives and the general hostility to frank talk about illegal immigration, ballot propositions led by unelected partisans and enacted through popular vote, rather than through legislative debate, have become the chief mechanisms of addressing this issue. Embittered Californians give tacit approval to therapeutic bromides in their schools and state agencies—and then flock to the polls to vent their rage by voting to end what they see as special consideration for those who broke the law in coming here. In the last decade, California majorities have voted against state aid to illegal immigrants, affirmative action and bilingual education, but far fewer than a majority will admit to taking part. It is not a healthy thing to have a voting population of millions thinking privately what they won't express publicly.

In the recent California recall election, a first-generation immigrant from Austria—a candidate who arrived here penniless and has a heavy accent that seems right out of a bad

World War II movie, but who became an up-by-his-bootstraps business success—was caricatured as a nativist and near-racist for supporting legal and measured immigration. Meanwhile, a third-generation Hispanic candidate—a man who grew up as Mike, not Cruz, Bustamante, speaking English in a California suburb—reinvented himself as the emblem of the Mexican Diaspora. Only in the poisonous atmosphere of today's identity politics could the immigrant be slandered as the nativist and the native deified as the immigrant.

Meanwhile Mexico, a richly endowed but nearly failed state, continues to refuse to do the political, cultural and economic restructuring that is needed to turn itself around. Indeed, why should it bother making these reforms when it can export potential dissidents from its hinterland to the U.S., gaining in the process $12 billion in remittances from expatriates? (These remittances constitute the second largest source of foreign exchange to the Mexican economy.) Not only that, but as noted previously, Mexico finds that the longer its expatriates stay away from Mexico and in the U.S., the more they come to love Mexico.

Unintended Consequences

Illustrating the law of unintended consequences, today's illegal immigration crisis was not quite what any of the stakeholders in this immigration had anticipated. In addition to its cheap labor, tax-conscious business interests are responsible for masses of unassimilated residents who eventually plugged into the state's near-bankrupt entitlement industry. In addition to a larger bloc vote, the pro-labor Left discovered that the wages of its own impoverished domestic constituencies were eroded by the influx of less expensive and more industrious alien workers. A full 50 percent of real wage labor losses was recently attributed by the Labor Department to the influx of cheap immigrant labor. While we continue to import this labor, millions of second-generation Hispanic and other legal laborers are making not much more than the minimum wage. Of course, few of the professors and politicians who support illegal immigration—whether for continuance of cheap labor or for the sake of the entitlement industries—live in California's new apartheid communities like Orange Cove, Mendota or Parlier, communities where Mexican immigrants make up the vast majority of the population and struggle with dismal schools, high crime, little revenue and other social problems akin to those in Mexico.

In a time of war, under the threat of domestic terrorism and with their state budget tens of billions of dollars in the red, Californians are predictably restive and looking for answers. They cannot quite figure out how a state with Hollywood, the Silicon Valley, vast industrial and manufacturing sectors, great ports, timber, oil, tourism, a vast agricultural industry, an ideal climate—not to mention some of the nation's highest sales and income taxes—is broken and paralyzed with billions of dollars in annual deficit. They are considering what kind of future they want. In more placid times, this could be an academic exercise. Under current circumstances, it is an urgent necessity.

In the end, the immigration crisis is simple to understand, but it can also seem to involve an unsolvable calculus. Californians want a lot of their work done cheaply by illegal immigrants who, they wrongly assume, will transform themselves quickly into Americans. In turn, too many downtrodden Mexicans and their elite American advocates romanticize Mexico, a nation that has brought them misery and driven them to flight, and deprecate the U.S., which gave them sanctuary.

In a country where there may be anywhere from eight to fifteen million illegal immigrants, is there any hope for avoiding the nightmare of Balkanization? Perhaps. After all, we got into our present mess only during the last 30 years, and then only by doing almost everything wrong. Thus we need not do everything right, but simply return to what we used to do so well: insist that immigration be measured and legal, do more of our own unpleasant work, enforce all of our laws equally, emphasize assimilation and return to thinking and speaking of Americans as individuals rather than in terms of their racial or group identities.

Reprinted by permission from Imprimis, *the national speech digest of Hillsdale College, www.hillsdale.edu.*

National Guard Soldier on the U.S./Mexico Border

The Ten Commandments Controversy
Michael Novak

December 2003 *Imprimis*

Michael Novak is the George Frederick Jewett Scholar in Religion, Philosophy and Public Policy at the American Enterprise Institute. He was the winner of the 1994 Templeton Prize for Progress in Religion. Novak has served as Ambassador of the U.S. Delegation to the U.N. Human Rights Commission in Geneva (1981-82) and head of the U.S. Delegation to the Conference on Security and Cooperation in Europe (1986).

On August 27 of this year, under the direction of U.S. District Court Judge Myron Thompson, a small monument (not even four feet high) of the Ten Commandments was removed from the back end of the towering rotunda in the Alabama state courthouse. Judge Thompson's argument for removing the monument runs as follows: Any recognition by the Alabama Supreme Court of a special role for the God of Judaism and Christianity in this nation's understanding of civil and political rights represents an establishment of religion, and thus violates the First Amendment.

Opposing this argument, now-suspended [and later removed] Alabama Chief Justice Roy S. Moore pointed out that the Virginia Declaration of Rights, James Madison's "Memorial and Remonstrance" and the Virginia Act for Establishing Religious Freedom—founding-era documents defining the idea of religious liberty that is embodied in the First Amendment—all appeal to a particular concept of God, with a fairly narrow range of characteristics. This God is almighty, and created the mind free. Further, He wishes to be worshiped by men and women who do so freely, under no duress or coercion, and solely according to the light of their own conscience. Any abuse of the right to religious liberty will have to be answered directly to Him in judgment, for it is an abuse against Him, not solely against humans. To worship Him, but solely as conscience directs, is a duty owed to Him as Creator and Judge. This duty owed Him grounds a personal responsibility and, therefore, a right. No one else can perform this responsibility in our place; therefore, the right is inalienable. In creating our minds both duty-bound and yet free, in other words, the Creator endowed us with certain rights, among them the right to religious liberty.

It is a matter of inference whether any other God except the God of Judaism and Christianity fits this required range of characteristics. Undoubtedly, from the founding generation until about 50 years ago, American institutions and courts supposed that this God was the God of the Jewish and Christian Bible, to whom the Founders usually referred as "Creator," "Judge," "Providence," and "Divine Governor of the universe."

Judge Thompson explained this historical fact by asserting that such usage may have been fitting when most American citizens were Christians or Jews. Nowadays, however, that inference goes too far, because we see more clearly that rights are endowed also in Muslims, Buddhists, atheists, and indeed all humans. (Of course, the Founders expressly affirmed this universality too; it is also implicit in the doctrine of "natural rights.") Among the many and varied religions, furthermore, Supreme Court precedents of the past half-century insist that the federal government ought not to show favoritism; not even to religion over non-religion. Indeed, the Court has developed an extreme, non-historical version of what constitutes "establishment." Thus, either the Supreme Court jurisprudence of the past 50 years needed to be overhauled, or the monument had to be moved.

In thinking about who is right on this issue, it might be useful, first, to make some distinctions concerning the particulars of the case. For instance, on the outside wall of the federal courthouse in Montgomery is a much larger statue of Artemis, described in the Court's brochure as the Greek goddess of justice. No one asserts that that statue represents an establishment of religion. Perhaps that is because no one still believes that Artemis is a real goddess. In any case, the mere stone embodiment of her image obliges no one's conscience. But then, in similar fashion, Chief Justice Moore's stone embodiment of a portion of a page from the Book of Exodus also puts no obligation upon the conscience of anyone who chooses not to accept that text as authoritative.

Second, the controversial text is from the Old Testament, not the New Testament. That made it less sectarian and broader. Furthermore, even if one does not take the Ten Commandments literally, as a gift by the Almighty to Moses, one may take them as a symbol of that higher law ("of Nature and Nature's God") reached by reason itself. Such a higher law has traditionally been seen (by Americans from the signers of the Declaration of Independence through Martin Luther King, Jr.) as infusing all man-made law, on the one hand, and upholding a standard beyond the power of governments to alter or abrogate, on the other. Only such a law is a sure foundation for our rights against the changing tempests of political fortune.

Third, the monument stood at least 90 feet distant, maybe more, from the front entrance of the Alabama state courthouse, all the way across the rotunda at the opposite wall. It was impossible at that distance even to make out what it was, let alone what was written upon it. No one was obliged to approach the small marble block close enough to be able to make out the words.

And finally, all 15 of the texts upon its sides were either already familiar or readily recognizable as classics of U.S. or Alabama law, or quotations from major American Founders. In the sense that Americans are expected to venerate the law, an air of veneration was present, but rather in the form of a history lesson on the American link between religion and law. The four dominant texts came from the Declaration of Independence, the Pledge of Allegiance, the Judiciary Act of 1789, and the U.S. Code.

History Lesson or Establishment?

Still, the main point in this case was the unique character of the Jewish and Christian God. The God of Abraham, Isaac, Jacob and Jesus is unlike any other God known to the ancient religions of Greece, Rome or the Middle East, or any other religion known to our Founders. Uniquely, this God wishes to be worshiped in spirit and truth, in whatsoever manner conscience directs, without coercion of any sort. This God reads hearts, and is satisfied only with purity of conscience and conviction. Those who belong to any other religion or tradition, or who count themselves among agnostics or atheists, are thereby given by this God equal freedom. They, too, must follow their individual consciences. This God wishes to be worshiped by men and women who are free, not under duress. Arising from His sovereignty, the rights He endows cannot be abrogated by a tyrannical majority among the people, or by the actions of the state in any of its branches.

This conception of religious liberty is spelled out directly in the founding-era documents mentioned above. For example, the Virginia Declaration of Rights affirms that religion, or the duty which we owe to our Creator and the manner of discharging it, can be directed only by reason and conviction, not by force or violence; and therefore, all men are equally entitled to the free exercise of religion, according to the dictates of conscience; and that it is the mutual duty of all to practice Christian forbearance, love, and charity towards each other.

This summarizes the classic American definition of religion and the foundation for religious liberty. To this definition, some make one or more objections. For instance, some point out that Christians (and Jews) have not always respected this principle, and thus try to discredit its Jewish and Christian origins. But human failure is no argument against the principle; human weakness is measured by it.

Second, one can say (as did Judge Thompson) that among Muslims, Hindus, Buddhists and others there have been examples of generations of "tolerance." But tolerance is a different (and less profound) concept than the right to religious liberty. Tolerance may arise merely from a temporary lack of power to enforce conformity; it does not by itself invoke a natural right. The concept of religious liberty, on the other hand, depends upon a particular conception of God, a particular conception of the human person, and a particular conception of liberty. Reaching these conceptions took Jews and Christians many centuries. They had to be learned through failure and sin and error, and at great cost. But they were eventually learned.

Scholars today can easily point to texts in the American tradition for definitions of these concepts, but they would find it difficult to locate analogous texts in other traditions. Rightly did the authors of *Federalist* 14 call attention to their own originality, even as they exerted themselves to pay due respect to the opinions of past ages. For this reason, calling the attention of the public to the Jewish and Christian conception of God's sovereignty, which grounds the principle of religious liberty, is not necessarily the same as "establishing" the Jewish or Christian religions.

In the first place, this conception is by its very nature public, not private, and has historically been invoked in the practice of existing public institutions in countless forms. The public life of our nation has been and is still remarkably religious, as is visible on public occasions such as the inaugural speeches of presidents, the swearing-in of judges, Thanksgiving Day, Independence Day and Memorial Day. The notion that the foundation of our rights lies in God's work has been officially deployed in many congressional and presidential decrees and proclamations, which recommend religious observances such as fasting, prayers, thanksgiving and imploring pardon for the nation's sins.

In the second place, the principle of religious liberty (as witnessed to in countless founding documents and in the public practices of the founding era) requires two courses of action: First, one must enunciate the principle clearly, understand it fully, and express it publicly for public guidance. Second, one must not coerce the conscience nor obstruct the free exercise of religion of any.

The specifically American principle of religious liberty, in and of itself, demands that each person's decision about how (if at all) to worship God is inalienable, for it belongs to each alone in his or her own conscience. Everyone must be free in conscience and in public exercise to accept, or to reject, the Judeo-Christian God. Even if unbelievers choose not to recognize this conception of God, conscience and liberty, but rather to concentrate upon abuses of the principle committed by Christians or others, this particular conception guarantees their freedom of conscience. It is also precious for believers, who are obliged by it to grant to all others exactly the same right to religious liberty that they claim for themselves.

This was exactly the point made by Chief Justice Moore in his oral testimony at last year's trial. He said again and again that he stood for two things, both of them derived from America's founding principles. First, human rights are guaranteed by the sovereignty of God, with the result that any abuse of them will have to be answered for before God in Judgment (as Madison had pointed out). Second, he neither intended to nor could demand that others share these beliefs, since that would violate the principle of religious liberty itself. He wished only "to recur to fundamental principles" (a phrase from the Virginia Declaration of Rights) by calling attention again to the Founders' beliefs about the grounding of our rights.

It is the special virtue of the Jewish and Christian conception of God that it allows us to make a twofold claim: to recognize in public the beliefs on which our rights are founded, and to refuse to mandate for others that they must hold the same beliefs. Thus we should be counted free to call public attention to the moral foundation of our rights, without by the same deed trying to force Jewish or Christian belief upon Muslims, Buddhists, atheists, agnostics, or anyone else.

Recurring to Fundamental Principles

In defense of his position on this matter, Chief Justice Moore has fittingly cited George Washington's Proclamation of General Thanksgiving (October 3, 1789), in which, in response to a request from both Houses of Congress, Washington notes:

It is the duty of all Nations [note: not only individuals] to acknowledge the providence of Almighty God, to obey his will, to be grateful for his benefits, and humbly to implore his protection and favor. . . .

If both houses of Congress and the President of the United States could go so far in 1789, why is it forbidden by the Constitution for a mere Chief Justice of the Supreme Court of Alabama to do even less?

Chief Justice Moore has also cited Abraham Lincoln's beautiful Decree of August 12, 1861, which also followed upon a resolution of both Houses of Congress: Recognizing that "it is fit and becoming in all people, at all times, to acknowledge and revere the Supreme Government of God," Lincoln proclaimed a National Fast Day to ask God's favor. If all this was not an establishment of religion in 1861, why does doing far less barely a century and a half later constitute an attempt to establish a religion? Clearly, the meaning of "establish" has now swollen far beyond its historic meaning.

Starting about 60 years ago, the Supreme Court took a half-truth about the meaning of "establishment" and carried it by tortuous logic to conclusions that go against the whole of its own prior tradition and against the tradition of American public life. In shifting its focus from the constitutional term "religious liberty" to the much more recent and polemical slogan "separation of church and state," the Court has come to seem radically anti-religious, and in particular, anti-Jewish and anti-Christian.

We should not want the Court to be pro-Jewish or pro-Christian. But we must insist that it show reverence for the moral foundations of the principle of religious liberty—foundations well located in Jewish and Christian conceptions by the classic documents of the American founding. It is not necessary to embrace these particular conceptions. Unavoidably, however, anyone wishing "to recur to fundamental principles" will have to measure rival conceptions by those historically agreed to in the founding era.

Chief Justice Moore is a profound believer in the principle of religious liberty, and an unusually thoughtful student of the origins and sources of that principle. Whatever one thinks of his early defiance of the Federal Court, the ideas he points to are public and traditional. He is a serious believer in the God who was written of with palpable reverence by our nation's founders and later forebears. All he has sought to do, in a manner fully respectful of the religious liberty of the many new citizens who are of different faiths and traditions, is to underline the originality of America's Founders in the matter of religious liberty—a principle which is not, after all, understood or accepted in all cultures of this planet. This idea of religious liberty is part of a precious conceptual heritage that needs to be set forth publicly so that all new immigrants might come easily to learn of it, even as they develop equivalent conceptions from the materials of their own traditions.

Someone might counter that although Chief Justice Moore is correct about the history of the American conception of religious liberty, he went too far by giving witness to the truth of this conception—thus to the truth of the sovereignty of God. But how does his official action differ from the official exercise of religion shown by Washington in his Proclamation of 1789 and Lincoln in his Decree of 1861?

The beauty of our forebears' conception of religious liberty is that it can be held as a truth by most Americans, respected by all, commended to newcomers as a model, yet never forced upon the conscience of anyone. That is precisely what the principle of religious liberty demands: Cherish it, teach it, but do not force it upon anyone. In light of this, it seems clearly unreasonable to have equated the silent monument that stood in the Alabama state courthouse with an establishment of religion.

Reprinted by permission from Imprimis, *the national speech digest of Hillsdale College, www.hillsdale.edu.*

Ten Commandments Illustration, c. 1876

Rolling Back Government:
Lessons from New Zealand
Maurice P. McTigue

April 2004 *Imprimis*

Maurice McTigue has been a member of the New Zealand Parliament and held several Cabinet positions in the New Zealand government. He also served as that country's ambassador to Canada. In more recent years he has lived in the United States, served as a visiting scholar at George Mason University, and advised several government agencies.

If we look back through history, growth in government has been a modern phenomenon. Beginning in the 1850s and lasting until the 1920s or '30s, the government's share of GDP in most of the world's industrialized economies was about six percent. From that period onwards—and particularly since the 1950s—we've seen a massive explosion in government share of GDP, in some places as much as 35-45 percent. (In the case of Sweden, of course, it reached 65 percent, and Sweden nearly self-destructed as a result. It is now starting to dismantle some of its social programs to remain economically viable.) Can this situation be halted or even rolled back? My view, based upon personal experience, is that the answer is "yes." But it requires high levels of transparency and significant consequences for bad decisions—and these are not easy things to bring about.

New Zealand

What we're seeing around the world at the moment is what I would call a silent revolution, reflected in a change in how people view government accountability. The old idea of accountability simply held that government should spend money in accordance with appropriations. The new accountability is based on asking, "What did we get in public benefits as a result of the expenditure of money?" This is a question that has always been asked in business, but has not been the norm for governments. And those governments today that are struggling valiantly with this question are showing quite extraordinary results. This was certainly the basis of the successful reforms in my own country of New Zealand.

New Zealand's per capita income in the period prior to the late 1950s was right around number three in the world, behind the United States and Canada. But by 1984, its per capita income had sunk to 27th in the world, alongside Portugal and Turkey. Not only that, but our unemployment rate was 11.6 percent, we'd had 23 successive years of deficits (sometimes ranging as high as 40 percent of GDP), our debt had grown to 65 percent of GDP, and our credit ratings were continually being downgraded. Government spending was a full 44 percent of GDP, investment capital was exiting in huge quantities, and government controls and micromanagement were pervasive at every level of the economy. We had foreign exchange controls that meant I couldn't buy a subscription to *The Economist* magazine without the permission of the Minister of Finance. I couldn't buy shares in a foreign company without surrendering my citizenship. There were price controls on all goods and services, on all shops and on all service industries. There were wage controls and wage freezes. I couldn't pay my employees more—or pay them bonuses—if I wanted to. There were import controls on the goods that I could bring into the country. There were massive levels of subsidies on industries in order to keep them viable. Young people were leaving in droves.

Spending and Taxes

When a reform government was elected in 1984, it identified three problems: too much spending, too much taxing and too much government. The question was how to cut spending and taxes and diminish government's role in the economy. Well, the first thing you have to do in this situation is to figure out what you're getting for dollars spent. Towards this end, we implemented a new policy whereby money wouldn't simply be allocated to government agencies; instead, there would be a purchase contract with the senior executives of those agencies that clearly delineated what was expected in return for the money. Those who headed up government agencies were now chosen on the basis of a worldwide search and received term contracts—five years with a possible extension of another three years. The only ground for their removal was non-performance, so a newly-elected government couldn't simply throw them out as had happened with civil servants under the old system. And of course, with those kinds of incentives, agency heads—like CEOs in the private sector—made certain that the next tier of people had very clear objectives that they were expected to achieve as well.

The first purchase that we made from every agency was policy advice. That policy advice was meant to produce a vigorous debate between the government and the agency heads about how to achieve goals like reducing hunger and homelessness. This didn't mean, by the way, how government could feed or house more people—that's not important. What's important is the extent to which hunger and homelessness are actually reduced. In other words, we made it clear that what's important is not how many people are on welfare, but how many people get off welfare and into independent living.

As we started to work through this process, we also asked some fundamental questions of the agencies. The first question was, "What are you doing?" The second question was, "What should you be doing?" Based on the answers, we then said, "Eliminate what you shouldn't be doing"—that is, if you are doing something that clearly is not a responsibility of the government, stop doing it. Then we asked the final question: "Who should be paying— the taxpayer, the user, the consumer, or the industry?" We asked this because, in many instances, the taxpayers were subsidizing things that did not benefit them. And if you take the cost of services away from actual consumers and users, you promote overuse and devalue whatever it is that you're doing.

When we started this process with the Department of Transportation, it had 5,600 employees. When we finished, it had 53. When we started with the Forest Service, it had 17,000 employees. When we finished, it had 17. When we applied it to the Ministry of Works, it had 28,000 employees. I used to be Minister of Works, and ended up being the only employee. In the latter case, most of what the department did was construction and engineering, and there are plenty of people who can do that without government involvement. And if you say to me, "But you killed all those jobs!"—well, that's just not true. The government stopped employing people in those jobs, but the need for the jobs didn't disappear. I visited some of the forestry workers some months after they'd lost their government jobs, and they were quite happy. They told me that they were now earning about three times what they used to earn—on top of which, they were surprised to learn that they could do about 60 percent more than they used to! The same lesson applies to the other jobs I mentioned.

New Zealand Currency

Some of the things that government was doing simply didn't belong in the government. So we sold off telecommunications, airlines, irrigation schemes, computing services, government printing offices, insurance companies, banks, securities, mortgages, railways, bus services, hotels, shipping lines, agricultural advisory services, etc. In the main, when we sold those things off, their productivity went up and the cost of their services went down, translating into major gains for the economy. Furthermore, we decided that other agencies should be run as profit-making and tax-paying enterprises by government. For instance, the air traffic control system was made into a stand-alone company, given instructions that it had to make an acceptable rate of return and pay taxes, and told that it couldn't get any investment capital from its owner (the government). We did that with about 35 agencies. Together, these used to cost us about one billion dollars per year; now they produced about one billion dollars per year in revenues and taxes.

We achieved an overall reduction of 66 percent in the size of government, measured by the number of employees. The government's share of GDP dropped from 44 to 27 percent. We were now running surpluses, and we established a policy never to leave dollars on the table: We knew that if we didn't get rid of this money, some clown would spend it. So we used most of the surplus to pay off debt, and debt went from 63 percent down to 17 percent of GDP. We used the remainder of the surplus each year for tax relief. We reduced income tax rates by half and eliminated incidental taxes. As a result of these policies, revenue increased by 20 percent. Yes, Ronald Reagan was right: lower tax rates do produce more revenue.

Subsidies, Education, and Competitiveness

. . . What about invasive government in the form of subsidies? First, we need to recognize that the main problem with subsidies is that they make people dependent; and when you make people dependent, they lose their innovation and their creativity and become even more dependent.

Let me give you an example: By 1984, New Zealand sheep farming was receiving about 44 percent of its income from government subsidies. Its major product was lamb, and lamb in the international marketplace was selling for about $12.50 (with the government providing another $12.50) per carcass. Well, we did away with all sheep farming subsidies within one year. And of course the sheep farmers were unhappy. But once they accepted the fact that the subsidies weren't coming back, they put together a team of people charged with figuring out how they could get $30 per lamb carcass. The team reported back that this would be difficult, but not impossible. It required producing an entirely different product, processing it in a different way and selling it in different markets. And within two years, by 1989, they had succeeded in converting their $12.50 product into something worth $30. By 1991, it was worth $42; by 1994 it was worth $74; and by 1999 it was worth $115. In other words, the New Zealand sheep industry went out into the marketplace and found people who would pay higher prices for its product. You can now go into the best restaurants in the U.S. and buy New Zealand lamb, and you'll be paying somewhere between $35 and $60 per pound.

Needless to say, as we took government support away from industry, it was widely predicted that there would be a massive exodus of people. But that didn't happen. To give you one example, we lost only about three-quarters of one percent of the farming enterprises—and these were people who shouldn't have been farming in the first place. In addition, some predicted a major move towards corporate as opposed to family farming. But we've seen exactly the reverse. Corporate farming moved out and family farming expanded, probably because families are prepared to work for less than corporations. In the end, it was the best thing that possibly could have happened. And it demonstrated that if you give people no choice but to be creative and innovative, they will find solutions.

New Zealand had an education system that was failing as well. It was failing about 30 percent of its children—especially those in lower socio-economic areas. We had put more and more money into education for 20 years, and achieved worse and worse results.

It cost us twice as much to get a poorer result than we did 20 years previously with much less money. So we decided to rethink what we were doing here as well. The first thing we did was to identify where the dollars were going that we were pouring into education.

We hired international consultants (because we didn't trust our own departments to do it), and they reported that for every dollar we were spending on education, 70 cents was being swallowed up by administration. Once we heard this, we immediately eliminated all of the Boards of Education in the country. Every single school came under the control of a board of trustees elected by the parents of the children at that school, and by nobody else. We gave schools a block of money based on the number of students that went to them, with no strings attached. At the same time, we told the parents that they had an absolute right to choose where their children would go to school. It is absolutely obnoxious to me that anybody would tell parents that they must send their children to a bad school. We converted 4,500 schools to this new system all on the same day.

But we went even further: We made it possible for privately owned schools to be funded in exactly the same way as publicly owned schools, giving parents the ability to spend their education dollars wherever they chose. Again, everybody predicted that there would be a major exodus of students from the public to the private schools, because the private schools showed an academic advantage of 14 to 15 percent. It didn't happen, however, because the differential between schools disappeared in about 18-24 months. Why? Because all of a sudden teachers realized that if they lost their students, they would lose their funding; and if they lost their funding, they would lose their jobs. Eighty-five percent of our students went to public schools at the beginning of this process. That fell to only about 84 percent over the first year or so of our reforms. But three years later, 87 percent of the students were going to public schools. More importantly, we moved from being about 14 or 15 percent below our international peers to being about 14 or 15 percent above our international peers in terms of educational attainment.

Now consider taxation and competitiveness: What many in the public sector today fail to recognize is that the challenge of competitiveness is worldwide. Capital and labor can move so freely and rapidly from place to place that the only way to stop business from leaving is to make certain that your business climate is better than anybody else's. Along these lines, there was a very interesting circumstance in Ireland just two years ago. The European Union, led by France, was highly critical of Irish tax policy—particularly on corporations—because the Irish had reduced their tax on corporations from 48 percent to 12 percent and business was flooding into Ireland. The European Union wanted to impose a penalty on Ireland in the form of a 17 percent corporate tax hike to bring them into line with other European countries. Needless to say, the Irish didn't buy that. The European community responded by saying that what the Irish were doing was unfair and uncompetitive. The Irish Minister of Finance agreed: He pointed out that Ireland was charging corporations 12 percent, while charging its citizens only 10 percent. So Ireland reduced the tax rate to 10 percent for corporations as well. There's another one the French lost!

When we in New Zealand looked at our revenue gathering process, we found the system extremely complicated in a way that distorted business as well as private decisions. So we asked ourselves some questions: Was our tax system concerned with collecting revenue? Was it concerned with collecting revenue and also delivering social services? Or was it concerned with collecting revenue, delivering social services and changing behavior, all three? We decided that the social services and behavioral components didn't have any place in a rational system of taxation. So we resolved that we would have only two mechanisms for gathering revenue—a tax on income and a tax on consumption—and that we would simplify those mechanisms and lower the rates as much as we possibly could. We lowered the high income tax rate from 66 to 33 percent, and set that flat rate for high-income earners. In addition, we brought the low end down from 38 to 19 percent, which became the flat rate for low-income earners. We then set a consumption tax rate of 10 percent and eliminated all other taxes—capital gains taxes, property taxes, etc. We carefully designed this system to produce exactly the same revenue as we were getting before and presented it to the public as a zero sum game. But what actually happened was that we received 20 percent more revenue than before. Why? We hadn't allowed for the increase in voluntary compliance. If tax rates are low, taxpayers won't employ high priced lawyers and accountants to find loopholes. Indeed, every country that I've looked at in the world that has dramatically simplified and lowered its tax rates has ended up with more revenue, not less.

What about regulations? The regulatory power is customarily delegated to non-elected officials who then constrain the people's liberties with little or no accountability. These regulations are extremely difficult to eliminate once they are in place. But we found a way: We simply rewrote the statutes on which they were based. For instance, we rewrote the environmental laws, transforming them into the Resource Management Act—reducing a law that was 25 inches thick to 348 pages. We rewrote the tax code, all of the farm acts, and the occupational safety and health acts. To do this, we brought our brightest brains together and told them to pretend that there was no pre-existing law and that they should create for us the best possible environment for industry to thrive. We then marketed it in terms of what it would save in taxes. These new laws, in effect, repealed the old, which meant that all existing regulations died—the whole lot, every single one.

Thinking Differently About Government

What I have been discussing is really just a new way of thinking about government. Let me tell you how we solved our deer problem: Our country had no large indigenous animals until the English imported deer for hunting. These deer proceeded to escape into the wild and become obnoxious pests. We then spent 120 years trying to eliminate them, until one day someone suggested that we just let people farm them. So we told the farming community that they could catch and farm the deer, as long as they would keep them inside eight-foot high fences. And we haven't spent a dollar on deer eradication from that day onwards. Not one. And New Zealand now supplies 40 percent of the world market in venison. By applying simple common sense, we turned a liability into an asset.

Let me share with you one last story: The Department of Transportation came to us one day and said they needed to increase the fees for driver's licenses. When we asked why, they said that the cost of relicensing wasn't being fully recovered at the current fee levels. Then we asked why we should be doing this sort of thing at all. The transportation people clearly thought that was a very stupid question: Everybody needs a driver's license, they said. I then pointed out that I received mine when I was fifteen and asked them: "What is it about relicensing that in any way tests driver competency?" We gave them ten days to think this over. At one point they suggested to us that the police need driver's licenses for identification purposes. We responded that this was the purpose of an identity card, not a driver's license. Finally they admitted that they could think of no good reason for what they were doing—so we abolished the whole process! Now a driver's license is good until a person is 74 years old, after which he must get an annual medical test to ensure he is still competent to drive. So not only did we not need new fees, we abolished a whole department. That's what I mean by thinking differently.

There are some great things happening along these lines in the United States today. You might not know it, but back in 1993 Congress passed a law called the Government Performance and Results Act. This law orders government departments to identify in a strategic plan what it is that they intend to achieve, and to report each year what they actually did achieve in terms of public benefits. Following on this, two years ago President Bush brought to the table something called the President's Management Agenda, which sifts through the information in these reports and decides how to respond. These mechanisms are promising if they are used properly. Consider this: There are currently 178 federal programs designed to help people get back to work. They cost $8.4 billion, and 2.4 million people are employed as a result of them. But if we took the most effective three programs out of those 178 and put the $8.4 billion into them alone, the result would likely be that 14.7 million people would find jobs. The status quo costs America over 11 million jobs. The kind of new thinking I am talking about would build into the system a consequence for the administrator who is responsible for this failure of sound stewardship of taxpayer dollars. It is in this direction that the government needs to move.

Reprinted by permission from Imprimis, *the national speech digest of Hillsdale College, www.hillsdale.edu.*

Something Higher Than Incumbency
James E. Rogan

June 2001 *Imprimis*

> *James E. Rogan was elected to the U.S. House of Representatives in 1996 from the 27th District of California. He served on the House Commerce and Judiciary committees, and in 1999 was one of the thirteen House managers to prosecute the impeachment trial of President Clinton. Mr. Rogan was defeated in his bid for re-election in 2000.*

I'm a conservative Republican who represented a liberal Democratic district where most of the Hollywood studios are located. Impeaching President Clinton was not a popular cause there. During that proceeding, many friends called to encourage me by saying, "It's two years until the next election. Nobody will remember." Larry Arnn, who has since become your president here at Hillsdale, called one day with a far different message. He said, "I know a lot of your friends are telling you that you're going to be all right in the next election. I'm your friend, and I'm telling you that you may not be all right." Then he added, "You know, congressmen lose elections all the time. It's very rare, though, that congressmen have the privilege of losing an election in defense of the Constitution." Those words carried me through that difficult period, and through my recent unsuccessful re-election campaign.

My dream as a kid was to serve in Congress, because I had read biographies of people from humble backgrounds, like mine, who had gone on to make a difference in their communities through politics and public service. That idea was so appealing to me that in 1994, I gave up a relatively secure job as a judge to run for state assembly. Two years later, I won my congressional seat with a 50.1 percent majority in a county where Bob Dole lost by about twenty points. My childhood dream had come true.

When I got to Congress, Henry Hyde asked me to serve on the Judiciary Committee. I turned him down because I preferred and had a shot at the Commerce Committee. Later he got me interested by pointing out that the sub-committee responsible for protecting intellectual property—the life blood of the high-tech and entertainment industries in my district—is in Judiciary. And when my friend Sonny Bono, who sat on that subcommittee, was killed in a tragic skiing accident in January 1998, Chairman Hyde submitted my name to replace him. I became a member of the Judiciary Committee on January 20, and on the very next day the Monica Lewinsky story broke. Needless to say, I felt the opposite of someone who had just won the lottery.

Over the next year, I concluded that the President's constitutional problem boiled down to the violation of his oath. Of all our federal officials, only presidents are constitutionally required to vow to "preserve, protect, and defend the Constitution." Of

208

course they are also charged by the Constitution with "tak[ing] care that the laws [are] faithfully executed." President Clinton had therefore violated his oath when he committed perjury in a civil rights action, obstructed justice, suborned perjury, and conspired to do the same. For me, as a former judge, the seriousness of this violation was never in question. The presidential oath was not an afterthought of America's Founders. No matter how popular a president-elect might be, he has to swear to uphold the Constitution before taking office. It is the oath, and not a politician's poll numbers, that gives legitimacy and continuity to that high office.

During the Judiciary Committee impeachment inquiry, a woman doctor testified. She was one of a host of witnesses, but her testimony was most powerful. She had been a medical doctor and an attorney, and worked at a veterans hospital. . . . [Later this woman] lied in a deposition in a civil case—exactly what President Clinton had done. But here the similarity ends, because the Clinton Justice Department prosecuted her. As a result she lost her medical license, she lost her law license, and she was sentenced to jail. When she testified before our committee, she was wearing an electronic monitoring device around her ankle because she was still under an incarceration order. And she was one of some 135 people then in federal prison who had been prosecuted for perjury by the Clinton Justice Department. How could we in Congress, representing the American people, hold that the law applies differently to the powerful? This was not a position that I was prepared to take.

Profiles In Weakness

When I and my twelve colleagues were sent over to present our case to the Senate on behalf of the House of Representatives, we ran into a wall. Although only one president had previously been impeached, Congress had a history of impeaching federal judges and

Dome of the United States Capitol

Cabinet members going back to the 1790s. In our case the Senate ignored all precedent, however, and for the first time in history refused to allow House Managers to call witnesses. Individual senators would often tell us, in effect, that poll numbers trumped precedent. "Americans don't want the President removed," they said, "so we're not going to remove him." We responded, "The Constitution gives the House the power to impeach, and the Senate the power to remove. If you don't vote to remove, that's fine. But let us present the evidence so that you can at least make an informed decision." I argued to my colleagues that we should decline to proceed unless the Senate followed precedent and allowed us to present evidence. But most felt that the train was too far down the track.

Over 60,000 pages of evidence had been deposited with Congress, and we on the House Judiciary Committee had taken months going through them. Shortly before the final vote in the House, the votes were not there for impeachment. We had Republican members who had announced on nationwide television that they were going to vote against it. But at a late-night caucus, we asked these members at least to go over to the Ford Building and review the evidence. Most of those who did so changed their minds. Jack Quinn, for example, represented a big union district in New York where impeachment was tremendously unpopular. But after looking at the evidence, he was no longer able to oppose it. Very few of the House Democrats ever went over and looked at the evidence. And I am told that not a single member of the United States Senate—not one—went over to do so. The Senators wouldn't look at the evidence; they wouldn't let us present the evidence; and then many of them justified their "no" votes by saying there wasn't enough evidence.

One night near the end of the trial, I walked my little girls to Baskin-Robbins to get ice cream cones. I was sitting there in a baseball cap and old jeans when a general attached to the Pentagon walked over to me and said, "You're Congressman Rogan. You're prosecuting my Commander-in-Chief." At this point I thought I should at least stand up. I didn't know what to expect. Then the general said, "The man you are prosecuting is unfit to command the men and women of the United States Armed Forces." He reached into his pocket, handed me his card and said, "I am General so-and-so. If you wish to report this conversation to the Secretary of Defense tomorrow morning, that will be your right and your privilege, and I will immediately resign my commission. Good evening, sir." And he saluted and walked off. I tore up the card. Here was a man prepared to risk his lifelong career in order to speak up for principle. It was a powerful experience.

Lessons Drawn

In my prepared closing argument before the Senate, I had tried to summarize for my children and my grandchildren what the trial was about. But the Chief Justice called a break just before I was up, and while in the back room I heard some remarks on television that called for an immediate response. When I rose to speak, then, I jettisoned most of my prepared text. But I'd like to read a few excerpts from it now:

> [T]he idea that no person is above the law . . . is not our inheritance automatically. The ghosts of patriots past cannot compel us to preserve this sacred bequest. Each generation of Americans must elect to adopt this standard. Once again, there is a time for choosing. How will the Senate respond? . . . The

cry has been raised that to remove the President is to create a constitutional crisis by undoing an election. But there is no constitutional crisis when the simple process of the Constitution is called into play. Listen to the words of Dr. Larry Arnn: "Elections have no higher standing under our Constitution than the impeachment process. Both stem from provisions of the Constitution. The people elect the President to do a constitutional job. They act under the Constitution when they do it. At the same time, they elect a Congress to do a different constitutional job. If the President is guilty of acts justifying impeachment, then he, and not the Congress, will have overturned the election. He will have acted in a way that betrays the purpose of his election. He will have acted, not as a constitutional representative, but as a monarch, above the law. If the great powers given the President are abused, then to impeach him defends not only the results of elections, but that higher thing of which elections are in service—the preeminence of the Constitution."

When I was a little boy, I used to write to retired legislators and ask their advice about a potential career in politics. A former U.S. Senator from Texas, a Democrat named Ralph Yarborough, wrote me a wonderful response when I was about twelve years old. He said that of all the political advice he could give, the best was to put principle and honor above incumbency. I closed my speech by telling the Senate that I now returned that sentiment to the body from which it came.

My recent race for re-election was the most expensive House race in American history, and it hurt to lose. But I'll never regret my vote for impeachment. It is easy for elected officials to succumb to the illusion that the greater good is served by their self-perpetuation in office. Seniority, of course, often brings promotion and power of a sort. But something larger gets lost. And here I'm not even talking about integrity or political soul. I'm really just talking about the ability to lead. The moment a politician decides that it's more important to be re-elected than to stand his ground, he becomes weak and ineffective. The willingness to lose elections is a necessary prerequisite of statesmanship. That, I believe, is one of the chief and enduring lessons of the Clinton impeachment trial.

Reprinted by permission from Imprimis, *the national speech digest of Hillsdale College, www.hillsdale.edu.*

Statesmanship and Its Betrayal
Mark Helprin

April 1998 *Imprimis*

Mark Helprin is a journalist and author of works of fiction.

When Marco Polo entered Xanadu, the capital of the Great Khan, he crossed ring after ring of outer city, each more splendid and interesting than the one that had come before. He was used to greatness of scale, having traveled to the limits of the ordered world and then doubled that distance into the unknown, where no European had ever set foot, over the Hindu Kush and beyond the Pamir, and through the immense empty deserts of Central Asia. And yet after passing through the world's most ethereal regions he was impressed above all by Xanadu, a city of seemingly infinite expanse, the end of which he could not see, no matter in which direction he looked.

For almost a thousand years, this city floated at the peak of Western imagination. Unlike Jerusalem, it had vanished. Unlike Atlantis, someone had actually seen it. Even during the glory of the British Empire, Coleridge held it out for envy. But no more. Now it has been eclipsed, with ease, by this, our country, founded not as a Xanadu but with the greatest humility, and on the scale of yeomen and their small farms, and as the cradle of simple gifts.

This country was not expected to be what it became. It was expected to be infinite seeming in its rivers, prairies, and stars, not in cities with hundreds of millions of rooms, passages, and halls, and buildings a quarter-mile high. It was expected to be rich in natural silence and the quality of light rather than in uncountable dollars. It was expected to be a place of unfathomable numbers, but of blades of grass and grains of wheat and the crags of mountains rather than millions upon millions of motors spinning and humming at any one time, and wheels turning, fires burning, voices talking, and lights shining.

But this great inventory of machines, buildings, bridges, vehicles, and an incomprehensible number of smaller things, is what we have. A nation founded according to a vision of simplicity has become complex. A nation founded with disdain for power has become the most powerful nation. When letters took a month by sea and the records of the United States government could be moved in a single wagon pulled by two horses, we had great statesmanship. We had men of integrity and genius: Washington, Hamilton, Franklin, Jefferson, Adams, Madison, and Monroe. These were men who were in love with principle as if it were an art, which, in their practice, they made it. They studied empires that had fallen, for the sake of doing what was right in a small country that had barely risen, and were able to see things so clearly that they surpassed in greatness each and every one of the classical models that they had approached in awe.

Now, lost in the sins and complexity of a Xanadu, when we desperately need their high qualities of thought, their patience for deliberation, and their unerring sense of balance, we have only what we have. Which is a political class that in the main has abandoned the essential qualities of statesmanship, with the excuse that these are inappropriate to our age. They are wrong. Not only do they fail to honor the principles of statesmanship, they fail to recognize them, having failed to learn them, having failed to want to learn them.

In the main, they are in it for themselves. Were they not, they would have a higher rate of attrition, falling with the colors of what they believe rather than landing always on their feet—adroitly, but in dishonor. In light of their vows and responsibilities, this constitutes not merely a failure but a betrayal. And it is a betrayal not only of statesmanship and principle but of country and kin.

Why is that? It is because things matter. Even though it be played like a game, by men who excel at making it a game, our life in this country, our history in this country, the sacrifices that have been made for this country, the lives that have been given to this country, are not a game. My life is not a game. My children's lives are not a game. My parents' lives were not a game. Your life is not a game.

Yes, it is true, we do have great accumulated stores—of power, and wealth, and decency—against which those who pretend to lead us can draw when, as a result of their vanities and ineptitudes, they waste and expend the gifts of previous generations. The margin of error bequeathed to them allows them to present their failures as successes. They say, as we are still standing, and a chicken is in the pot, what does it matter if I break the links between action and consequence, work and reward, crime and punishment, merit and advancement? I myself cannot imagine a military threat (and never could), so what does it matter if I weld shut the silo hatches on our ballistic missile submarines? What does it matter if I weld shut my eyes to weapons of mass destruction in the hands of lunatics who are building long-range missiles? Our jurisprudence is the envy of the world, so what does it matter if, now and then, I perjure myself, a little? What is an oath? What is a pledge? What is a sacred trust? Are not these things the province of the kinds of people who were foolish enough to do without all their lives, to wear the ruts into the Oregon Trail, to brave the seas, to die on the beaches of Normandy and Iwo Jima and on the battlefields of Shiloh and Antietam, for me, so that I can draw from America's great accounts, and look good, and be presidential, and have fun, in all kinds of ways?

That is what they say, if not in words then, indelibly, in actions. They who, in robbing Peter to pay Paul, present themselves as payers and forget that they are also robbers. They who, with studied compassion, minister to some of us at the expense of others. They who make goodness and charity a public profession, depending for their election upon a well-manured embrace of these things and the power to move them not from within themselves or by their own sacrifices but, by compulsion, from others. They who, knowing very little or next to nothing, take pride in eagerly telling everyone else what to do. They who believe absolutely in their recitation of pieties not because they believe in the pieties but because they believe in themselves.

Nearly four hundred years of America's hard-earned accounts—the principles we established, the battles we fought, the morals we upheld for century after century, our very humility before God—now flow promiscuously through our hands, like blood onto sand, squandered and laid waste by a generation that imagines history to have been but a prelude for what it would accomplish. More than a pity, more than a shame, it is despicable. And yet, this parlous condition, this agony of weak men, this betrayal and this disgusting show, are not the end of things.

Principles are eternal. They stem not from our resolution or lack of it but from elsewhere where, in patient and infinite ranks, they simply wait to be called. They can be read in history. They arise as if of their own accord when in the face of danger natural courage comes into play and honor and defiance are born. Things such as courage and honor are the mortal equivalent of certain laws written throughout the universe. The rules of symmetry and proportion, the laws of physics, the perfection of mathematics, even the principle of uncertainty, are encouragement, entirely independent of the vagaries of human will, that not only natural law but our own best aspirations have a life of their own. They have lasted through far greater abuse than abuses them now. They can be neglected, but they cannot be lost. They can be thrown down, but they cannot be broken.

Each of them is a different expression of a single quality, from which each arises in its hour of need. Some come to the fore as others stay back, and then, with changing circumstance, those that have gone unnoticed rise to the occasion.

The principle suggests itself from a phrase, and such principles suggest easily and flow generously. You can grab them out of the air, from phrases, from memories, from images. A statesman must rise to the occasion. Even Democrats can do this. Harry Truman had the discipline of plowing a straight row ten, twelve, and fourteen hours a day, of rising and retiring with the sun, of struggling with temperamental machinery, of suffering heat and cold and one injury after another. After a short time on a farm, presumptions about ruling others tend to vanish. It is as if you are pulled to earth and held there.

The man who works the land is hard put to think that he would direct armies and nations. Truman understood the grave responsibility of being the president of the United States, and that it was a task too great for him or for anyone else to accomplish without doing a great deal of injury–if not to some, then to others. He understood that, therefore, he had to transcend himself. There would be little enjoyment of the job, because he had to be always aware of the enormous consequences of everything he did. Contrast this with the unspeakably vulgar pleasure in office of President Clinton.

Truman, absolutely certain that the mantle he assumed was far greater than he could ever be, was continually and deliberately aware of the weight of history, the accomplishments of his predecessors, and, by humble and imaginative projection, his own inadequacy. The sobriety and care that derived from this allowed him a rare privilege for modern presidents, to give to the presidency more than he took from it. It is not possible to occupy the Oval Office without arrogantly looting its assets or nobly adding to them. . . .

America would not have come out of the Civil War as it did had it not been led by Lincoln and Lee. The battles raged for five years, but for a hundred years the country, both North and South, modeled itself on their character. They exemplified almost perfectly Churchill's statement, "Public men charged with the conduct of the war should live in a continual stress of soul." This continual stress of soul is necessary as well in peacetime, because for every good deed in public life there is a counterbalance. Benefits are given only after taxes are taken. That is part of governance. The statesman, who represents the whole nation, sees in the equilibrium for which he strives a continual tension between victory and defeat. If he did not understand this, he would have no stress of soul, he would be merely happy—about money showered upon the orphan, taken from the widow. About children sent to day care, so that they may be long absent from their parents. About merciful parole of criminals, who kill again. Whereas a statesman knows continual stress of soul, a politician is happy, for he knows not what he does.

It is difficult for individuals or nations to recognize that war and peace alternate. But they do. No matter how long peace may last, it will end in war. Though most people cannot believe at this moment that the United States of America will ever again fight for its survival, history guarantees that it will. And, when it does, most people will not know what to do. They will believe of war, as they did of peace, that it is everlasting.

The statesman, who is different from everyone else, will, in the midst of common despair, see the end of war, just as during the peace he was alive to the inevitability of war, and saw it coming in the far distance, as if it were a gray wave moving quietly across a dark sea. The politician will revel with his people and enjoy their enjoyments. The statesman, in continual stress of soul, will think of destruction. As others move in the light, he will move in darkness, so that as others move in darkness he may move in the light. This tenacity, that is given to those of long and insistent vision, is what saves nations.

A statesman must have a temperament that is suited for the Medal of Honor, in a soul that is unafraid to die. Electorates rightly favor those who have endured combat, not as a matter of reward for service, as is commonly believed, but because the willingness of a soldier to give his life is a strong sign of his correct priorities, and that in future he will truly understand that statesmen are not rulers but servants. It seems clear even in these years of squalid degradation that having risked death for the sake of honor is better than having risked dishonor for the sake of life.

No matter what you are told by the sophisticated classes that see virtue in every form of corruption and corruption in every form of virtue, I think you know, as I do, that the American people hunger for acts of integrity and courage. The American people hunger for a statesman magnetized by the truth, unwilling to give up his good name, uninterested in calculation only for the sake of victory, unable to put his interests before those of the nation. What this means in practical terms is no focus groups, no polls, no triangulation, no evasion, no broken promises, and no lies. These are the tools of the chameleon. They are employed to cheat the American people of honest answers to direct questions. If the average politician, for fear that he may lose something, is incapable of even a genuine yes or no, how is he supposed to rise to the great occasions of state? How is he supposed to face a destructive and implacable enemy? How is he supposed to understand the rightful destiny of his country, and lead it there?

At the coronation of an English monarch, he is given a sword. Elizabeth II took it last, and as she held it before the altar, she heard these words:

> Receive this kingly Sword, brought now from the altar of God and delivered to you by us, the Bishops and servants of God, though unworthy. With this Sword do justice, stop the growth of iniquity, protect the holy Church of God, help and defend widows and orphans, restore the things that are gone to decay, maintain the things that are restored, punish and reform what is amiss, and confirm what is in good order; that doing these things you may be glorious in all virtue; and so faithfully serve our Lord.

Would that we in America come once again to understand that statesmanship is not the appetite for power but—because things matter—a holy calling of self-abnegation and self-sacrifice. We have made it something else. Nonetheless, after and despite its betrayal, statesmanship remains the manifestation, in political terms, of beauty, and balance, and truth. It is the courage to tell the truth, and thus discern what is ahead. It is a mastery of the symmetry of forces, illuminated by the genius of speaking to the heart of things.

Statesmanship is a quality that, though it may be betrayed, is always ready to be taken up again merely by honest subscription to its great themes. Have confidence that even in idleness its strengths are growing, for it is a providential gift given to us in times of need. Evidently we do not need it now, but as the world is forever interesting the time will surely come when we do. And then, so help me God, I believe that, solely by the grace of God, the corrupt will be thrown down and the virtuous will rise up.

Reprinted by permission from Imprimis, *the national speech digest of Hillsdale College, www.hillsdale.edu.*

Image Credits

Department of Defense: 77, 79, 83, 121, 169, 173, 175, 187, 194, 213

Department of State: 84

Images of American Political History: 99

Mary Evelyn Notgrass: 134

Nova Development Corporation: 76, 93, 137, 208, cover image of U.S. Capitol

Library of Congress, Prints and Photographs Division: 10, 18, 37, 39, 51, 73, 98, 100, 101, 113, 136, 139, 145, 154, 200, cover images of John Quincy Adams, President and Mrs. Calvin Coolidge, Judge Joseph Story, Group photograph of Democratic Members of Congress, First Prayer in Congress

Ronald Reagan Presidential Library: 163